STUDY GUIDE AND WORKING PAPERS

for use with

A SURVEY OF FINANCIAL AND MANAGERIAL

ACCOUNTING

James Don Edwards, Ph.D., CPA
J. M. Tull Professor of Accounting
University of Georgia

Roger H. Hermanson, Ph.D., CPA
Ernst & Whinney Alumni Professor
Regents' Professor of Accounting
Georgia State University

R. F. Salmonson, Ph.D., CPA
Professor Emeritus
Michigan State University

1989 Fifth Edition

Homewood, IL 60430
Boston, MA 02116

ISBN 0-256-06977-8

Printed in the United States of America.

2 3 4 5 6 7 8 9 0 VK 6 5 4 3 2 1 0

Contents

Note to Student

This workbook contains for each chapter:

(1) Understanding the learning objectives and a repeat of the glossary from the text.

(2) Short-answer questions, exercises, and multiple-choice questions covering the basic content of the chapter. Answers are supplied immediately following the questions in each chapter.

(3) Working papers to be used in solving the problems assigned. Many of them are partially filled in to reduce the amount of writing you will have to do. Also, the format gives you assistance in knowing how to approach the solution of each problem.

Accounting truly is the language of business. We wish you success in mastering the content of accounting. It will be useful to you the rest of your life.

The Authors

Introduction

The Accounting Environment

Understanding the Learning Objectives

1. Define accounting.

    *   Accounting is "the process of identifying, measuring, and communicating economic information to permit informed judgments and decisions by users of the information."

2. Describe the functions performed by accountants.

    *   Accountants observe many events and identify and measure in financial terms (dollars) those events considered evidence of economic activity.

    *   The economic events are recorded, classified into meaningful groups, and summarized for conciseness.

    *   Accountants report on business activity by preparing financial statements and special reports. And accountants are often asked to interpret these statements and reports for various groups such as management and creditors.

3. Describe employment opportunities in accounting.

    *   An accountant may be employed in public accounting and specialize in auditing, tax, or management consulting.

    *   Management accountants are employed by a single company and may specialize in measuring and controlling costs, budgeting, accounting systems, or some other function.

    *   Some accountants are employed in government agencies, universities, or other not-for-profit organizations.

4. Differentiate between financial and managerial accounting.

    *   Financial accounting is meant primarily for external use; it provides information for groups such as owners and prospective owners, creditors, employees, customers, governmental units, and the general public.

    *   Managerial accounting is meant for internal use; it provides special information for the managers of the company.

5. Identify the five organizations that have a role in the development of financial accounting standards.

    *   American Institute of Certified Public Accountants (AICPA)—made up of persons holding the CPA certificate. The Accounting Principles Board (APB) was under the AICPA.

    *   Financial Accounting Standards Board (FASB)—issues FASB Statements, which are the "rules" of financial accounting.

* Governmental Accounting Standards Board (GASB)—issues GASB Statements, which are the "rules" of governmental accounting.

* Securities and Exchange Commission (SEC)—a government agency that has legislative authority over financial accounting standards. To date, the SEC has allowed the private sector to set the standards.

* American Accounting Association (AAA)—academic members perform research, publish the results, and teach accounting courses.

6. Define and use correctly the new terms in the glossary.

The new terms used in the Introduction are as follows:

Accounting—"The process of identifying, measuring, and communicating eonomic information to permit informed judgments and decisions by the users of the information."

Accounting Principles Board (APB)—An organization created in 1959 by the AICPA and empowered to speak for it on matters of accounting principle; replaced in 1973 by the Financial Accounting Standards Board.

American Accounting Association (AAA)—A professional organization of accountants, many of whom are college or university professors of accounting.

American Institute of Certified Public Accountants (AICPA)—A professional organization of certified public accountants, many of whom are in public accounting practice.

Annual report—A pamphlet or document of varying length containing audited financial statements and other information about a company, distributed annually to its owners.

Audit (independent)—Performed by independent auditors to determine whether the financial statements of a business fairly reflect the economic performance of the business.

Audit (internal)—Performed by accounting employees of a company to determine if company policies and procedures are being followed.

Certified Internal Auditor (CIA)—An accountant who has passed an examination prepared and graded by the Institute of Internal Auditors and who has met certain other requirements.

Certified Management Accountant (CMA)—Awarded to accountants who pass an examination prepared and graded by the Institute of Certified Management Accountants, an affiliate of the National Association of Accountants, and who meet certain other requirements.

Certified Public Accountant (CPA)—An accountant who has passed an examination prepared and graded by the American Institute of Certified Public Accountants (AICPA) and who has met certain other requirements, such as work experience in accounting and specified courses in accounting. The accountant is then awarded a CPA certificate and may be licensed by the state to practice as an independent professional.

Controller—The executive officer in charge of a company's accounting activity.

Financial accounting—Relates to the process of supplying financial information to parties external to the reporting entity.

Financial Accounting Standards Board (FASB)—The highest-ranking nongovernmental authority on the development of accounting standards or principles.

Financial statements—Formal reports providing information on a company's financial position (solvency), changes in this position, and the results of operations (profitability).

Generally Accepted Accounting Principles (GAAP)—Accounting standards and principles that have been developed largely in accounting practice or have been established by an authoritative organization.

Governmental Accounting Standards Board (GASB)—This body issues statements on accounting and financial reporting in the governmental area.

Governmental or other not-for-profit accounting—Governmental accountants are employed by government agencies at the federal, state, and local levels. Other not-for-profit accountants record and account for receipts and disbursements for churches, charities, fraternities, and universities. Accountants in the academic segment of the accounting profession teach accounting to students and conduct research on accounting issues.

Independent audit—See Audit (independent).

Independent auditors—Certified public accountants who perform audits to determine whether the financial statements of businesses fairly reflect the economic performance of these businesses.

Independent auditor's opinion or report—The formal written statement by a certified public accountant that states whether or not the client's financial statements fairly reflect the economic performance of the business.

Internal audit—See Audit (internal).

Internal auditors—Private accountants employed to see that the policies and procedures established by the business are followed in its divisions and departments.

Managerial accounting—Relates to the process of supplying financial information for internal management use.

Private or industrial accountants—Accountants who provide accounting services for a single business and who are employees of that business.

Public accounting—Pertains to accounting and related services offered for a fee to companies, other organizations, and the general public.

Securities and Exchange Commission (SEC)—A governmental agency created by Congress to administer acts dealing with interstate sales of securities and having the authority to prescribe the accounting and reporting practices of firms under its jurisdiction.

Completion and Exercises

1. Accounting is primarily an information system with two objectives—to _____ and _____ financial information that is relevant to users for their decision-making needs.

2. Accounting deals primarily with information expressed in terms of _____ about _____ resources and their use.

3. An independent, professional accountant, licensed by the state to practice as a certified public accountant (CPA), may offer his clients three types of services, namely, _____ , _____ _____ , and _____ services.

4. An accountant who offers his services solely to a single profit-seeking organization is said to be in _____ accounting. A third major area of employment for accountants is generally described as _____ accounting.

5. The decisions that must be made by the management of a business generally fall into four major categories: (a) _____ , (b) _____ _____ , (c) _____ , and (d) _____ decisions. That part of the accounting discipline called upon to provide information for such internal decision making is called _____ accounting.

6. Although many external users of accounting information exist, such as the general public, governmental agencies, customers, and employees, the most important external users probably are _____ and _____ .

7. Financial accounting information generally relates to a company as a _____ and is usually _____ in nature.

8. The dominant influence over the past half century in the development of financial accounting standards is the _____ _____ _____ _____ _____ _____ .

9. A governmental agency having the power to prescribe the accounting practices of most large business corporations is the _____ _____ _____ _____ .

Multiple-Choice Questions

For each of the following questions, indicate the single best answer by circling the appropriate letter.

1. Which of the following activities is *not* a part of the accounting function?

    a. Measurement of economic activity in monetary terms
    b. Classification of recorded events into meaningful groups
    c. Creation of economic activity for recognition by the business
    d. Interpretation of financial statements and reports

2. Accounting is concerned with each of the following activities *except*:

    a. cost studies of managerial effectiveness.
    b. long-range financial planning.
    c. design of management information systems.
    d. executive recruitment.

3. Which of the following is generally performed only by certified public accountants?

    a. Preparing budgets and financial forecasts of future results of operations
    b. Rendering an opinion on the fairness of published financial information
    c. Preparing income tax returns for SEC-regulated corporations
    d. Providing management advisory consulting services about the installation of a computer system

4. Implementing a decision causes:

    a. a change in the preferred outcome of the decision.
    b. new events and problems to occur.
    c. a decision maker to justify his decision.
    d. the correction of the perceived alternatives.

5. Managerial accounting information:

    a. is historical in nature.
    b. must be prepared using generally accepted accounting principles.
    c. describes the results of operations or profitability of a firm.
    d. is not required and should only be prepared when it is useful.

4

6. Which of the following organizations has had the least influence on the development of generally accepted accounting principles?

   a. The American Institute of CPAs
   b. The Securities and Exchange Commission
   c. The Internal Revenue Service
   d. The Financial Accounting Standards Board

   Now compare your answers to the correct ones on page 6.

Solutions/Introduction

Completion and Exercises

1. measure; report

2. money; economic

3. auditing; management advisory; tax

4. private; governmental

5. financing; resource allocation; production; marketing; managerial

6. owners and prospective owners; creditors and prospective creditors

7. whole; historical

8. American Institute of Certified Public Accountants

9. Securities and Exchange Commission

Multiple-Choice Questions

1. c. Accounting does not normally create economic activity; it merely processes such activity in an information system after it has occurred.

2. d. Although such activity could be undertaken by a CPA, it is not an accounting function. All of the others involve financial information and are regularly engaged in by accountants.

3. b. Generally, the right to express an opinion on the fairness of published financial information is restricted by law to CPAs (and a few other public accountants in some states). All of the other activities can be undertaken by both CPAs and non-CPAs.

4. b. The implementation of a decision causes activity to occur that, in turn, causes new problems and new decisions.

5. d. Two basic requirements of managerial accounting information is that it be useful and that its cost not exceed its benefit. Items a, b, and c are related to financial accounting information.

6. c. The Internal Revenue Service has only limited effect on the development of generally accepted accounting principles. This is because the goals of financial accounting and tax laws may be substantially different and, therefore, the methods by which information is developed are also different. There are numerous variations between how economic activity is reported for financial accounting and tax accounting; what is appropriate for one item (such as a tax return) is not necessarily appropriate for another item (such as an income statement).

Accounting—A Source of Financial Information

Understanding the Learning Objectives

1. Identify and describe the three basic forms of business organizations.

    * A single proprietorship is an unincorporated business owned by an individual and often managed by that same individual.

    * A partnership is a business owned by two or more persons associated as partners and is often managed by those same persons.

    * A corporation is a business that may be owned by a few persons or by thousands of persons and is incorporated under the laws of one of the fifty states.

2. Distinguish among the three types of business activities performed by business organizations.

    * Service companies perform services for a fee.

    * Merchandising companies purchase goods that are ready for sale and then sell them to customers.

    * Manufacturing companies buy materials, convert them into products, and then sell the products to other companies or to final customers.

3. Describe the content and purposes of the balance sheet, income statement, and statement of retained earnings.

    * The balance sheet shows the assets, liabilities, and stockholders' equity of a business firm at a specific moment in time.

    * The income statement reports the profits of a business organization for a stated period of time.

    * The statement of retained earnings explains the changes in retained earnings that occurred between two balance sheet dates.

4. State the basic accounting equation and describe its relationship to the balance sheet.

    * The accounting equation is: Assets = Liabilities + Stockholders' Equity.

    * The left-hand side of the equation represents the left-hand side of the balance sheet.

    * The right-hand side of the equation represents the right-hand side of the balance sheet.

5. Analyze business transactions and determine their effects on items in the financial statements.

    * Illustration 1.5 shows the effects of business transactions on the accounting equation.

6. Prepare a balance sheet and income statement.

    * The balance sheet is shown in Illustration 1.8.

    * The income statement is shown in Illustration 1.9.

7. Define and use correctly the new terms in the glossary.

The new terms introduced in the chapter are as follows:

Accounting equation—Basically, Assets = Equities; in slightly expanded form for a corporation, Assets = Liabilities + Stockholders' Equity.

Accounts payable—Amounts owed to suppliers for goods or services purchased on credit.

Accounts receivable—Amounts owed to a business by its customers.

Assets—Things of value; they constitute the resources of the firm. Examples include money, machines, and buildings. Assets possess service potential or utility to their owner that can be measured and expressed in money terms.

Balance sheet—Financial statement that lists a company's assets, liabilities, and stockholders' equity (including dollar amounts) as of a specific moment in time. Also called a statement of financial position.

Business entity concept—The separate existence of the business organization.

Capital stock—The title given to an equity account showing the investment in a business corporation by its stockholders.

Continuity (going concern)—The assumption by the accountant that unless specific evidence exists to the contrary, a business firm will continue to operate into the indefinite future.

Corporation—Business that may be owned by a few persons or by thousands of persons and is incorporated under the laws of one (1) of the 50 states.

Cost—The sacrifice made or the resources given up to acquire some desired thing; the basis of valuation of the bulk of the assets of a business.

Dividend—Payment (usually of cash) to the owners of the business; it is a distribution of income to owners rather than an expense of doing business.

Duality—The two-sided effect of every transaction.

Entity—A unit that is deemed to have an existence separate and apart from its owners, creditors, employees, and other interested parties and for which accounting records are maintained.

Equities—Broadly speaking, all claims to or interests in assets.

Expenses—The sacrifice made, usually measured in terms of the cost of the assets surrendered or consumed, to generate revenues.

Income statement (earnings statement)—Financial statement showing the revenues and expenses of an organization for a specified period of time.

Liabilities—Debts or obligations that usually possess a known or determinable amount, maturity date, and party to whom payment is to be made.

Manufacturing companies—Companies that buy materials, convert them into products, and then sell the products to other companies or to final customers.

Merchandising companies—Companies that purchase goods that are ready for sale and then sell them to customers.

Money measurement—Expression of a property of an object in terms of a number of units of a standard monetary medium, such as the dollar.

Net income—The amount by which the revenues of a period exceed the expenses of the same period.

Net loss—The amount by which the expenses of a period exceed the revenues of the same period.

Notes payable—Written promises to pay to other parties definite sums of money at certain or determinable dates, usually with interest at a specified rate.

Partnership—Business owned by two or more persons associated as partners.

Periodicity—An assumption that an entity's life can be subdivided into time periods for purposes of reporting the economic activities.

Profitability—Ability to generate income. The income statement reflects a company's profitability.

Retained earnings—Accumulated net income less dividend distributions to stockholders.

Revenues—The inflows of assets resulting from the sale of goods or the providing of services to customers.

Service companies—Companies that perform services (such as accounting firms, law firms, repair shops, or dry-cleaning establishments) for a fee.

Single proprietorship—Business owned by an individual and often managed by that same individual.

Solvency—Ability to pay debts as they become due. The balance sheet reflects a company's solvency.

Source document—Any written or printed evidence of a business transaction that describes the essential facts of that transaction.

Statement of retained earnings—Statement used to explain the changes in retained earnings that occurred between two balance sheet dates.

Stockholders or shareholders—Owners of the corporation; they buy shares of stock, which are units of ownership in the corporation.

Stockholders' equity—The owners' interest in a corporation.

Transactions—Recordable happenings or events (usually exchanges) that affect the assets, liabilities, stockholders' equity, revenues, or expenses of an entity.

Completion and Exercises

1. The balance sheet of a business corporation usually will show three classes of items; these are: (a) _____ , (b) _____ , and (c) _____ _____, while its income statement will show two classes, namely, (a) _____ and (b) _____ .

2. In its most basic form, the accounting equation is simply _____ = _____ . This equation is usually expanded to _____ = _____ + _____ _____ .

3. Changes in the financial position of an organization are brought about by events, exchanges, and other real-world happenings that the accountant measures and records and that are called _____ _____ .

4. To show your understanding of the effects of each of the named transactions upon the assets, liabilities, and stockholders' equity of a business, fill in each blank in each column with either + (for increase), − (for decrease), or 0 (for no change):

	Assets	Liabilities	Stockholders' Equity
a. Issued capital stock for cash..............	_____	_____	_____
b. Borrowed money from a bank	_____	_____	_____
c. Purchased equipment on credit	_____	_____	_____
d. Rendered services for cash	_____	_____	_____
e. Paid creditor in (c)	_____	_____	_____
f. Paid monthly rent........................	_____	_____	_____
g. Sold merchandise on credit at a profit	_____	_____	_____
h. Rendered services for which the customer promised to pay at a later date	_____	_____	_____

9

5. Refer to Question 4 and indicate, by letter, which of the transactions would be reported in the income statement _____ _____ _____ _____ .

6. The total flow of services rendered or goods delivered (as measured by the assets received from customers) is called _____ while the assets surrendered or consumed in this process are called _____ . A corporation rewards its stockholders for providing capital by the payment of _____ .

7. The statement that summarizes the changes in retained earnings is called _____ _____ _____ _____ _____ _____ .

8. The specific unit or organization for which accounting information is accumulated and reported is called the _____ . The basis of valuation of assets in accounting is _____ .

9. The _____ concept in accounting refers to the fact that every transaction has a two-sided effect upon both parties entering into it.

10. If expenses for a period exceed revenues for the same period, the entity is deemed to have suffered a _____ _____ .

11. An income statement is prepared for a _____ , while a balance sheet is prepared as of a specific _____ .

12. Under the _____ concept, the accountant assumes that a business will continue more or less indefinitely and therefore that assets that will be consumed in future operations can be reported at _____ rather than at _____ values.

Multiple-Choice Questions

For each of the following questions, indicate the single best answer by circling the appropriate letter.

1. Which of the following would not generally be included in a partnership agreement?
   a. Initial investment of each partner
   b. Method of dividing income and losses
   c. Settlement procedures upon death or withdrawal of a partner
   d. Amount of dividends to be granted to each partner each year

2. The corporate form of business is generally used when:
   a. small amounts of money are needed to start the business organization.
   b. the owners wish to manage and control the organization.
   c. the owners wish to limit their personal liability for debts of the organization.
   d. ownership is to be restricted to a very limited group of individuals.

3. The financial statement that presents the assets and equities of a business at a particular moment in time is the:
   a. statement of changes in financial position.
   b. statement of retained earnings.
   c. balance sheet.
   d. income statement.

4. Resources of a firm are referred to as:

    a.   liabilities.
    b.   entities.
    c.   assets.
    d.   revenues.

5. If a company has stockholders' equity of $20,000:

    a.   a total of $20,000 was invested by stockholders.
    b.   revenues less expenses equals $20,000.
    c.   the business has total assets of $20,000.
    d.   total business assets less total liabilities equals $20,000.

6. Company K has assets of $30,000 and liabilities of $5,000. The company buys delivery equipment on credit for $4,000. What immediate effect would this transaction have on the balance sheet?

    a.   Assets increase $4,000 and expenses increase $4,000.
    b.   Assets increase $4,000 and liabilities increase $4,000.
    c.   Expenses increase $4,000 and liabilities increase $4,000.
    d.   Expenses increase $4,000 and stockholders' equity increases $4,000.

7. Revenue is:

    a.   the inflow of assets from products or services provided to customers.
    b.   the difference between the selling price of a product or service and the cost of providing such product or service.
    c.   the same as net income.
    d.   a decrease in stockholders' equity.

8. Little Corporation collected $500 of its $2,000 of accounts receivable. How is the balance sheet affected?

    a.   Assets increase by $500 and stockholders' equity increases by $500.
    b.   Accounts receivable is decreased by $500 and liabilities are increased by $500.
    c.   Total assets are increased, but liabilities and stockholders' equity remain the same.
    d.   There is no change in total assets, liabilities, or stockholders' equity.

9. Which of the following statements is *incorrect*?

    a.   An income statement shows how much net income or net loss was generated for a period of time.
    b.   An income statement summarizes revenue and expense transactions for a period of operations between two balance sheet dates.
    c.   The income statement shows the changes in assets and liabilities that occurred during the period of operations covered by the statement.
    d.   The income statement heading should disclose the name of the company and the period of time that the statement covers.

10. Which of the following is usually *not* recorded by the accountant?

    a.   The purchase of a machine by giving a note payable for its full selling price
    b.   The collection of an account receivable
    c.   The issuance of a purchase order by a business for supplies
    d.   The payment of $2,000 of rent for the following year

11. Most assets are reported in the balance sheet at:

    a.   what it would cost to replace the asset.
    b.   the amount that the asset is worth to the managers of the business.
    c.   the historical cost incurred to acquire the asset.
    d.   the amount that would be received upon the sale of the asset.

12. Which of the following is an appropriate format for the balance sheet equation?

    a.   Assets + Liabilities = Stockholders' Equity
    b.   Assets + Liabilities = Revenues − Expenses
    c.   Assets + Liabilities = Liabilities + Expenses
    d.   Assets − Liabilities = Stockholders' Equity

13. Which of the following would increase assets and liabilities?

    a.   Received payment from a customer for services rendered
    b.   Borrowed money to purchase a piece of equipment
    c.   Received cash as additional investment by stockholders
    d.   Received a utility bill for the month but have not paid it

14. A payment to the owners of a business as a return on the investment they provided is called a(n):

    a.   expense.
    b.   revenue.
    c.   account receivable.
    d.   dividend.

15. If total assets of Q Corporation are $100,000, total liabilities are $34,000, and capital stock is $40,000, how much are the retained earnings of Q Corporation?

    a. $ 26,000
    b. $ 94,000
    c. $106,000
    d.   Cannot be determined from the above information

16. The _____ assumption means that a business is deemed to have an existence separate and distinct from its owners.

    a.   equity
    b.   going concern
    c.   cost
    d.   entity

17. The payment of an account payable:

    a.   increases an expense and decreases a liability.
    b.   increases a liability and decreases an asset.
    c.   decreases an asset and increases a liability.
    d.   decreases an asset and decreases a liability.

18. If a service is provided, but cash is not received, a business would:

    a.   increase an asset and increase a revenue.
    b.   increase an asset and increase a liability.
    c.   decrease a liability and increase capital stock.
    d.   increase an asset and increase an expense.

19. An increase in an expense:

    a.   increases an asset.
    b.   increases stockholders' equity.
    c.   decreases a liability.
    d.   decreases retained earnings.

20. Palmer Company has assets of $50,000, liabilities of $24,000, and capital stock of $8,000 at the end of a month. During the month, Palmer had $30,000 of revenues, $10,000 of expenses, and paid dividends of $6,000. Net income for the month was:

    a. $14,000.
    b. $18,000.
    c. $20,000.
    d. $26,000.

21. Using the above information for Palmer Company, retained earnings at the end of the month would be:

    a. $12,000.
    b. $18,000.
    c. $26,000.
    d. $32,000.

22. Connie Corporation showed the following information at the beginning of June 1989:

Assets	$16,000
Liabilities............	2,000
Capital Stock	3,000

During the month of June, Connie Corporation generated $10,000 of revenues, incurred $4,000 of expenses, and paid dividends of $1,000. Retained earnings at the end of June would be:

    a. $ 5,000.
    b. $ 6,000.
    c. $16,000.
    d. $17,000.

Now compare your answers with the correct ones beginning on page 14.

Solutions/Chapter 1

Completion and Exercises

1. assets; liabilities, stockholders' equity; revenues; expenses

2. Assets = Equities; Assets = Liabilities + Stockholders' Equity

3. transactions

4.

	Assets	Liabilities	Stockholders' Equity
a	+	0	+
b	+	+	0
c	+	+	0
d	+	0	+
e	−	−	0
f	−	0	−
g	+	0	+
h	+	0	+

5. (d), (f), (g), and (h)

6. revenue; expenses; dividends

7. the statement of retained earnings

8. entity; cost

9. duality

10. net loss

11. period; date

12. continuity; cost; market (or liquidation)

Multiple-Choice Questions

1. d. Dividends are not given in a partnership situation, only in corporations. The amounts that may be withdrawn from the partnership may be specified, but usually only as related to income distribution.

2. c. Since single proprietorships and partnerships do not limit personal responsibility for debts of the business, a corporate form of organization (being a separate legal entity) is used for this purpose. This is one of the major strengths of this form of organization as compared to the other forms.

3. c. The balance sheet is like a snapshot of the business at a point in time.

4. c. The assets of a business are its resources, or items of value that are owned.

5. d. The balance sheet equation is Assets = Liabilities + Stockholders' Equity, so Assets − Liabilities = Stockholders' Equity.

6. b. The purchase of delivery equipment increases assets by $4,000 and the fact that it was purchased on credit means that the company has incurred a debt or liability for the amount.

7. a. Revenue is properly defined as the total inflow of assets from products or services delivered to or performed for customers by an entity. Net income is the difference between revenues and expenses. Revenues increase stockholders' equity.

Name _____

(a)

SPRINGFIELD COMPANY
Summary of Transactions

Date	Explanation	Assets			=	Liabilities	+	Stockholders' Equity	
		Cash	Accounts Receivable	Equipment	=	Notes Payable	+	Capital Stock	Retained Earnings
		$	$	$		$		$	$
		$	$	$		$		$	$
		$	$	$		$		$	$
		$	$	$		$		$	$
		$	$	$		$		$	$
		$	$	$		$		$	$
		$	$	$		$		$	$
		$	$	$		$		$	$

Name _____

_____

(b) _____ SPRINGFIELD COMPANY _____

Balance Sheet

June 30, 1990

Name _____

_____

DANIELS COMPANY

Income Statement

For the Month Ended May 31, 1990

Name _____

_____

EWING COMPANY

Income Statement

For the Year Ended June 30, 1990

2

The Basic Accounting System

Understanding the Learning Objectives

1. Use the account as the basic classifying and storage unit for information.

    *   An account is a storage unit used to classify and summarize money measurements of business activity of a similar nature.

    *   An account will be established whenever the data to be recorded in it are believed to be useful to some party having a valid interest in the business.

2. Express the effects of business transactions in terms of debits and credits to six different types of accounts.

    *   A T-account resembles the letter T.

    *   Debits are entries on the left-hand side of a T-account.

    *   Credits are entries on the right-hand side of a T-account.

    *   Asset, expense, and Dividends accounts are increased by debits.

    *   Liability, stockholders' equity, and revenue accounts are increased by credits.

3. Record the effects of business transactions in a journal.

    *   A journal contains a chronological record of the transactions of a business.

    *   An example of a general journal is shown in Illustration 2.1.

    *   Journalizing is the process of entering a transaction in a journal.

4. Post journal entries to the accounts in the ledger.

    *   Posting is the process of transferring information recorded in the journal to the proper place in the ledger.

    *   Cross-indexing is the placing of the account number in the journal and the placing of the journal page number in the ledger account.

    *   An example of cross-indexing appears in Illustration 2.2.

5. Prepare a trial balance to test the equality of debits and credits in the journalizing and posting process.

    *   A trial balance is a listing of the accounts and their debit or credit balances.

    *   If the trial balance does not balance, the accountant should work backwards to discover the error.

    *   A trial balance is shown in Illustration 2.3.

6. Define and use correctly the new terms in the glossary.

    The new terms introduced in the chapter are as follows:

    Account—An element in an accounting system that is used to classify and summarize measurements of business activity. The three-column account is normally used. It contains columns for debit, credit, and balance.

Charge—Means the same as the word *debit*.

Chart of accounts—The complete listing of the titles and account numbers of all of the accounts in the ledger; somewhat comparable to a table of contents.

Compound journal entry—A journal entry with more than one debit and/or credit.

Credit—The right side of any account; when used as a verb, to enter a dollar amount on the right side of an account; credits increase liability, stockholders' equity, and revenue accounts and decrease asset, expense, and dividends accounts.

Credit balance—The balance in an account when the sum of the credits to the account exceeds the sum of the debits to that account.

Credit entry—An entry on the right side of an account.

Cross-indexing—The placing of the account number in the journal and the placing of the journal page number in the ledger account.

Debit—The left side of any account; when used as a verb, to enter a dollar amount on the left side of an account; debits increase asset, expense, and dividends accounts and decrease liability, stockholders' equity, and revenue accounts.

Debit balance—The balance in an account when the sum of the debits to the account exceeds the sum of the credits to that account.

Debit entry—An entry on the left side of an account.

Double-entry procedure—The accounting requirement that every transaction be recorded in an entry that has equal debits and credits.

Journal—A chronological (arranged in order of time) record of business transactions; the simplest form of journal is the two-column general journal.

Journal entry—Shows all of the effects of a business transaction as expressed in terms of debit(s) and credit(s) and may include an explanation of the transaction.

Journalizing—A step in the accounting recording process that consists of entering a transaction in a journal.

Ledger—The complete collection of all of the accounts of a company; often referred to as the general ledger.

Nominal accounts—Income statement accounts—revenues and expenses.

Posting—Recording in the ledger the information contained in the journal.

Real accounts—Balance sheet accounts (assets, liabilities, and stockholders' equity).

T-account—An account resembling the letter *T*, which is used for illustrative purposes only. Debits are entered on the left side of the account and credits are entered on the right side of the account.

Trial balance—A listing of the ledger accounts and their debit or credit balances to determine that debits equal credits in the recording process.

Completion and Exercises

1. The basic unit in which data are stored in an accounting system is called an _____ . These storage units should be so constructed as to readily receive money measurements of the

    _____ or _____ in the items for which they are established.

2. Whether or not an account is established is determined largely by whether or not it will provide

    _____ _____ .

28

3. The difference between the amounts entered as increases in an account and those entered as decreases is called the _____ of the account.

4. For each of the following T-accounts indicate on which side increases are recorded and on which side decreases are recorded:

Assets	Liabilities	Stockholders' Equity

5. From (4) it follows that assets, which appear on the left side of a balance sheet, will have balances on the _____ side of the account. Conversely, liabilities and stockholders' equity items will appear on the right side of the balance sheet and have balances on the _____ side of the account.

6. Since revenues increase stockholders' equity, and stockholders' equity increases are recorded on the _____ side of the account, it follows that increases in revenues are recorded on the _____ side of the account.

7. Since expenses decrease stockholders' equity and such decreases are recorded on the _____ side of the account, it follows that increases in expenses are recorded on the _____ side of the account.

8. Accountants do not speak in terms of increases and decreases. Rather, they use technical terminology. Thus, to _____ an account means to place an entry on the left side of the account; to _____ an account means to place an entry on the right side of the account.

9. Fill in the blanks below with the word *debits* or *credits*:

Type of Account	Increased by	Decreased by
Asset......................................	_____	_____
Liability	_____	_____
Stockholders' equity.......................	_____	_____
Revenue...................................	_____	_____
Expense...................................	_____	_____

10. Collectively, all of the accounts in the accounting system are referred to as the _____ . The list of accounts in an accounting system (often together with their numbers) is called the _____ _____ _____ .

11. A _____ is often called a book of original entry and contains a chronological record of the transactions of a business. Before a transaction can be entered in this book of original entry its effects upon the business must be determined and encoded into terms of _____ and _____ .

12. The act of entering a transaction in a journal is called _____ . After a transaction is so entered it is _____ from the journal to the _____ at which time a process known as _____ also takes place in order that amounts in accounts can be readily traced to the original record of the transactions giving rise to them.

13. The statement prepared as a proof of the arithmetic accuracy of the recording process and which contains a list of the accounts and their debit or credit balances is called a _____

_____ .

14. Prepare journal entries for the company that engaged in the following transactions:

January   1—Issued capital stock for $50,000 cash.
January 10—Paid the rent for January, $400.
January 13—Performed services for customers who promised to pay later, $600.
January 20—Purchased equipment, $4,000, promised to pay later.
January 30—Received payment for the services rendered on January 13.

GENERAL JOURNAL

DATE	ACCOUNT TITLES AND EXPLANATION	POST. REF.	DEBIT	CREDIT

15. Post to the ledger the journal entries prepared in Question 14.

DATE	EXPLANATION	POST. REF.	DEBIT	CREDIT	BALANCE

DATE	EXPLANATION	POST. REF.	DEBIT	CREDIT	BALANCE

15. (concluded)

	DATE		EXPLANATION	POST. REF.	DEBIT	CREDIT	BALANCE

	DATE		EXPLANATION	POST. REF.	DEBIT	CREDIT	BALANCE

	DATE		EXPLANATION	POST. REF.	DEBIT	CREDIT	BALANCE

	DATE		EXPLANATION	POST. REF.	DEBIT	CREDIT	BALANCE

	DATE		EXPLANATION	POST. REF.	DEBIT	CREDIT	BALANCE

16. Thus far, the financial accounting process has been shown to consist of five steps, namely:

a. _____

b. _____

c. _____

d. _____

e. _____

Multiple-Choice Questions

For each of the following questions, indicate the single best answer by circling the appropriate letter.

1. An account:

   a. is established for every business transaction that occurs.
   b. is a storage unit for business activity of a similar nature.
   c. must be contained in a book of original entry so that transactions can be recorded in it as they occur.
   d. title should be as specific and detailed as possible to avoid confusion.

2. Credit entries increase:

   a. assets, expenses, and dividends and decrease revenues and stockholders' equity items.
   b. assets, liabilities, and stockholders' equity items and decrease revenues, expenses, and dividends.
   c. liabilities, stockholders' equity items, and revenues and decrease assets, expenses and dividends.
   d. liabilities, expenses, and dividends and decrease assets, stockholders' equity items, and revenues.

3. Expense accounts:

   a. eventually increase the balance in retained earnings.
   b. usually have credit balances.
   c. show the costs of producing revenue during an accounting period.
   d. do all of the above.

4. Increases and decreases in a Dividends account are handled in the same manner as those in a(n):

   a. expense account because a dividend is, in reality, an expense of doing business.
   b. asset account because a dividend is something of value to the owners of the business.
   c. revenue account because a dividend provides revenue to the owners of the business.
   d. expense account because both expenses and dividends reduce the amount of retained earnings in a business.

5. Steno Service Company, Inc., performed services for customers during the month totaling $2,800, for which it billed the customers. What entry should be made?

   a. Debit Cash, $2,800; credit Service Revenue, $2,800
   b. Debit Accounts Receivable, $2,800; credit Service Revenue, $2,800
   c. Debit Accounts Receivable, $2,800; credit Cash, $2,800
   d. Debit Service Revenue, $2,800; credit Accounts Receivable, $2,800

6. Received a bill for newspaper advertising for $50. The bill will be paid in 15 days. What entry is required?

   a. Debit Advertising Expense, $50; credit Cash, $50
   b. Debit Accounts Payable, $50; credit Advertising Expense, $50
   c. Debit Accounts Payable, $50; credit Advertising Revenue, $50
   d. Debit Advertising Expense, $50; credit Accounts Payable, $50

7. Received $850 from customers in payment of bills sent to them for services performed last month. What entry is required?

   a. Debit Cash, $850; credit Service Revenue, $850
   b. Debit Accounts Receivable, $850; credit Cash, $850
   c. Debit Accounts Receivable, $850; credit Service Revenue, $850
   d. Debit Cash, $850; credit Accounts Receivable, $850

8. Welsch and Company, CPAs, purchased an electric calculator for $100 and new office chairs for $800. All items were purchased from the Office Equipment Supply Company on open account. The required entry for this purchase is which of the following?

   a. Debit Office Machines, $900; credit Accounts Payable, $900
   b. Debit Office Equipment Supply Company, $900; credit Accounts Payable, $900
   c. Debit Office Machines, $100; debit Office Furniture, $800; credit Accounts Payable, $900
   d. Debit Accounts Payable, $900; credit Office Machines, $100; credit Office Furniture, $800

9. Which of the following statements regarding debits and credits is *incorrect*?

   a. If debits exceed credits in a given account, that account will have a debit balance.
   b. The term debit refers to the right side of an account and the term credit refers to the left side of an account.
   c. Each journal entry will have equal debit and credit amounts.
   d. When an asset is debited, another asset may be credited.

10. A ledger is defined as:

    a. a collection of all business transactions.
    b. a listing of all account titles and account numbers.
    c. a collection of all accounts and their balances.
    d. a book of original entry from which transactions are posted.

11. Which of the following statements is *incorrect*?

    a. When making entries in the general journal, the accountant need not concern himself with the equality of debits and credits because this will be proven when the trial balance is prepared.
    b. The general journal is a record of business transactions in chronological sequence.
    c. Each general journal entry includes the date of the transaction, the titles of all accounts affected, and the amounts of the debits and credits related to each account affected.
    d. The use of a general journal promotes the division of labor in a business organization because one person may prepare entries, while another person posts entries to the ledger.

12. Posting is the act of:

    a. recording entries in the journal.
    b. transferring the balances in the ledger to the trial balance.
    c. tracing amounts from the journal to the ledger in order to find errors.
    d. entering amounts in the accounts in the ledger as indicated by entries in the journal.

13. Cross-indexing:

    a. provides a link between the journal and the ledger accounts.
    b. facilitates the finding of errors.
    c. reduces the likelihood of double posting or forgetting to post an item.
    d. does all of the above.

14. Debits:

    a.   increase all balance sheet accounts and decrease all income statement accounts.
    b.   increase assets and decrease dividends.
    c.   will always equal credits in a particular account.
    d.   increase expenses and decrease liabilities.

15. Which of the following statements regarding a trial balance is *incorrect*?

    a.   A trial balance is a test of the equality of the debit and credit balances in the ledger.
    b.   A trial balance is a list of all open accounts in the ledger with their balances as of a given date.
    c.   A trial balance proves that no errors have been made in the accounts during the accounting period.
    d.   A trial balance helps to localize errors within an identifiable time period.

16. Which of the following sequences of events reflects the accounting process?

    a.   Analyzing economic activities, journalizing transactions, posting, preparing a trial balance, and preparing financial statements
    b.   Analyzing economic activities, posting transactions, journalizing transactions, preparing a trial balance, and preparing financial statements
    c.   Analyzing economic activities, preparing financial statements, journalizing transactions, posting transactions, and preparing a trial balance
    d.   Analyzing economic activities, preparing a trial balance, posting transactions to a journal, and preparing financial statements

17. Dividends are shown on:

    a.   the balance sheet as assets.
    b.   the income statement as expenses.
    c.   the balance sheet as expenses.
    d.   none of the above.

18. Which of the following accounts would normally have a credit balance?

    a.   Accounts receivable
    b.   Salary expense
    c.   Dividends
    d.   Capital stock

19. Which of the following errors would cause a trial balance *not* to balance?

    a.   Not recording a transaction during the period
    b.   Recording the purchase of delivery equipment as an expense
    c.   Recording the collection of an account receivable as a debit to Cash and a credit to Accounts payable
    d.   Posting a credit of $100 as a credit of $1,000

20. Collins Corporation paid the rent for June on June 1 and made the following journal entry: debit Rent Expense and credit Cash, both for $400. When this entry was posted to the accounts, the debit was posted in the correct amount, but the credit was posted as $40. Which of the following statements is *correct*?

    a.   The trial balance will not balance and the debits will be $400 larger than the credits.
    b.   The trial balance will balance because the entry was journalized properly even though it was posted wrong.
    c.   The trial balance will not balance and the credits will be larger than the debits by $360.
    d.   The trial balance will not balance and the debits will be larger than the credits by $360.

Now compare your answers with the correct ones beginning on page 36.

Solutions/Chapter 2

Completion and Exercises

1. account; increases; decreases

2. useful information

3. balance

4.

Assets		Liabilities		Stockholders' Equity	
increases	decreases	decreases	increases	decreases	increases

5. left; right

6. right; right

7. left; left

8. debit; credit

9.

Type of Account	Increased by	Decreased by
Asset	Debits	Credits
Liability	Credits	Debits
Stockholders' Equity	Credits	Debits
Revenue	Credits	Debits
Expense	Debits	Credits

10. ledger; chart of accounts

11. journal; debit(s); credit(s)

12. journalizing; posted; ledger; cross-indexing

13. trial balance

DATE		ACCOUNT TITLES AND EXPLANATION	POST. REF.	DEBIT	CREDIT
19— Jan.	1	Cash		5 0 0 0 0 00	
		Capital Stock			5 0 0 0 0 00
		Cash invested in business.			
	10	Rent Expense		4 0 0 00	
		Cash			4 0 0 00
		Rent for January, 19—.			
	13	Accounts Receivable		6 0 0 00	
		Fees Earned			6 0 0 00
		To record fees earned for services.			
	20	Equipment		4 0 0 0 00	
		Accounts Payable			4 0 0 0 00
		Purchased equipment on credit.			
	30	Cash		6 0 0 00	
		Accounts Receivable			6 0 0 00
		Received cash on account.			

15.

Cash   ACCOUNT NO.

DATE		EXPLANATION	POST. REF.	DEBIT	CREDIT	BALANCE
19— Jan.	1		G-1	50 0 0 0 00		50 0 0 0 00
	10		G-1		4 0 0 00	49 6 0 0 00
	30		G-1	6 0 0 00		50 2 0 0 00

Accounts Receivable   ACCOUNT NO.

DATE		EXPLANATION	POST. REF.	DEBIT	CREDIT	BALANCE
19— Jan.	13		G-1	6 0 0 00		6 0 0 00
	30		G-1		6 0 0 00	0

15. (concluded)

Equipment | ACCOUNT NO.

DATE		EXPLANATION	POST. REF.	DEBIT	CREDIT	BALANCE
19— Jan.	20		G-1	4 0 0 0 00		4 0 0 0 00

Accounts Payable | ACCOUNT NO.

DATE		EXPLANATION	POST. REF.	DEBIT	CREDIT	BALANCE
19— Jan.	20		G-1		4 0 0 0 00	4 0 0 0 00

Capital Stock | ACCOUNT NO.

DATE		EXPLANATION	POST. REF.	DEBIT	CREDIT	BALANCE
19— Jan.	1		G-1		50 0 0 0 00	50 0 0 0 00

Fees Earned | ACCOUNT NO.

DATE		EXPLANATION	POST. REF.	DEBIT	CREDIT	BALANCE
19— Jan.	13		G-1		6 0 0 00	6 0 0 00

Rent Expense | ACCOUNT NO.

DATE		EXPLANATION	POST. REF.	DEBIT	CREDIT	BALANCE
19— Jan.	10		G-1	4 0 0 00		4 0 0 00

16. analyzing business transactions, journalizing transactions, posting to the ledger, taking a trial balance, and preparing financial statements.

Multiple-Choice Questions

1. b. This is the definition of an account.

2. c. Since liabilities and stockholders' equity are both equity items, they are treated in the same manner. Revenues also increase stockholders' equity and are therefore credited to show increases. All other accounts are handled in the opposite manner.

3. c. Revenues, not expenses, bring about an increase in retained earnings. Expense accounts generally have debit balances and represent the costs of producing revenue in an accounting period. They are disclosed on the income statement.

4. d. A dividend is not an expense of doing business, but increases and decreases are handled in the same manner as those of expenses, because both expenses and dividends serve to reduce the amount of retained earnings in a business organization.

5. b. An asset (Accounts Receivable) is increased because the customers are obligated to pay for the work performed and the company earned revenue, and therefore the increase in revenue is recorded as a credit to that account.

6. d. An expense has been incurred, and therefore an increase to that account is recorded with a debit. The bill has not yet been paid, but is owed (a liability) by the business (an additional liability, therefore, a credit).

7. d. Cash (an asset) has increased and is therefore debited, while another asset, Accounts Receivable, has decreased which is recorded by a credit to that account.

8. c. Both the amount of Office Equipment and the amount of Office Furniture is important, so an account will be maintained for both pieces of data. These are both assets and are debited when increased in amount. The firm owes for the items on open account, so a liability has also increased, and Accounts Payable is credited to reflect that fact.

9. b. The term debit refers to the left side of an account and the term credit refers to the right side.

10. c. All accounts and their respective balances appear in the ledger. Entries are posted to these accounts which, in turn, change the balances.

11. a. Although the inequality of debits and credits will be reflected when a trial balance is prepared, if the accountant pays attention on an ongoing basis while recording transactions there is less likelihood that such an inequality will exist.

12. d. Posting always goes from the journal to the ledger. The entries in the journal indicate the appropriate accounts and amounts affected by a transaction.

13. d. Cross-indexing accomplishes a, b, and c, and indexing is done in both the journal (indexed to place of posting in the ledger) and the ledger (place information is found in journal).

14. d. Debits increase assets, expenses, and dividends, and decrease liabilities, stockholders' equity items, and revenues. Although debits and credits will be equal in amount in each transaction, they will not be equal in each account because the debit and credit are each posted to separate accounts. If all accounts had equal debits and credits, no account could have a balance.

15. c. A trial balance that is in-balance fails to prove that no errors have been made in the accounts. For instance, if a debit were made to the wrong account, the trial balance would not aid in discovering the error. Total debits would still be equal to total credits.

16. a. This is not the entire sequence of events, however. Additional items will be covered in later chapters. This is the sequence of events up to this point in time.

17. d. Dividends are shown on the statement of retained earnings.

18. d. Stockholders' equity accounts generally have credit balances and capital stock is a stockholders' equity account.

19. d. Since the credit was made $900 larger than the debit, the trial balance would not balance. Items a, b, and c would cause the trial balance to be incorrect, but it would still be in balance.

20. d. Since the debit was posted for $400 and the credit was posted for only $40, the trial balance will be out-of-balance by the difference of $360. Debits would be larger than credits, because the larger posting was made as a debit.

Name _____

_____

(a)

COLE COMPANY
T-Accounts

Cash

Capital Stock

Accounts Receivable

Dividends

Service Revenue

Truck

Wages Expense

Accounts Payable

Supplies Expense

Notes Payable

Gas and Oil Expense

(b)   COLE COMPANY
_____ Trial Balance _____
                                        August 31, 1990

		DEBITS	CREDITS	
	Cash			

Name _____

_____

(a)

ROBIN COMPANY
T-Accounts

Cash	Capital Stock

Accounts Receivable	Fee Revenue

Office Furniture	Advertising Expense

	Wages Expense

Accounts Payable	

	Rent Expense

(b)   ROBIN COMPANY

                                         Trial Balance

                                        July 31, 1990

		DEBITS	CREDITS
	Cash		
	Accounts receivable		

Name _____

_____

TATE COMPANY
GENERAL JOURNAL   Page 1

DATE	ACCOUNT TITLES AND EXPLANATION	POST. REF.	DEBIT	CREDIT

TATE COMPANY
GENERAL JOURNAL

Page 2

DATE	ACCOUNT TITLES AND EXPLANATION	POST. REF.	DEBIT	CREDIT	

Name _____

_(a)_   GUYSON COMPANY

Income Statement

For the Year Ended December 31, 1990

_(b)_   GUYSON COMPANY

Statement of Retained Earnings

For the Year Ended December 31, 1990

Name _____

_____

MOSS COMPANY
GENERAL JOURNAL

(b)   Page 1

DATE	ACCOUNT TITLES AND EXPLANATION	POST. REF.	DEBIT	CREDIT

(b) (concluded)

MOSS COMPANY
GENERAL JOURNAL

Page 2

DATE	ACCOUNT TITLES AND EXPLANATION	POST. REF.	DEBIT	CREDIT

(a) (c)

	Cash				ACCOUNT NO. 1
DATE 1990	EXPLANATION	POST. REF.	DEBIT	CREDIT	BALANCE

	Accounts Receivable				ACCOUNT NO. 2
DATE 1990	EXPLANATION	POST. REF.	DEBIT	CREDIT	BALANCE

	Office Equipment				ACCOUNT NO. 11
DATE 1990	EXPLANATION	POST. REF.	DEBIT	CREDIT	BALANCE

Name _____

_(a) (c)_ (continued)

Trucks   ACCOUNT NO. _12_

DATE 1990		EXPLANATION	POST. REF.	DEBIT	CREDIT	BALANCE

ACCOUNT NO.

DATE 1990		EXPLANATION	POST. REF.	DEBIT	CREDIT	BALANCE

ACCOUNT NO.

DATE 1990		EXPLANATION	POST. REF.	DEBIT	CREDIT	BALANCE

ACCOUNT NO.

DATE 1990		EXPLANATION	POST. REF.	DEBIT	CREDIT	BALANCE

(a)(c) (continued)

ACCOUNT NO. _____

DATE 1990	EXPLANATION	POST. REF.	DEBIT	CREDIT	BALANCE

ACCOUNT NO. _____

DATE 1990	EXPLANATION	POST. REF.	DEBIT	CREDIT	BALANCE

ACCOUNT NO. _____

DATE 1990	EXPLANATION	POST. REF.	DEBIT	CREDIT	BALANCE

ACCOUNT NO. _____

DATE 1990	EXPLANATION	POST. REF.	DEBIT	CREDIT	BALANCE

(a) (c) (continued)

ACCOUNT NO. ____

DATE 1990	EXPLANATION	POST. REF.	DEBIT	CREDIT	BALANCE

ACCOUNT NO. ____

DATE 1990	EXPLANATION	POST. REF.	DEBIT	CREDIT	BALANCE

ACCOUNT NO. ____

DATE 1990	EXPLANATION	POST. REF.	DEBIT	CREDIT	BALANCE

ACCOUNT NO. ____

DATE 1990	EXPLANATION	POST. REF.	DEBIT	CREDIT	BALANCE

(a) (c) (concluded)

ACCOUNT NO.

DATE 1990	EXPLANATION	POST. REF.	DEBIT	CREDIT	BALANCE

ACCOUNT NO.

DATE 1990	EXPLANATION	POST. REF.	DEBIT	CREDIT	BALANCE

ACCOUNT NO.

DATE 1990	EXPLANATION	POST. REF.	DEBIT	CREDIT	BALANCE

(d) _____ MOSS COMPANY _____

Trial Balance

December 31, 1990

ACCT. NO.	ACCOUNT TITLE	DEBITS	CREDITS
1	Cash		
2	Accounts receivable		

Name _____

_____

(e)

MOSS COMPANY

Income Statement

For the Year Ended December 31, 1990

(f)

MOSS COMPANY

Statement of Retained Earnings

For the Year Ended December 31, 1990

(g)   MOSS COMPANY
                                        Balance Sheet
                                     December 31, 1986

ASSETS

LIABILITIES AND STOCKHOLDERS' EQUITY

(a)

(b)   *Exhibit A*
                              Approximate Income Statement for 1990

3

Adjusting Entries and Completion of the Accounting Cycle

Understanding the Learning Objectives

1. Identify why adjusting entries must be made.

    *   Adjusting entries are needed to convert the amounts that are actually in the accounts to the amounts that should be in the accounts for proper financial reporting.

    *   Many business events such as the using up of insurance coverage are known as continuous events. Continuous events are usually recorded periodically in adjusting entries before financial statements are to be prepared.

2. Describe the basic characteristics of the cash basis and the accrual basis of accounting.

    *   Under the cash basis of accounting, expenses and revenues usually are not recorded until cash is paid out or received.

    *   Under the accrual basis of accounting, revenues are recognized when sales are made or services are rendered, and expenses are recognized as incurred.

    *   The accrual basis is more generally accepted than the cash basis because it provides a better matching of revenues and expenses.

3. Identify the classes and types of adjusting entries.

    *   Deferred items consist of those entries that relate to data previously recorded in the accounts. Adjusting entries in this class normally involve moving data from asset and liability accounts to expense and revenue accounts. The two types of adjustments within this deferred items class are asset/expense adjustments and liability/revenue adjustments.

    *   Accrued items consist of entries relating to activities on which no data have been previously recorded in the accounts. These entries involve the initial recording of assets and liabilities and the related revenues and expenses. The two types of adjustments within this accrued items class are asset/revenue adjustments and liability/expense adjustments.

4. Prepare adjusting entries.

    *   Entries for deferred items and accrued items are illustrated in the chapter.

5. Prepare closing entries.

* Closing entries are necessary to reduce the balances of expense and revenue accounts to zero so they are ready to receive data for the next accounting period.

* Expense accounts are closed by crediting them and debiting Income Summary.

* Revenue accounts are closed by debiting them and crediting Income Summary.

* The Income Summary account is closed by debiting the account if there is net income for the period and crediting Retained Earnings.

* If a separate Dividends account is used, it must be closed by crediting Dividends and debiting Retained Earnings.

6. Prepare a classified balance sheet.

* A classified balance sheet subdivides the major categories on the balance sheet into subcategories. For instance, assets are subdivided into current assets; long-term investments; property, plant, and equipment; and intangible assets. Liabilities are subdivided into current liabilities and long-term liabilities.

7. Prepare a work sheet for a service company.

* A work sheet for a service company is shown in Illustration 3.4.

8. Define and use correctly the new terms in the glossary.

The new terms introduced in the chapter are as follows:

Accounting period—A time period normally of one month, one quarter, or one year into which an entity's life is arbitrarily divided for financial reporting purposes.

Accounting year (fiscal year)—An accounting period of one year. The accounting year may or may not coincide with the calendar year.

Accounts payable—Amounts owed to creditors for items purchased from them.

Accounts receivable—Amounts owed to a business by customers (debtors).

Accrual basis of accounting—Recognizes revenues when sales are made or services are performed, regardless of when cash is received. Recognizes expenses as incurred whether or not cash has been paid out.

Accrued—A claim that comes into existence over time.

Accrued assets and liabilities—Assets and liabilities that exist at the end of an accounting period but have not yet been recorded; they represent rights to receive, or obligations to make, payments that are not legally due at the balance sheet date. Examples are accrued fees receivable and salaries payable.

Accrued items—See accrued assets and liabilities.

Accrued wages payable—Amounts owed to employees for services rendered.

Accumulated depreciation account—A contra asset account that shows the total of all depreciation on the asset up to the balance sheet date.

Adjusting entries—Journal entries made at the end of an accounting period to change the balance of certain accounts; they reflect economic activity that has taken place but has not yet been recorded. Adjusting entries are made to bring the accounts to their proper balances before financial statements are prepared.

Bonds payable—Written promises to pay a definite sum at a certain date as evidenced by formal printed certificates that are sometimes secured by liens on property, such as mortgages.

Book value—For depreciable assets, book value equals cost less accumulated depreciation.

Buildings—Structures in which business is carried out.

Calendar year—The normal year ending on December 31.

Capital stock—Shows the capital paid in to the company as the stockholders' investment.

Cash—Includes deposits in banks available for current operations at the balance sheet date, plus cash on hand consisting of currency, undeposited checks, drafts, and money orders.

Cash basis of accounting—Recognizes revenues when cash is received and recognizes expenses when cash is paid out.

Classified balance sheet—Subdivides at least some of the major categories (assets, liabilities, and stockholders' equity) in order to provide useful information for interpretation and analysis by users of financial statements.

Closing process—The act of transferring the balances in the revenue and expense accounts to a clearing account called Income Summary and then to the Retained Earnings account.

The balance in the Dividends account is also transferred to the Retained Earnings account.

Contra account—An account that is directly related to another account.

Contra asset account—An account shown as a deduction from the asset to which it relates in the balance sheet; used to give interested parties more complete financial information.

Copyright—Grants the owner the exclusive privilege of publication of written material.

Current assets—Cash and other assets that will be converted into cash or used up by the business during a relatively short period of time, usually a year or less.

Current liabilities—Debts, usually due within one year, the payment of which normally will require the use of current assets.

Deferred items—Those items involving data previously recorded in the accounts. Data are transferred from asset and liability accounts to expense and revenue accounts. Examples are prepaid expenses, depreciation, and unearned revenues.

Delivery equipment—Trucks used to deliver goods to customers.

Depreciable asset—A building, machine, vehicle, or equipment on which depreciation expense is recorded.

Depreciable cost—The difference between an asset's cost and its estimated salvage value.

Depreciation accounting—The process of recording depreciation expense.

Depreciation expense—The amount of asset cost assigned as an expense to a particular time period.

Depreciation formula (straight-line)—

$$\frac{\text{Asset cost} - \text{Estimated scrap value}}{\text{Estimated number of years of useful life}} = \text{Annual depreciation}$$

Dividends payable—Amounts declared payable to stockholders that represent a distribution of income.

Fiscal year—An accounting year of 12 consecutive months that may or may not coincide with the calendar year. For example, a company may have an accounting or fiscal year that runs from April 1 of one year to March 31 of the next.

Goodwill—An intangible value attaching to a business evidenced by the ability to earn larger net income per dollar of investment than that earned by competitors within the same industry.

Income Summary Account—A clearing account used only at the end of an accounting period to summarize revenues and expenses for the period.

Intangible assets—Noncurrent, nonphysical assets of a business.

Interest payable—Arises when interest has been incurred but not yet paid at the balance sheet date because the amount is not due until later.

Interest receivable—Arises when interest has been earned but has not been collected at the balance sheet date.

Land—Ground on which the business buildings of the company are located.

Leaseholds—Rights to use leased properties.

Long-term investment—Usually securities of another company that the owner expects to hold over long periods of time, usually more than one year.

Long-term liabilities—Liabilities not due for a relatively long period of time, usually more than one year.

Machinery—Heavy equipment used in manufacturing a product or performing a service for a customer.

Marketable securities—Readily salable securities acquired with temporarily unneeded cash.

Matching principle—An accounting principle requiring that expenses incurred in producing revenues be deducted from the revenues they generated during the accounting period.

Note payable—An unconditional written promise to pay a definite sum of money at a certain or determinable date, usually with interest at a specified rate.

Office equipment (office fixtures)—Items such as file cabinets, calculators, typewriters, computers, desks, and chairs.

Patent—A right granted by the federal government to an inventor or the owner of an invention whereby he or she alone has the authority to manufacture a product or to use a process for a period of time.

Prepaid expense—An asset that is awaiting assignment to expense. An example is prepaid insurance. Assets such as cash and accounts receivable are not prepaid expenses.

Property, plant, and equipment—They are acquired for use in a business rather than for resale; also called plant assets or fixed assets.

Retained earnings—Show the cumulative income of the company less the amounts distributed to the owners in the form of dividends.

Scrap value (salvage value)—The amount for which an asset can probably be sold at the end of its estimated useful life.

Service potential—The benefits that can be obtained from assets. The future services that assets can render make assets "things of value" to a business.

Stockholders' equity—Shows the owners' interest (equity) in the business.

Store equipment (store fixtures)—Items such as showcases, counters, tools, chairs, and cash registers.

Taxes withheld from employees—Income taxes and social security taxes withheld from employees.

Unclassified balance sheet—Has only major categories labeled assets, liabilities, and stockholders' equity.

Unearned revenue—Assets received from customers before services are performed for them. Since the revenue has not been earned, it is a liability, often called *revenue received in advance,* or *advances by customers.*

Useful life—The estimated number of periods that a company can make use of an asset.

Work sheet—A columnar sheet of paper on which accountants have summarized information needed to make the adjusting and closing entries and to prepare the financial statements.

Completion and Exercises

1. Because economic activity occurs continuously, not solely in the transactions that the accountant records, _____ _____ usually must be prepared prior to the preparation of financial statements.

2. Some small businesses, especially those rendering services, may employ _____ basis accounting. But most business firms use _____ basis accounting.

3. Assume that a consulting company rendered services for a client in 1989 and collected cash for those services in 1990. Under cash basis accounting, revenue would be recognized in _____ , while under accrual basis accounting revenue would be recognized in _____ . Generally speaking, under cash basis accounting, revenue is recognized _____

   _____ .

4. Assume that a company received services from its employees in 1989 for which it had previously agreed it would pay $6,000. This sum was paid in 1990. The $6,000 would be treated as an expense of the year

   _____ under cash basis accounting and of the year _____ under accrual basis accounting. Generally speaking, under cash basis accounting, expenses are recognized in the account-

   ing system when _____ .

5. One expense that would probably be recognized in the same period under both the cash and accrual bases of accounting is _____ .

6. The two major classes of adjusting entries are _____ and _____ .

7. The four major types of adjusting entries are:

   (a) _____ , (b) _____ ,

   (c) _____ , and (d) _____ .

   But every adjusting entry will involve one account that is reported in the _____

   _____ and another account that is reported in the _____ .

8. The process whereby the cost (less scrap value) of a long-lived asset used in a business is allocated to the periods in which it is used is called _____ . The amount of cost allocated to each period is called _____ .

9. When depreciation is recorded it is credited to a contra account called _____

   _____ and reported in the _____

   _____ as a _____ from the depreciable asset to which it relates.

10. Depreciation expense is an _____ expense that is closed, at the end of the accounting year, to the _____ _____ account.

11. The Ross Company has a monthly payroll of $200,000 and its employees are paid monthly on the 1st. The adjusting entry required on December 31 (the end of the company's fiscal year) would involve a debit of

    $_____ to the _____ _____ account and a credit of

    $_____ to the _____ _____ _____ account.

12. The Hall Company owns a warehouse that it leases to others for $2,000 per month that is collected in semiannual installments on March 31 and September 30. The preferred entry required to record the receipt of the advance payment of rent on September 30 would involve a debit of $ _____ to the _____ account and a credit of $ _____ to the _____ _____ _____ _____ account.

13. Refer to the data in (12). If monthly adjusting entries are made, the entry required on October 31 would consist of a debit to _____ _____ _____ _____ _____ and a credit to _____ _____ in the amount of $ _____ .

14. Assume that the six basic elements in accounting consist of assets, liabilities, stockholders' equity, revenues, expenses, and net income. If the Ross Company, in (11) above, failed to make the required adjusting entry, its financial statements for the period ending December 31 would show too much _____ _____ and _____ _____ and too little _____ and _____ .

15. Refer to the data in (13) above. If financial statements are to be prepared for the period ending October 31 and if the Hall Company failed to make the required adjusting entry, it would have overstated its _____ _____ and understated its _____ , _____ _____ , and _____ _____ .

16. Apex Company purchased store supplies costing $450 during the quarter that were charged to an asset account. Its beginning inventory of store supplies was $150. The end-of-quarter balance sheet showed store supplies on hand of $75. The amount charged to Store Supplies Expense and credited to Store Supplies on Hand was _____ .

17. A theater offered theater ticket books for use at future performances to its patrons at $50 per book for 5 tickets per book. During the year, 1,200 books were sold and this amount was erroneously credited to Theater Revenue. At the end of the period it was determined that 2,400 tickets of the book sales had been used at the box office. The appropriate adjusting entry at the end of the period would be:

17. (concluded) GENERAL JOURNAL

DATE	ACCOUNT TITLES AND EXPLANATION	POST. REF.	DEBIT	CREDIT

18. Baker Company started operations on December 1, 19—. Employees earn $85 per day and work a six-day week. There are twenty-seven work days in December. By the last pay period in December (December 27), the employees had been paid $1,955.

Required:

Prepare the adjustment needed on December 31.

GENERAL JOURNAL

DATE	ACCOUNT TITLES AND EXPLANATION	POST. REF.	DEBIT	CREDIT

19. State the effect that each of the following would have on the amount of net income reported for 1990 and 1991 and assets and liabilities as of December 31, 1990. The firm's accounting period ends on December 31.

a. A collection in 1990 of $700 for services rendered in 1989 was credited to a revenue account in 1990.

19. (concluded)

    b. The collection of $400 for services not yet performed as of December 31, 1990, is credited to a revenue account and not adjusted. The services are to be performed next year in 1991.

    c. No adjustment is made for accrued salaries of $1,000 as of December 31, 1990.

20. Given the following account balances, prepare the closing entries:

	Dr.	Cr.
Service revenue		$1,950
Salaries expense	$600	
Insurance expense	150	
Utilities expense	90	
Miscellaneous expense	30	
Supplies expense	120	
Rent expense	180	
Depreciation expense-equipment	45	

GENERAL JOURNAL

DATE	ACCOUNT TITLES AND EXPLANATION	POST. REF.	DEBIT	CREDIT

21. A balance sheet that separates the assets and liabilities into categories is called a _____ balance sheet.

(Based on appendix.)

22. Use the information given below to complete the work sheet for the Barney Company.

    a. Supplies on hand at December 31, 1990: $60.
    b. Rent expense for 1990: $180.
    c. Depreciation on equipment for 1990: $45.

BARNEY COMPANY
Work Sheet
For the Year Ended December 31, 1990

Account Title	Unadjusted Trial Balance		Adjustments		Adjusted Trial Balance		Income Statement		Statement of Retained Earnings		Balance Sheet	
	Dr.	Cr.	Dr.	Cr.	Dr.	Cr.	Dr.	Cr.	Dr.	Cr.	Dr.	Cr.
Cash	300											
Accounts receivable	600											
Supplies on hand	180											
Prepaid rent	240											
Equipment	600											
Accumulated depr.—equip.		180										
Accounts payable		270										
Capital stock		300										
Retained earnings, 1/1/90		90										
Service revenue		1,950										
Salaries expense	600											
Insurance expense	150											
Utilities expense	90											
Miscellaneous expense	30											
	2,790	2,790										

Multiple-Choice Questions

For each of the following questions, indicate the single best answer by circling the appropriate letter.

1. Which of the following statements is *incorrect*?

   a. The cash basis of accounting is appropriate if the results approximate those that would be achieved under the accrual basis of accounting.

   b. The accrual basis of accounting recognizes revenues when sales are made or services are rendered rather than when cash is received.

   c. The accrual basis of accounting provides a better measure of net income of a business due to proper matching of revenues and expenses.

   d. The accrual basis of accounting must be applied on a calendar year basis from January 1 to December 31 as the reporting period.

2. Adjusting entries:

   a. record economic activity that has not yet taken place, but that is expected to occur within the next accounting period.

   b. are based in part upon estimates of future events.

   c. will be recorded at the end of each day's business activities.

   d. all of the above are true regarding adjusting entries.

3. A major class of adjusting entries is adjustments for accrued items. Such adjustments include which of the following types of entries?

   a. Asset/revenue and liability/expense adjustments

   b. Asset/expense and liability/revenue adjustments

   c. Asset/liability and revenue/expense adjustments

   d. Asset/cash and liability/expense adjustments

4. On December 31, the end of an annual accounting period, interest in the amount of $1,000 has been earned but has not been received. The correct entry on December 31 is:

   a. No entry

   b. Cash 1,000
      Interest Revenue   1,000

   c. Accrued Interest Receivable 1,000
      Interest Revenue   1,000

   d. Accounts Receivable 1,000
      Interest Expense   1,000

5. Robbie's Restaurant paid a two-year insurance premium of $2,400 on September 1, 1990. The appropriate journal entry on December 31, 1990 (Robbie's is a calendar year company), is:

   a. Prepaid Insurance 400
      Insurance Expense   400

   b. Insurance Expense 1,200
      Prepaid Insurance............   1,200

   c. Prepaid Insurance 2,400
      Cash   2,400

   d. Insurance Expense 400
      Prepaid Insurance............   400

6. On October 1, 1990, Fred's Flower Corporation prepaid rent for a year amounting to $6,000. At that time, the bookkeeper debited Rent Expense. At the end of 1990, Fred's prepared adjusting entries. What entry would be necessary in regard to the rent?

   a. Rent Expense 1,500
        Prepaid Rent.................   1,500
   b. Prepaid Rent 4,500
        Rent Expense   4,500
   c. Rent Expense 4,500
        Prepaid Rent.................   4,500
   d. No entry is necessary

7. On June 30, the close of the monthly accounting period, employees of the O'Callaghan Company have earned salaries totaling $1,200 payable on the payday of July 3. The entry required on June 30 is:

   a. Salary Expense................... 1,200
        Accrued Salaries Payable   1,200
   b. Accrued Salaries Payable 1,200
        Salary Expense   1,200
   c. Salary Expense................... 1,200
        Cash   1,200
   d. No entry is necessary

8. Morris Corporation had $1,500 of office supplies at the beginning of 1990. During the year, Morris purchased $6,000 of office supplies. On December 31, 1990, a physical inventory of supplies was taken and it was determined that there were $2,000 of office supplies on hand at that time. If Morris debited an asset account upon the purchase of the office supplies during the year, what journal entry should be made related to office supplies at year-end?

   a. Supplies on Hand 2,000
        Supplies Expense   2,000
   b. Supplies on Hand 5,500
        Supplies Expense   5,500
   c. Supplies Expense 2,000
        Supplies on Hand   2,000
   d. Supplies Expense 5,500
        Supplies on Hand   5,500

9. Office furniture is purchased on October 1, 1990, at a cost of $3,400. Estimated scrap value is $200 and its estimated useful life is four years. The entry to record depreciation on December 31 at the close of the annual accounting period is:

   a. Depreciation Expense—Office Furniture 800
        Accumulated Depreciation—Office Furniture   800
   b. Depreciation Expense—Office Furniture 200
        Accumulated Depreciation—Office Furniture   200
   c. Depreciation Expense—Office Furniture 200
        Office Furniture   200
   d. Accumulated Depreciation—Office Furniture 800
        Office Furniture   800

10. Myra's Boutique purchased $9,000 of store equipment on January 1, 1989. The estimated scrap value is $1,000 and the estimated useful life is four years. After the adjusting entry in *1990*, the balance in the Accumulated Depreciation account will be:

    a. $9,000.
    b. $8,000.
    c. $4,000.
    d. $2,000.

79

11. Business World magazine received 100 subscriptions to its publication on May 31, 1990. Each subscription was accompanied by a check for $36 that represented a monthly subscription amount of $3. Business World prepares adjusting entries on December 31. Before adjustment in 1990, the company showed a liability account related to these subscriptions with a balance of $3,600. What adjusting entry should be made on December 31, 1990?

    a.   Unearned Subscription Revenue   1,500
               Magazine Subscription Revenue   1,500
    b.   Unearned Subscription Revenue   2,100
               Magazine Subscription Revenue   2,100
    c.   Magazine Subscription Revenue   1,500
               Unearned Subscription Revenue   1,500
    d.   Magazine Subscription Revenue   2,100
               Unearned Subscription Revenue   2,100

12. Using the same information as above, except that on December 31, 1990, Business World showed a balance in a revenue account related to these subscriptions of $3,600, what adjusting entry would be made?

    a.   Unearned Subscription Revenue   2,100
               Magazine Subscription Revenue   2,100
    b.   Unearned Subscription Revenue   1,500
               Magazine Subscription Revenue   1,500
    c.   Magazine Subscription Revenue   2,100
               Unearned Subscription Revenue   2,100
    d.   Magazine Subscription Revenue   1,500
               Unearned Subscription Revenue   1,500

13. Prior to the recording of adjusting entries, the revenues of X Company exceeded its expenses by $45,000. Adjusting entries were made at year-end to record commissions receivable of $5,000, depreciation of $6,000, and accrued wages of $3,000. X Company's net income for the year is:

    a. $31,000.
    b. $41,000.
    c. $49,000.
    d. $53,000.

14. Which of the following accounts is closed by an entry which includes a debit to Income Summary?

    a.   Service Revenue
    b.   Accounts Payable
    c.   Dividends
    d.   Rent Expense

15. After the accounts have been closed:

    a.   the Asset, Liability, and Stockholders' Equity accounts have zero balances.
    b.   the Revenue, Expense, Income Summary, and Retained Earnings accounts have zero balances.
    c.   the Revenue, Expense, Income Summary, and Stockholders' Equity accounts have zero balances.
    d.   the Revenue, Expense, Income Summary, and Dividends accounts have zero balances.

16. Which of the following would *not* be classified as a current asset?

    a.   Accounts Receivable
    b.   Prepaid insurance covering a one-year policy
    c.   Note receivable due in 6 months
    d.   Note receivable due in 18 months

(The remaining questions are based on the appendix.)

17. Which of the following statements is *true* concerning the work sheet?

    a.   It is a formal accounting statement that is distributed to owners and managers.
    b.   The accounting process could not be completed without the preparation of a work sheet.
    c.   The work sheet must contain either 11 or 12 columns.
    d.   The accountant can use any format he or she wishes in designing a work sheet.

18. Which of the following items would *not* be useful in determining what adjusting entries need to be made at the end of a period?

    a.   The work sheet of the prior period
    b.   The financial statements of the current period
    c.   The accounts appearing in the trial balance of the current period
    d.   Various business documents

19. Supplies on Hand are shown at $315 in the Unadjusted Trial Balance columns of the work sheet. The Adjustments columns show that $290 of these supplies were used during the month. The amount shown as supplies on hand in the Balance Sheet columns is a:

    a. $25 debit.
    b. $315 debit.
    c. $290 debit.
    d. $25 credit.

20. On a work sheet, a net loss would appear in the:

    a.   Income Statement debit column only.
    b.   Income Statement credit column only.
    c.   Income Statement debit column and Retained Earnings credit column.
    d.   Income Statement credit column and Retained Earnings debit column.

Now compare your answers with the correct ones beginning on page 82.

Solutions/Chapter 3

Completion and Exercises

1. adjusting entries

2. cash; accrual

3. 1990; 1989; when cash is received

4. 1990; 1989; they are paid in cash

5. depreciation expense

6. deferrals; accruals

7. asset/expense adjustments (prepaid assets); liability/revenue adjustments (unearned revenues); asset/revenue adjustments (accrued assets); liability/expense adjustments (accrued liabilities); balance sheet; income statement

8. depreciation accounting; depreciation (or depreciation expense)

9. Accumulated Depreciation; balance sheet; deduction

10. operating; Income Summary

11. $200,000; Wages Expense; $200,000; Accrued Wages Payable

12. $12,000; Cash; $12,000; Rent Received in Advance (Unearned Rent)

13. Rent Received in Advance; Rent Revenue; $2,000

14. stockholders' equity; net income; liabilities; expenses

15. liabilities; revenues; net income; stockholders' equity

16. $525; $150 + $450 purchases = $600 available for use − $75 ending inventory = $525.

17. Theater Revenue 36,000
        Unearned Theater Revenue   36,000

    1,200 × $50 = $60,000 credited to Theater Rev.
            − 24,000 Rev. earned
            $36,000 Unearned Theater Rev.

18. Salary Expense....................... 340
        Accrued Salaries Payable..........   340

            $2,295 (27 days × $85)
        − 1,955 paid to employees
          $ 340 adjustment

19. a. Net income is overstated in 1990 by $700. Accounts Receivable (an asset) would be overstated as of 12-31-90 by $700 because the claim against the customer was not credited at the time of collection in 1990. There is no effect on liabilities or on 1991 net income.
    b. Revenue for 1990 is overstated, causing net income to be overstated by $400. In the following year, 1991 revenue and net income will be understated by $400 assuming the services are performed in that year. Liabilities are understated by $400 as of 12-31-90. There is no effect on assets.
    c. Net income for 1990 would be overstated by $1,000 because salaries expense is understated. The following year, 1991, net income would be understated by $1,000 since salaries expense would be overstated assuming all other salaries incurred in 1991 are correctly recognized. Salaries Payable (a liability) would be understated by $1,000 as of 12-31-90. There is no effect on assets.

20. a.   Service Revenue 1,950
           Income Summary   1,950

    b.   Income Summary 1,215
           Salaries Expense......................   600
           Insurance Expense   150
           Utilities Expense   90
           Miscellaneous Expense   30
           Supplies Expense   120
           Rent Expense   180
           Depreciation Expense—Equipment......   45

    c.   Income Summary 735
           Retained Earnings.....................   735

21. classified

22.

BARNEY COMPANY
Work Sheet
For the Year Ended December 31, 1990

Account Title	Unadjusted Trial Balance Dr.	Unadjusted Trial Balance Cr.	Adjustments Dr.	Adjustments Cr.	Adjusted Trial Balance Dr.	Adjusted Trial Balance Cr.	Income Statement Dr.	Income Statement Cr.	Statement of Retained Earnings Dr.	Statement of Retained Earnings Cr.	Balance Sheet Dr.	Balance Sheet Cr.
Cash	300				300						300	
Accounts receivable	600				600						600	
Supplies on hand	180			(a) 120	60						60	
Prepaid rent	240			(b) 180	60						60	
Equipment	600				600						600	
Accumulated depr.—equip.		180		(c) 45		225						225
Accounts payable		270				270						270
Capital stock		300				300						300
Retained earnings, 1/1/90		90				90				90		
Service revenue		1,950				1,950		1,950				
Salaries expense	600				600		600					
Insurance expense	150				150		150					
Utilities expense	90				90		90					
Miscellaneous expense	30				30		30					
	2,790	2,790										
Supplies expense			(a) 120		120		120					
Rent expense			(b) 180		180		180					
Depreciation exp.—equip.			(c) 45		45		45					
			345	345	2,835	2,835	1,215	1,950				
Net income							735		-0-	735		
							1,950	1,950	825	825		
Retained earnings, 12/31									825			825
											1,620	1,620

Multiple-Choice Questions

1. d. The accrual basis of accounting can be applied to any fiscal year or any other shorter reporting period used by a business.

2. b. Adjusting entries record activity that has already taken place but that has not yet been recorded. Many estimates are used, including the scrap and life estimates necessary to record depreciation expense.

3. a. Accruals include adjustments for asset/revenue items (such as recording unbilled revenues) and liability/expense items (such as recording salaries earned by employees but unpaid at the end of the period).

4. c. Two items are missing prior to the adjusting entry in the accounting records: the amount of interest earned and the amount of interest which we have the right to receive. Therefore, to reflect the appropriate assets and income of the period, the receivable is debited and the revenue is credited.

5. d. Each month would have an insurance cost of $100 ($2,400/24 months). Therefore, four months of insurance have expired as of December 31 and need to be reflected as an expense with a corresponding reduction in the value of the asset.

6. b. Each month would have a rent expense of $500 ($6,000/12 months). Therefore, since all rent was reflected as an expense when paid, the adjusting entry needs to reflect the proper amount of the asset (9 months left × $500) while correspondingly reducing the expense.

7. a. The O'Callaghan Company needs to accrue the salaries by increasing an expense account and increasing a liability account. Since the amount is for employees' salaries, the appropriate account title for the liability should indicate this.

8. d. During the year, Morris Corporation had a total of $7,500 available for use ($1,500 at the beginning plus $6,000 purchased). If only $2,000 were on hand at the end of the year, Morris Corporation must have used up $5,500 of supplies. Since an asset account was used to record the purchase, the $5,500 needs to be reflected as an expense and a reduction in asset value.

9. b. The office furniture was owned by the business for only three months, or one fourth of the year. Therefore, only one fourth of annual depreciation amount can be shown as an expense. Annual depreciation = ($3,400 − $200)/4 years = $800; the depreciation from October–December is $200. An expense account is increased and the contra asset account Accumulated Depreciation is used to reflect the decrease in asset value. Due to the use of estimates for scrap and life, it is more appropriate to credit a contra account than the asset account directly.

10. c. After the adjusting entry in 1986, there will be two years of depreciation shown in the Accumulated Depreciation account. Depreciation per year = ($9,000 − $1,000)/4 = $2,000.

11. b. When the magazine received the subscriptions, it debited Cash and credited Unearned Subscription Revenue (a liability). Seven months have passed since the receipt of the subscriptions, so $3 per month × 100 subscriptions × 7 months equals the earning of $2,100 of revenue. Business World needs to reduce the liability and increase the revenue.

12. d. In this instance, Cash was debited and Magazine Subscription Revenue was credited when the subscriptions were received. Business World, on December 31, needs to recognize the amount of subscriptions that have *not* been earned, or $3 per month × 100 subscriptions × 5 months, or $1,500. The revenue account needs to be reduced by this amount and the liability recognized.

13. b. The amount is computed as follows: excess of revenues over expenses before adjusting entries of $45,000 plus commissions earned of $5,000 minus depreciation and wages expenses of $9,000 equals net income of $41,000.

14. d. Since Rent Expense is a debit balanced account, to close it, Income Summary is debited and the expense account is credited. Although Dividends is also debit balanced, it is *not* closed to Income Summary; it is closed directly to Retained Earnings.

15. d. These are accounts that are closed. The balance sheet accounts remain open after closing entries have been posted.

16. d. A note payable is considered a current asset only if it will be converted into cash within one year.

17. d. The work sheet is an informal schedule. The accounting process could (although not as easily) be completed without preparing a work sheet. The work sheet may contain as many columns as the accountant wishes to use. The work sheet must contain an even number of columns so as to have debit and credit columns in each major set of columns.

18. b. The financial statements for the current period would be of no help in determining which adjusting entries should be made, because in order to prepare the financial statements of the current period the adjusting entries would have already been made.

19. a. Since Supplies on Hand had a debit balance of $315 and the adjustment recognized the using up of supplies through a $290 credit, the remaining debit balance of $25 would appear in the Balance Sheet Columns.

20. d. A net loss occurs if the total of the Income Statement debit column exceeds the total of the Income Statement credit column. The net loss is entered in the Income Statement credit column as the balancing figure as well as in the Statement of Retained Earnings debit column to reduce the amount of Retained Earnings in the business.

KRAFT COMPANY
GENERAL JOURNAL

(a)

DATE	ACCOUNT TITLES AND EXPLANATION	POST. REF.	DEBIT	CREDIT
	Case 1			
	Case 2			
	Case 3			

Name _____

_____

(b)

Case 1

Depreciation Expense—Equipment	Dr.	Cr.	Bal.

Accumulated Depreciation—Equipment	Dr.	Cr.	Bal.

Case 2

Salaries Expense	Dr.	Cr.	Bal.

Accrued Salaries Payable	Dr.	Cr.	Bal.

Case 3

Insurance Expense	Dr.	Cr.	Bal.

Prepaid Insurance	Dr.	Cr.	Bal.

(a)

JACKSON COMPANY
GENERAL JOURNAL

DATE	ACCOUNT TITLES AND EXPLANATION	POST. REF.	DEBIT	CREDIT

(b)

Office Supplies on Hand   ACCOUNT NO.

DATE	EXPLANATION	POST. REF.	DEBIT	CREDIT	BALANCE

Prepaid Insurance   ACCOUNT NO.

DATE	EXPLANATION	POST. REF.	DEBIT	CREDIT	BALANCE

Buildings   ACCOUNT NO.

DATE	EXPLANATION	POST. REF.	DEBIT	CREDIT	BALANCE

SANCHO COMPANY
GENERAL JOURNAL

DATE	ACCOUNT TITLES AND EXPLANATION	POST. REF.	DEBIT	CREDIT

Name _____

GENERAL JOURNAL

DATE	ACCOUNT TITLES AND EXPLANATION	POST. REF.	DEBIT	CREDIT

Name _____

HANLEY COMPANY
GENERAL JOURNAL

(a)

DATE	ACCOUNT TITLES AND EXPLANATION	POST. REF.	DEBIT	CREDIT

Name _____

(b)

DATE		ACCOUNT TITLES AND EXPLANATION	POST. REF.	DEBIT	CREDIT

Name _____

_____

(a)

ISAAC COMPANY
GENERAL JOURNAL

DATE	ACCOUNT TITLES AND EXPLANATION	POST. REF.	DEBIT	CREDIT

(b)   ISAAC COMPANY
                                      Balance Sheet
                                   December 31, 1990

ASSETS

LIABILITIES AND STOCKHOLDERS' EQUITY

4

Sales, Cost of Goods Sold, and Inventories

Understanding the Learning Objectives

1. Record journal entries for sales on account.

    * Sales on account are recorded by debiting Accounts Receivable and crediting Sales.

2. Describe accounting for inventories, returns and allowances, and cash discounts.

    * Under perpetual inventory procedure all purchases of merchandise are debited to Merchandise Inventory.

    * Under periodic inventory procedure all purchases of merchandise are debited to Purchases.

    * A return is when the purchaser of goods is dissatisfied with the merchandise and returns it to the seller.

    * An allowance is when the purchaser of goods is dissatisfied with the merchandise and is granted a reduction in the price of the goods.

    * A cash discount is a reduction in the amount of payment due granted for paying the invoice within the discount period.

3. Prepare adjusting and closing entries.

    * At the end of the accounting period one adjusting entry is prepared to transfer the existing balances in the inventory, transportation-in, and purchase-related accounts to the Cost of Goods Sold Account. Another adjusting entry debits Inventory for the ending inventory balance and credits Cost of Goods Sold.

    * Then all revenue and expense accounts are closed to Income Summary, and, finally, Income Summary is closed to Retained Earnings.

4. Account for Uncollectible Accounts.

    * Uncollectible Accounts Expense is debited and Allowance for Uncollectible Accounts is credited.

    * The percentage of sales method or the percentage of accounts receivable method may be used.

5. Calculate which costs are properly included in inventory.

    * Cost includes the net invoice price of the goods plus insurance in transit; transportation charges; receiving, handling, and storage costs; and duties.

6. Calculate cost of ending inventory, cost of goods sold, and effects on net income under the four major inventory costing methods.

    * The four methods are specific identification; first-in, first-out (FIFO); last-in, first-out (LIFO); and weighted-average method.

7. Apply the lower-of-cost-or-market method to inventory.

   * This method may be applied to each item in the inventory, to each class in the inventory, or to the total inventory.

8. Estimate cost of ending inventory using the gross margin method and the retail inventory method.

   * The gross margin method is based on the assumption that the rate of gross margin realized is highly stable from period to period.

   * Under the retail inventory method, beginning inventory and purchases are shown at both cost and retail prices. Transportation-in is added in the cost column. The cost/retail price ratio is applied to the ending inventory at retail to reduce it to cost.

9. Define and use correctly the new terms in the glossary.

   The new terms introduced in the chapter are as follows:

   Aging schedule—A means of classifying accounts receivable according to their age, used to determine the necessary balance in an Allowance for Uncollectible Accounts. A different uncollectibility rate is used for each age category.

   Allowance for Uncollectible Accounts—A contra asset account to the Accounts Receivable account; it reduces accounts receivable to their net realizable value. Also called Allowance for Doubtful Accounts or Allowance for Bad Debts.

   Bad debts expense—See uncollectible accounts expense.

   Cash discount—A deduction from the gross invoice price that can be taken only if the invoice is paid within a specified period of time; to the seller, it is a sales discount, to the buyer, it is a purchase discount.

   Cost of goods sold—Shows the cost to the seller of the goods sold to customers; under periodic procedure cost of goods sold is computed as Beginning inventory + Net cost of purchases − Ending inventory.

   FIFO (first-in, first-out)—A method of pricing inventory under which the costs of the first goods purchased are the first costs charged to cost of goods sold when goods are actually sold.

   Gross margin—Net sales − Cost of goods sold; identifies the number of dollars available to cover expenses; may be expressed as a percentage rate.

   Gross margin method—A procedure for estimating inventory cost in which estimated cost of goods sold (determined using an estimated gross margin) is deducted from the cost of goods available for sale to determine estimated ending inventory. The estimated gross margin is calculated using gross margin rates (in relation to net sales) of prior periods.

   Gross price method—The recording of merchandise purchases at gross invoice price.

   Gross profit—Net sales − Cost of goods sold.

   LIFO (last-in, first-out)—A method of pricing inventory under which the costs of the most recent purchases are the first costs charged to cost of goods sold when goods are actually sold.

   Lower-of-cost-or-market (LCM) method—An inventory pricing method that values inventory at the lower of its historical cost or its current market (replacement) cost.

   Merchandise inventory—The quantity of goods on hand and available for sale at any given time.

   Net realizable value—Estimated selling price of an item less the estimated costs that will be incurred in preparing the item for sale and selling it.

   Percentage of accounts receivable method—A method for determining the desired size of the Allowance for Uncollectible Accounts by basing the calculation on the Accounts Receivable balance at the end of the period.

   Percentage of sales method—A method of estimating uncollectible accounts from a given period's credit sales.

Periodic inventory procedure—A method of accounting for merchandise acquired for sale to customers wherein the cost of merchandise sold and the cost of merchandise on hand are determined only at the end of the accounting period by taking a physical inventory.

Perpetual inventory procedure—A method of accounting for merchandise acquired for sale to customers wherein the Merchandise Inventory account is debited for each purchase and credited for each sale so that the current balance is shown in the account at all times.

Retail inventory method—A procedure for estimating the cost of the ending inventory by applying a cost/retail price ratio to ending inventory stated at retail prices.

Specific identification—An inventory pricing method that attaches the actual cost to an identifiable unit of product.

Stock cards (perpetual inventory cards)—Records that show the dates, quantities, and prices of goods received and goods issued, and the quantities and prices of the goods on hand at any given time.

Transportation-In account—An account used under periodic inventory procedure to record transportation costs incurred in the acquisition of merchandise; a part of cost of goods sold.

Uncollectible accounts expense—An operating (usually a selling) expense a business incurs as a result of customers not paying their bills when the company sells on credit.

Weighted-average method—A method of pricing ending inventory using a weighted-average unit cost, determined by dividing the total number of units purchased plus those in beginning inventory into total cost of goods available for sale. Units in the ending inventory are carried at this per unit cost.

Completion and Exercises

1. Generally, a sale consists of transfer of _____ _____ to goods accompanied

    by actual _____ to the customer.

2. The sales revenue (or net sales revenue) of a firm is usually equal to sales less _____

    _____, _____ _____, and _____ _____.

    Its amount is important because it represents an approximate measure of the flow of _____ into a firm from its operations.

3. Suppose that A sold $10,000 of merchandise to B on July 26 under terms of 3/10, n/30. State exactly what is meant by these terms in these circumstances.

    _____

    _____

    _____

    _____

    _____

    _____

4. Use the data in Question 3 and assume that B returned $2,000 of the merchandise to A and then paid the balance of the invoice within the discount period. In the space below, give the necessary entries on B's books for the purchase, the return, and the payment. (Assume B uses periodic inventory procedure.)

DATE	ACCOUNT TITLES AND EXPLANATION	POST. REF.	DEBIT	CREDIT

5. Although cash discounts are considered as being offered to induce prompt payment of an account, they are theoretically viewed as _____ of recorded revenue by the seller and of recorded cost by the buyer.

6. If a high degree of control is desired over relatively high unit value goods, a company probably should use _____ inventory procedure. Under such procedure, an entry is required (in addition to the debit to Accounts Receivable or Cash and the credit to Sales) to record the _____ _____ _____ _____ and the reduction in _____ _____ for every sale.

(Note: In answering the remaining questions, assume use of periodic inventory procedure.)

7. Using the following information, prepare the necessary adjusting entries to establish cost of goods sold in the accounts:

Merchandise inventory 1/1	$20,000
Merchandise inventory 12/31	26,000
Purchases	55,000
Purchase discounts..............	1,000
Purchase returns	2,000
Transportation-in................	3,000

112

DATE	ACCOUNT TITLES AND EXPLANATION	POST. REF.	DEBIT	CREDIT

8. When using periodic inventory procedure, how is the amount of the ending inventory determined?

_____

_____

_____

9. Use the information in Question 7 and assume that sales for the period amounted to $85,000. Prepare a partial income statement.

10. Assume that $1,500 of accounts receivable is estimated to be uncollectible and there is a zero balance in the allowance account. The _____ _____ _____ account should be debited, and the _____ _____ _____ _____ account should be credited for $_____ in the end-of-period adjusting entry.

11. If an account for $300 is deemed to be uncollectible, the _____ _____ _____ _____ account should be debited and the _____ _____ account should be credited for $_____ .

12. If $100 of the amount written off in Question 11 is collected (with no prospect of collecting the remainder) what entry(ies) would be made?

DATE	ACCOUNT TITLES AND EXPLANATION	POST. REF.	DEBIT	CREDIT

13. When is the specific identification method of inventory valuation most applicable?

_____

_____

_____

14. Both _____-_____ , _____-_____ and _____-_____ , _____-_____ methods of inventory valuation make assumptions as to the flow of costs.

15. Following is a summary of beginning inventory and purchases. If a physical count at December 31 revealed that there were 3,000 units on hand, at what amount would the ending inventory be priced assuming the first-in, first-out method is used?

Inventory on January 1	1,200 units at $8.00
Purchases:	
January 8	2,800 units at $7.70
March 15	1,000 units at $8.25
July 28	1,400 units at $8.10
November 30	200 units at $8.50

16. At what amount would the ending inventory in Question 15 be priced if the last-in, first-out method were used?

17. Under FIFO, net income exists if revenues are sufficient to cover the _____ cost of the units of inventory sold (assuming the physical flow of goods is FIFO).

18. Under LIFO, net income exists if revenues are sufficient to cover the _____ cost of the units of inventory sold provided new units are acquired before the end of the accounting period.

19. The principal argument for _____ says that it more precisely matches costs and revenues in current terms.

20. During a period of rising prices, _____ will give a higher net income figure.

21. Below is a record of beginning inventories and purchases. Compute the ending inventory under the weighted-average method assuming periodic inventory procedure if a physical count showed 200 units on hand at the end of the month.

Inventory on May 1	150 units at $10.00	=	$1,500.00
Purchases:			
May 10	100 units at $10.25	=	1,025.00
May 15	50 units at $10.15	=	507.50
May 25	200 units at $10.05	=	2,010.00
	500 units	=	$5,042.50

22. What is the cost of goods sold in the example in Question 21?

23. The lower-of-cost-or-market method uses market values only to the extent that these values are _____ than cost.

24. The Engstrom Company has three different products in its inventory at December 31, 1990, that have costs and current market values as follows:

Item	Cost	Market
X	$ 4,000	$ 4,400
Y	12,000	11,800
Z	10,000	10,300

If each product is priced at the lower of cost or market, the inventory is $ _____ .

If the total inventory is priced at the lower of cost or market, the inventory is _____ .

25. Concerning the gross margin method of estimating inventory, what assumption must be correct for this method to be satisfactory?

_____

_____

26. To apply the gross margin method, the rate of gross margin on sales is multiplied by _____ to arrive at gross margin. The gross margin is then subtracted from sales to arrive at _____ _____ _____ _____ . This figure is then subtracted from _____ _____ _____ _____ _____ _____ to arrive at ending inventory.

27. Use the following information and the retail inventory method to estimate the ending inventory at cost:

	Cost	Retail
Beginning inventory	$ 7,440	$ 12,000
Purchases, net	93,000	150,000
Sales		152,000

Multiple-Choice Questions

For each of the following questions, indicate the single best answer by circling the appropriate letter.

1. All of the following are contra (or reduction) accounts except:

   a. Sales Discounts.
   b. Purchase Discounts.
   c. Transportation-In.
   d. Sales Returns and Allowances.

2. Periodic inventory procedure (choose the incorrect statement):

   a. determines cost of goods sold at the end of the accounting period.
   b. provides close control over inventory.
   c. buries losses from shrinkage and shoplifting in cost of goods sold.
   d. is appropriate for merchandise having a low individual unit value.

3. Given the following information:

Beginning inventory	$ 5,000
Sales	15,900
Ending inventory	3,000
Purchases	9,000
Sales returns and allowances	600
Transportation-in	700
Sales discounts	300
Purchase discounts	200
Purchase returns and allowances	400

Which of the following statement(s) is(are) correct?

a. Net purchases are $9,100.
b. Cost of goods available for sale is $14,100.
c. Cost of goods sold is $11,100.
d. All of the above are true.

4. On July 1, the following entry was made to record an invoice received on that date:

Purchases	1,000	
Accounts Payable		1,000
To record purchase on which the terms were 2/10, n/30.		

What entry would be correct if the invoice were paid on July 10?

a.
Accounts Payable	1,000	
Cash		1,000

b.
Accounts Payable	980	
Purchase Discounts	20	
Cash		1,000

c.
Accounts Payable	980	
Cash		980

d.
Accounts Payable	1,000	
Cash		980
Purchase Discounts		20

5. If the ending inventory is overstated:

a. cost of goods sold is understated and net income for the period is overstated.
b. cost of goods sold is understated and net income for the period is understated.
c. cost of goods sold is overstated and net income is overstated.
d. cost of goods sold is overstated and net income is understated.

6. Which of the following correctly describes the makeup of the cost of goods sold section of the income statement under periodic inventory procedure?

a. Beginning inventory + Purchases − Transportation-in − Purchase returns and allowances − Purchase discounts − Ending inventory
b. Beginning inventory + Purchases − Transportation-in − Purchase returns and allowances − Purchase discounts + Ending inventory
c. Beginning inventory + Purchases + Transportation-in + Purchase returns and allowances − Purchase discounts − Ending inventory
d. Beginning inventory + Purchases + Transportation-in − Purchase returns and allowances − Purchase discounts − Ending inventory

7. Which of the following income statement relationships is true?

   a. Gross margin = Sales − Operating expenses
   b. Cost of goods sold = Net sales − Gross margin
   c. Net income = Gross margin − Cost of goods sold
   d. Net sales = Sales − Selling expenses

8. If periodic inventory procedure is used, then:

   a. The cost of merchandise on hand can be readily determined by referring to the merchandise inventory account.
   b. The cost of merchandise on hand can be readily determined by referring to the purchases account.
   c. The cost of goods sold can be determined only after a physical inventory is taken.
   d. The inventory items would most likely have a high individual unit value.

9. Which of the following is a characteristic of periodic inventory procedure?

   a. Can be used with low value units of merchandise
   b. Tight inventory control
   c. An account balance exists with which to compare the results of a physical inventory
   d. Cost of goods sold can be closely approximated prior to taking a physical inventory

10. If the cost of goods available for sale during the first quarter was $150,000, purchases were $125,000, and ending inventory was $100,000, what is the cost of goods sold to be reported on the interim financial statements?

   a. $ 50,000
   b. $175,000
   c. $125,000
   d. $150,000

11. Under periodic inventory procedure, which of the following statements about Cost of Goods Sold is *incorrect?*

   a. Cost of Goods Sold has a debit balance.
   b. Cost of Goods Sold is created during the adjusting process under periodic inventory procedure.
   c. Cost of Goods Sold is closed with the other expense accounts during the closing process.
   d. Cost of Goods Sold is increased by the amount of ending inventory.

12. Which of the following methods of determining uncollectible accounts expense most closely matches expense to revenue?

   a. Recording uncollectible accounts expense only as accounts are written off as uncollectible
   b. Recording estimated uncollectible accounts expense as a percentage of credit sales for the period
   c. Estimating the allowance for uncollectible accounts balance as a percentage of accounts receivable at period end
   d. Estimating the allowance for uncollectible accounts balance by aging the accounts receivable

13. In March 1990, after trying unsuccessfully to collect for nearly two years, Fred Company wrote the $95 account of Poole off as uncollectible. In August 1990, Poole sent a check for $50 "on account." Assuming Fred Company uses the allowance method, which of the following entries should it make upon receipt of the $50 check?

a. Cash 50.00
    Accounts Receivable (Poole) 50.00

b. Cash 50.00
    Allowance for Uncollectible Accounts ...   50.00

c. Accounts Receivable (Poole)................ 50.00
    Allowance for Uncollectible Accounts ...   50.00

    Cash 50.00
    Accounts Receivable (Poole) 50.00

d. Accounts Receivable (Poole)................ 95.00
    Allowance for Uncollectible Accounts ...   95.00

    Cash 50.00
    Accounts Receivable (Poole) 50.00

14. The accounts of the Hellois Company on December 31, 1990, show Accounts Receivable, $303,000; Allowance for Uncollectible Accounts (Cr.), $800; Sales, $890,000; and Sales Discounts, $13,500. At this time, the company decides to write off the account of the Bean Corporation, $3,000. The Allowance for Uncollectible Accounts account is then to be adjusted to 3 percent of the outstanding receivables. The amount of uncollectible accounts expense recognized for the year is:

a. $26,700.
b. $ 9,090.
c. $ 9,000.
d. $11,200.

15. A company has, for a given year, a beginning inventory of 600 units at $6; purchases of 1,400 units on May 1 at $8, and 2,400 units on September 5 at $9; and sales of 2,000 units and 1,800 units. What is the cost of the ending inventory under the FIFO method of pricing inventory?

a. $3,600
b. $5,400
c. $4,800
d. $4,600

16. Given the following data, which of the statements below is true? Assume there is no beginning inventory and periodic inventory procedure is used.

Purchases

Feb. 2 .... 1,800 units @ $3.00
   10 .... 1,200 units @ $3.75
   20 ....   600 units @ $4.15

Sales

Feb. 9 .... 1,050 units
  25 ....   900 units

a. Under the weighted-average method, the units sold on February 9 would have a unit cost of $3.00 each.
b. Under the LIFO method applied on a periodic basis, the 1,050 units sold on February 9 would be charged to cost of goods sold at $3.00 each.
c. Under the FIFO method, the 1,800 units purchased on February 2 would be included in cost of goods sold.

17. The Tiddle Company has three different products in its inventory at December 31, 1990, that have costs and current market values as follows:

Item	Cost	Market
X.........	$2,000	$1,900
Y.........	2,500	2,600
Z.........	4,000	3,900

With respect to the above inventory, which of the following statements is(are) true?

a. The inventory could be reported at $8,400 under the lower-of-cost-or-market method.
b. The inventory could be reported at $8,300 under the lower-of-cost-or-market method.
c. If item A has a selling price of $2,100 and additional costs of $250 will be incurred in disposing of this item, it should be included in inventory at $1,850 under the lower-of-cost-or-market method.
d. All of the above are true.

18. True/Blue Company for several years has maintained a 40 percent average gross margin rate on sales. Given the following data for 1990, what is the approximate cost of the inventory on December 31, 1990, computed using the gross margin method of estimating inventory?

	Cost
Inventory, January 1.......	$ 25,000
Purchases	115,000
Total	$140,000

Sales in 1990 were $180,000.

a. $84,000
b. $72,000
c. $32,000
d. $40,000

19. Given the following data, compute the cost of the ending inventory using the retail inventory method:

	Cost	Retail
July 16, inventory	$ 33,000	$ 60,000
Purchases	165,000	270,000
Sales...................		255,000

a. $ 45,000
b. $153,000
c. $ 45,833
d. $153,333

20. The Green Bond Company uses periodic procedure and the LIFO method of inventory costing. Following are inventory data for 1990:

Purchases

January 10	600 units at $4.00
March 15	800 units at $3.80
May 18	500 units at $4.20
December 30	700 units at $4.25

Sales

March 17	400 units
October 5	1,300 units

If there was no beginning inventory, the cost of the ending inventory is:

a. $4,015.
b. $3,540.
c. $6,700.
d. $3,440.

Now compare your answers with the correct ones beginning on page 122.

Solutions/Chapter 4

Completion and Exercises

1. legal title; delivery

2. sales discounts; sales returns; sales allowances; assets

3. B can deduct $30 (0.03 × $1,000) from the $1,000 amount of the invoice for these goods if B pays on or before August 5. If B pays later than this, B must pay $1,000.

4.

Purchases	10,000	
Accounts Payable		10,000
To record purchase on account.		
Accounts Payable	2,000	
Purchase Returns and Allowances		2,000
To record return of merchandise to vendor.		
Accounts Payable	8,000	
Purchase Discounts		240
Cash		7,760
To record payment of invoice.		

5. deductions or reductions

6. perpetual; cost of goods sold; Merchandise Inventory

7.

Cost of Goods Sold	75,000	
Purchase Discounts	1,000	
Purchase Returns	2,000	
Purchases		55,000
Transportation-In		3,000
Merchandise Inventory		20,000
To transfer net cost of purchases and beginning inventory to cost of goods sold.		
Merchandise Inventory	26,000	
Cost of Goods Sold		26,000
To set up ending inventory in the accounts.		

8. Quantities (obtained by physical counts) are multiplied by prices obtained from vendor's invoices and the extensions summed to arrive at the total cost of the inventory.

9.

Partial Income Statement
For the Year Ended December 31, 19—

Sales			$85,000
Cost of goods sold:			
Merchandise inventory 1/1		$20,000	
Purchases	$55,000		
Less: Purchase discounts	$1,000		
Purchase returns	2,000	3,000	
		$52,000	
Transportation-in		3,000	55,000
Goods available for sale			$75,000
Less: Merchandise inventory 12/31			26,000	49,000
Gross margin			$36,000

10. Uncollectible Accounts Expense; Allowance for Uncollectible Accounts; $1,500

11. Allowance for Uncollectible Accounts; Accounts Receivable; $300

12.
Accounts Receivable	100	
Allowance for Uncollectible Accounts		100

To record collection of $100 on account.

Cash	100	
Accounts Receivable		100

To reverse part of original entry to write off an account receivable.

13. The specific identification method is most applicable when the products bought and sold are large, readily identifiable, and of high unit value.

14. first-in, first-out; last-in, first-out

15.
200 units at $8.50 =	$ 1,700.00	
1,400 units at $8.10 =	11,340.00	
1,000 units at $8.25 =	8,250.00	
400 units at $7.70 =	3,080.00	
3,000 units	$24,370.00	

16.
1,200 units at $8.00 =	$ 9,600.00
1,800 units at $7.70 =	13,860.00
3,000 units	$23,460.00

17. historical

18. replacement

19. LIFO

20. FIFO

21. Weighted-average unit cost is $5,042.50 ÷ 500, or $10.085
Ending inventory is 200 × $10.085 = $2,017.00

22.
Cost of goods available for sale	$5,042.50
Less: Ending inventory...............................	2,017.00
Cost of goods sold	$3,025.50

23. less

24. $25,800; $26,000

25. The assumption that the rate of gross margin realized is highly stable from period to period must be correct.

26. sales; estimated cost of goods sold; cost of goods available for sale

27.
	Cost	Retail
Beginning inventory	$ 7,440	$ 12,000
Purchases, net	93,000	150,000
Goods available for sale	$100,440	$162,000

Cost/retail price ratio: $100,440/$162,000 = 62 percent

Sales		152,000
Cost of goods sold (62 percent of $152,000)	94,240	
Ending inventory (cost is 62 percent of $10,000)	$ 6,200	$ 10,000

1. c.   Transportation-in is an addition to the cost of purchases rather than a reduction from this cost. All of the other accounts are contra or reduction accounts.

2. b.   The major disadvantage of periodic inventory procedure is that it fails to provide an inventory amount in the books against which the cost of a physical inventory can be compared. Thus, the element of control is missing.

3. d.   All of the statements are correct. Net purchases are $9,100 ($9,000 + $700 − $400 − $200). Cost of goods available for sale is $14,100 ($9,100, net cost of purchase plus $5,000, beginning inventory). Cost of goods sold is $11,100 ($14,100, cost of goods available for sale, less $3,000, ending inventory).

4. d.   This entry correctly reduces the Accounts Payable account balance to zero, records the cash discount of $20 taken in the Purchase Discounts account, and records the decrease in the Cash account of $980.

5. a.   Ending inventory is a deduction from total goods available for sale to arrive at the cost of goods sold. If it is overstated, cost of goods sold will be understated. Cost of goods sold is a deduction from revenues in arriving at net income. If it is understated, net income will be overstated.

6. d.   Response (a) would be correct if it had indicated that transportation-in was added rather than subtracted. Response (b) is incorrect for two reasons. Transportation-in should be added rather than deducted. Ending inventory should be deducted rather than added. Response (c) is incorrect because purchase returns and allowances should be deducted rather than added in determining the cost of the goods sold.

7. b.   Since Net sales − Cost of goods sold = Gross margin is true, Cost of goods sold would be equal to Net sales − Gross margin.

8. c.   Since the books do not contain the correct inventory amount, it must be obtained by taking a physical inventory.

9. a.   Periodic procedure is generally used with merchandise of low unit value.

10. a. $150,000 − $100,000.

11. d.   Cost of goods available for sale is reduced by the amount of ending inventory. Since cost of goods available for sale is recorded in the Cost of Goods Sold account by the first adjusting entry, this account would be reduced by the amount of ending inventory in the second adjusting entry.

12. b.   This method of estimating uncollectible accounts is based on sales rather than a balance sheet amount. Thus, estimates of uncollectible accounts are directly related to revenues and the best matching possible is obtained. If uncollectible accounts are charged off when they are found to be bad, then the bulk of these accounts would be written off in the period following the period of sale.

13. c.   The entry to write off the account should be reversed, to the extent of the cash received. Then the amount received should be debited to the Cash account and credited to Accounts Receivable in the usual fashion. Mr. Poole indicates a willingness to pay, but so far has shown the ability to pay only to the extent of $50.

14. d,   After writing off the account of Bean Corporation, the accounts receivable total is $300,000 and the allowance has a debit balance of $2,200. Since the allowance is to be adjusted to a credit balance of $9,000, the amount of the credit to the allowance must be $11,200; this is the amount charged to bad debts expense.

15. b.   Since the inventory of 600 units is less than the 2,400 units acquired at $9.00 each in the most recent purchase, the 600 units are all priced at $9.00 each.

16. c. Only (c) of the three statements is true. Statement (a) is false because the weighted-average unit cost is $3.44 ($12,390/3,600). Statement (b) is false. Cost of goods sold includes 1,950 units of the latest costs: 600 units at $4.15 + 1,200 units at $3.75 + 150 units at $3.00. Note that only 150 of the units with a $3.00 unit cost are included in cost of goods sold. Statement (c) is true since the 1,950 units sold would, under FIFO, include the costs of the earliest units purchased—the 1,800 units acquired on February 2.

17. d. All of the statements are true. The method can be applied to total inventory or to individual items, so both (a) and (b) are true. A modification of the general rule is that goods should not be priced for inventory purposes at an amount in excess of their net realizable value, since this would entail inventorying losses.

18. c. The cost of the goods available for sale is $140,000. The cost of the goods sold is estimated at $108,000 ($180,000 less 40 percent of $180,000). Thus, the inventory is estimated at $32,000 ($140,000 less $108,000).

19. a. Inventory at retail = $75,000 ($330,000 − $255,000) × .6 (cost/price ratio: $198,000/$330,000) = $45,000.

20. b. 600 at $4.00 + 300 at $3.80 = $3,540.

Name _____

ERICKSON COMPANY
GENERAL JOURNAL

(a)

DATE	ACCOUNT TITLES AND EXPLANATION	POST. REF.	DEBIT	CREDIT

(b)

Name _____

(a)

DRAKE COMPANY
GENERAL JOURNAL

Entry Number DATE	ACCOUNT TITLES AND EXPLANATION	POST. REF.	DEBIT	CREDIT

Name _____

_____

(b)

Name _____

_(a)_

CRISSY CORPORATION

Partial Income Statement

under FIFO and under LIFO

	Per FIFO	Inventories	Per LIFO

(b)

Internal Control and Control of Cash

Understanding the Learning Objectives

1. Describe the necessity for and features of internal control.

    *   An internal control system is the plan of organization and all the procedures and actions taken by an entity to protect its assets against theft and waste, ensure compliance with company policies and federal law, evaluate the performance of all personnel in the company so as to promote efficiency of operations, and ensure accurate and reliable operating data and accounting reports.

    *   The purpose of internal control is to ensure the efficient operations of a business.

2. Define cash and list the objectives sought by management in handling a company's cash.

    *   Cash includes coins; paper money; certain undeposited negotiable instruments such as checks, bank drafts, and money orders; amounts in checking and savings accounts; and demand certificates of deposit.

    *   To protect its cash, companies should account for all cash transactions accurately, make sure there is enough cash available to pay bills as they come due, avoid holding too much idle cash, and prevent loss of cash due to theft or fraud.

3. Identify procedures for controlling cash receipts and disbursements.

    *   Procedures for controlling cash receipts include such basic principles as recording all cash receipts as soon as cash is received, depositing all cash receipts on the day they are received or on the next business day, and preventing the person who handles cash receipts from also recording the receipts in the accounting records or from disbursing cash.

    *   Procedures for controlling cash disbursements include, among others, making all disbursements by check or from petty cash, using checks that are serially numbered, requiring two signatures on each check, and having the person who authorizes payment of a bill be someone other than the person allowed to sign checks.

4. Prepare a bank reconciliation statement and make necessary journal entries based on that statement.

    *   A bank reconciliation statement is prepared to reconcile, or explain, the difference between the cash balance shown on the bank statement and the cash balance shown on the company's books.

    *   A bank reconciliation statement is shown in Illustration 5.8.

    *   Reconciling items to the balance per ledger necessitates journal entries to record that information.

5. Explain why a petty cash fund is used, describe its operations, and make the necessary journal entries.

   * Companies establish a petty cash fund to permit minor disbursements to be made in cash and still maintain adequate control over cash.

   * When the petty cash becomes low it should be replenished, and a journal entry is necessary to record the replenishment.

6. Apply the net price method of handling purchase discounts.

   * When the net price method is used, a purchase is recorded "net" of the discount.

   * If a discount is missed, the Discounts Lost account is debited. This procedure focuses management's attention on discounts missed rather than on discounts taken.

7. Describe the operation of the voucher system.

   * The voucher system is a set of procedures, special journals, and authorization forms designed to provide control over cash payments.

   * A voucher is a form with spaces provided for data about a liability that must be paid.

   * A voucher register is a multicolumn special journal; it contains a record of all vouchers prepared, listed in order by date and voucher number.

   * A check register is a special journal showing all checks issued, listed by date and check number.

8. Define and use correctly the new terms in the glossary.

   The new terms introduced in the chapter are as follows:

   Bank reconciliation statement—A statement the depositor prepares to "reconcile," or explain, the difference between the cash balance shown on the bank statement and the cash balance on the depositor's books.

   Bank statement—A statement issued (usually monthly) by a bank describing the activities in a depositor's checking account during the period.

   Cash—Includes coins; paper money; certain undeposited negotiable instruments such as checks, bank drafts, and money orders; amounts in checking and savings accounts; and demand certificates of deposit.

   Cashier's check—A check drawn by a bank made out to either the depositor or a third party after deducting the amount of the check from the depositor's account or receiving cash from the depositor.

   Certificate of deposit—An interest-bearing deposit in a bank that can be withdrawn at will (demand CD) or at a fixed date (time CD).

   Certified check—A check written, or drawn, by a depositor and taken to the depositor's bank for certification. The check is deducted from the depositor's balance immediately and becomes a liability of the bank. Thus, it usually will be accepted without question.

   Check—A written order on a bank to pay a specific sum of money to the party designated as the payee by the party issuing the check.

   Check register—A special journal showing all checks issued by date and check number.

   Checking account—A money balance maintained in the bank that is subject to withdrawal by the depositor, or owner of the money, on demand.

   Credit memo—A form used by a bank to explain an addition to the depositor's account.

   Debit memo—A form used by a bank to explain a deduction from the depositor's account.

   Deposit in transit—Typically a day's cash receipts recorded in the depositor's books in one period but recorded as a deposit by the bank in the succeeding period.

   Deposit ticket—A form that shows the date and the items that make up the deposit.

   Discounts Lost account—The account used to show the amount of discounts not taken when merchandise purchased is recorded at net invoice price.

Drawer—The party (depositor) writing a check.

Fidelity bonds—Insure an employer against loss up to a certain amount from fraud or theft by employees who are "bonded."

Internal auditing—Consists of investigating and evaluating compliance by employees with the company's policies and procedures. Internal auditing is performed by company personnel.

Internal control system—The plan of organization and all the procedures and actions taken by an entity to (1) protect its assets against theft and waste, (2) ensure compliance with company policies and federal law, (3) evaluate the performance of all personnel in the company so as to promote efficiency of operations, and (4) ensure accurate and reliable operating data and accounting reports.

Invoice—Bill sent from the supplier to the purchaser requesting payment for the merchandise shipped.

Net price method—An accounting procedure in which purchases and accounts payable are initially recorded at net invoice price—gross price less discount offered for prompt payment. Records discounts lost rather than discounts taken.

NSF check—A customer's check returned from the customer's bank because the customer's checking account balance was insufficient to cover the check.

Outstanding checks—Checks issued by a depositor that have not yet been paid by the bank on which they are drawn.

Paid voucher file—A permanent file used in a voucher system where paid vouchers are filed in numerical sequence.

Payee—The party to whom a check is made payable.

Petty cash fund—A nominal sum of money established as a separate fund from which minor cash disbursements for valid business purposes are made. The cash in the fund plus the vouchers covering disbursements must always equal the balance at which the fund was established and at which it is carried in the ledger accounts.

Petty cash voucher—A document or form that shows the amount of and reason for a petty cash disbursement.

Purchase order—A document sent from the purchasing department to a supplier requesting that merchandise or other items be shipped to the purchaser.

Purchase requisition—A written request from an employee inside the company to the purchasing department to purchase certain items.

Receiving report—A document prepared by the receiving department showing the descriptions and quantities of all items received from suppliers.

Remittance advice—Informs the payee why the drawer (or maker) of the check is making this payment.

Segregation of duties—Having the person responsible for safeguarding an asset be someone other than the person who maintains the accounting records for that asset.

Service charges—Charges assessed by the bank on the depositor to cover the cost of handling the checking account.

Signature card—Provides the signatures of persons authorized to sign checks drawn on an account.

Transfer bank accounts—Bank accounts set up so that local banks automatically transfer to a central bank (by written bank draft) all amounts on deposit in excess of a stated amount.

Unpaid voucher file—Contains all vouchers that have been prepared and approved as proper liabilities but have not yet been paid. Serves as an accounts payable subsidiary ledger under a voucher system; unpaid vouchers are filed according to their due dates.

Voucher—A form with spaces provided for data about a liability that must be paid. The data include items such as creditor's name and address, description of the goods or services received, invoice number, terms of payment, due date, and amount due. The voucher also has spaces for signatures of those approving the liability for payment.

Voucher register—A multicolumn special journal used in a voucher system; it contains a record of all vouchers prepared, listed in order by date and voucher number. A brief explanation of each transaction also may be included. In addition to a credit column for Vouchers Payable, it normally has various columns for debits such as Merchandise Purchases, Salaries, and Transportation-In.

Voucher system—A set of procedures, special journals, and authorization forms designed to provide control over cash payments.

Wire transfer of funds—Interbank transfer of funds (in the form of accounting debits and credits) by telephone.

Completion and Exercises

1. The purposes of internal accounting controls are to—

    a. _____

    b. _____

    c. _____

    d. _____

       _____

2. Control documents that are used in merchandise transactions include the following:

    a. _____

    b. _____

    c. _____

    d. _____

3. If _____ exists between employees, the system of internal control can be broken.

4. What is the composition of cash?

    _____

    _____

    _____

    _____

5. Why do most firms exercise special care in safeguarding cash?

    _____

    _____

    _____

    _____

    _____

6. State whether each of the following statements is true or false.

_____ a. Misappropriations of cash can occur just as easily before or after a record is made of a cash receipt.

_____ b. All cash receipts should be deposited intact in the bank.

_____ c. Cash disbursements should not be made from cash receipts.

_____ d. The person who receives the cash should also record cash transactions in the accounting records.

_____ e. Cash receipts and cash disbursements should be the function of one group to facilitate record keeping for cash.

_____ f. All cash disbursements except those out of petty cash should be by check.

_____ g. The person who authorizes the disbursement should also be the person who signs the checks.

7. What is the purpose of the bank reconciliation statement? _____

_____

_____

_____

_____

_____

8. From the following information prepare a bank reconciliation statement for the McCord Company in the space provided below:

Balance of Cash account on March 31, 1990	$12,155.45
Balance on March 31, 1990, bank statement	14,297.63
Deposits in transit	842.27
Outstanding checks	1,989.45

The bank statement also contained the following information that had not been recorded on the books of McCord Company:

The bank had collected a note for McCord Company for $1,000.00.
The bank had charged McCord Company $5.00 for servicing the account.

9. The Cash Short and Over account is a(n) _____ if it has a debit balance and a(n) _____ if it has a credit balance.

10. A _____ check becomes a liability of the bank.

11. A _____ _____ _____ should be prepared for each disbursement from the petty cash fund.

12. The petty cash fund is usually _____ when the amount of cash in the fund becomes low.

13. At the time for replenishing, the $200 petty cash fund had $24 remaining and the following petty cash vouchers:

Stamps .... $ 50
Transportation-in 100
Stationery 24

What entry would be made to record the replenishment of the fund?

DATE	ACCOUNT TITLES AND EXPLANATION	POST. REF.	DEBIT	CREDIT

14. A method of obtaining close control over cash disbursements is called a _____ system.

15. Two special journals used in a voucher system are the _____ _____ and _____ _____ .

16. The _____ _____ _____ serves as an accounts payable subsidiary ledger.

17. When a voucher is paid it is placed in the _____ _____ _____ .

Multiple-Choice Questions

For each of the following questions, indicate the single best answer by circling the appropriate letter.

1. Which of the following statements is true? Effective cash management includes:

   a. making all disbursements from cash receipts.
   b. having the same person authorize and sign checks.
   c. having one person who is responsible for both cash receipts and cash disbursements.
   d. avoiding the accumulation of excessive amounts of idle cash.

2. Which of the following items must be deducted from the bank statement balance in preparing a bank reconciliation statement that ends with adjusted cash balance?

   a. Bank service charges
   b. Outstanding checks
   c. Checks returned marked "not sufficient funds"
   d. Deposits in transit

3. Given the following information for N. Parkinson & Company, determine which of the journal entries shown is necessary to adjust the Cash account balance.

Balance per bank statement, October 31, 1990	$22,220
Balance per Cash account in ledger, October 31, 1990	19,993
Outstanding checks at October 31, 1990	13,000
Deposit in transit dated September 30, 1990	1,525
Deposit in transit dated October 31, 1990	3,670
Bank service charges for October	3
Check from a customer returned by bank marked NSF	1,100

a.
Accounts Receivable	1,100	
Cash in Bank		1,100

b.
Accounts Receivable	1,100	
Bank Service Charges	3	
Cash in Bank		1,103

c.
Cash in Bank	3,670	
Accounts Receivable		3,670

d.
Cash in Bank	1,103	
Accounts Receivable		1,100
Bank Service Charges		3

4. The accountant for the Anselman Company was able to prepare the bank reconciliation statement for August 31, 1990, using the unadjusted ledger balance for cash and the following information:

Deposit in transit	$1,200
Balance per bank statement	2,750
Bank service charges	5
Checks outstanding	1,625
NSF check returned	500
Deposit of $550 recorded by company as $505	45

What must have been the unadjusted balance in the Cash account in the ledger?

a. $2,325
b. $2,875
c. $2,830
d. None of the above

5. The Petty Cash account is debited:

a. only when the fund is established.
b. when the fund is established and every time it is replenished.
c. when the fund is established and when the size of the fund is increased.
d. when the fund is established, replenished, or increased in size.

153

6. J. F. Knauf Company has a petty cash fund in the amount of $200. On August 14, a count of the fund discloses the following:

Voucher for postage stamps	$ 36
Vouchers for transportation-In	72
Vouchers for sales returns	46
Currency	22
Coins	18
Total	$194

The correct entry to record replenishing the fund is:

a.
Postage Expense	36	
Transportation-In	72	
Sales Returns and Allowances	46	
Accounts Payable		154

b.
Postage Expense	36	
Transportation-In	72	
Sales Returns and Allowances	46	
Cash Short and Over	6	
Cash in Bank		160

c.
Petty Cash	160	
Cash in Bank...................		160

d.
Postage Expense	36	
Transportation-In	72	
Sales Returns and Allowances	46	
Cash Short and Over		6
Cash in Bank...................		148

7. Which of the following are characteristics of a petty cash fund?

    a. It is cash in the custody of a responsible person who administers the fund.
    b. It is periodically reimbursed.
    c. Cash in the fund plus the amount of payments made from the fund should equal the fixed fund total.
    d. All of the above are correct.

8. Which of the following bits of information from the bank statement requires an entry in the depositor's ledger?

    a. Outstanding checks
    b. NSF check
    c. Deposits in transit
    d. All of the above

9. Cash receipts of the last day of the month that have been recorded in the depositor's Cash account but which have not been mailed to the bank or placed in its night depository:

    a. should not be included in the cash reported in the balance sheet.
    b. may, as a practical matter, be treated as deposits in transit on the bank reconciliation statement.
    c. require a correcting entry on the bank's books.
    d. require a correcting entry on the depositor's books.

10. Sunshine Beach Company showed a cash balance of $4,299 on March 31, 1990. On the same date, the bank showed a balance of $4,649 in the company's account. This difference could be caused by:

    a. a $350 deposit in transit.
    b. $425 of outstanding checks and a customer's $75 NSF check.
    c. a $10 service charge by the bank and $340 of outstanding checks.
    d. a $200 note collected by the bank for the company and outstanding checks of $550.

11. The custodian of the petty cash fund presented the following vouchers for reimbursement:

No. 223 Transportation-In $62.35
No. 224 Postage expense 36.00
No. 225 Miscellaneous expense 7.96
No. 226 Transportation-In 25.50

The fund was set up for $200. The current cash balance of the fund is $67.99. The journal entry to record the reimbursement would be:

a. Miscellaneous Expense 131.81
    Cash 131.81

b. Transportation-In 87.85
    Miscellaneous Expense 7.96
    Postage Expense 36.00
    Cash 131.81

c. Transportation-In 87.85
    Postage Expense 36.00
    Miscellaneous Expense 7.96
    Cash Short and Over 20
    Petty Cash 132.01

d. Transportation-In 87.85
    Postage Expense 36.00
    Miscellaneous Expense 7.96
    Cash Short and Over 20
    Cash 132.01

12. A check issued by the depositor, paid by the depositor's bank, and returned to the depositor with the bank statement is called a(n):

a. cancelled check.
b. certified check.
c. NSF check.
d. outstanding check.

13. Which of the following would improve control over cash disbursements?

a. All disbursements should be made out of cash receipts.
b. The same person should approve the disbursement and sign the check.
c. Each check should be supported by a petty cash voucher.
d. The same person should not sign the checks and prepare the bank reconciliation statement.

14. The balance in the Tex Company's Cash account on October 31 was $5,613.49, before the bank reconciliation statement was prepared. After examining the October bank statement and items included with it, the company's accountant found:

Outstanding checks $1,519.81
NSF check 50.00
Note collected by bank for the Tex Company 500.00
Deposit in transit 632.95
Service charges 15.00

What is the amount of cash that should be reported in the balance sheet for October 31?

a. $4,726.63
b. $5,161.63
c. $6,048.49
d. $5,178.49

155

15. Which of the following might cause a depositor to receive a credit memorandum from the bank?

    a.   A service charge
    b.   A NSF check
    c.   A deposit in transit
    d.   A note collected by the bank for depositor

16. A petty cash fund is established at $300. At fiscal year-end the fund contains cash of $56.90, an IOU from an employee for $5, and petty cash vouchers totalling $239.10. The entry to reimburse the fund would include:

    a.   a credit to Advances to Employees of $5.
    b.   a debit to Cash Short and Over of $1.00.
    c.   a credit to Petty Cash of $239.10.
    d.   a credit to Cash of $243.10.

Now compare your answers with the correct ones beginning on page 157.

Solutions/Chapter 5

Completion and Exercises

1. (a) safeguard the assets against theft; (b) ensure that management's policies are being followed; (c) promote efficiency of operations; (d) ensure accurate and reliable operating data and accounting reports

2. (a) purchase requisition; (b) purchase order; (c) invoice; (d) receiving report

3. collusion

4. Cash is composed of those items commonly acceptable as a medium of exchange and also immediately convertible into money at face value. Cash includes the following: currency, coins, negotiable instruments, checking accounts, savings accounts, and demand certificates of deposit.

5. Cash can easily be misappropriated since it can be concealed and it is not readily identifiable. It can also be used to acquire anything else.

6. (a) F; (b) T; (c) T; (d) F; (e) F; (f) T; (g) F

7. The purpose of a bank reconciliation statement is to account for the difference between the cash balance on the books and the depositor's balance at the bank as shown on the bank statement. Such a statement concludes with the properly adjusted Cash account balance.

8.
McCORD COMPANY
Bank Reconciliation Statement
March 31, 1990

Balance per bank statement, March 31, 1990	$14,297.63	Balance per ledger, March 31, 1990	$12,155.45
Add: Deposit in transit	842.27	Add: Note collected by bank	1,000.00
	$15,139.90		$13,155.45
Less: Outstanding checks	1,989.45	Less: Bank charges	5.00
Corrected ledger balance, March 31, 1990	$13,150.45	Corrected ledger balance, March 31, 1990	$13,150.45

9. expense; revenue

10. Certified

11. petty cash voucher

12. replenished

13.
Stamps and Stationery	74.00	
Transportation-in	100.00	
Cash Short and Over	2.00	
Cash		176.00

To record check drawn to replenish petty cash fund.

14. voucher

15. voucher register; check register

16. unpaid voucher file

17. paid voucher file

Multiple-Choice Questions

1. d. Holding too much cash generally results in an opportunity loss—the revenue that could have been earned by investing the idle cash in productive assets.

2. b. Only those items which the bank has entered in error or has yet to record should be entered as additions to, or deductions from, the balance per the bank statement. Of those listed, only outstanding checks are yet to be recorded by the bank as deductions from the balance it carries in its records for the depositor.

3. b. Of the items listed, only two have not been recorded by the company: (1) the return of the NSF check deposited, and (2) the service charges deducted by the bank from the company's balance. Entry (b) correctly restores the balance in accounts receivable and recognizes the expense incurred.

4. d. The correct answer is $2,785. The solution to the problem is derived in the following manner:

Balance per bank statement	$2,750
Add: Deposit in transit..........	1,200
	$3,950
Less: Checks outstanding	1,625
Adjusted balance	$2,325

This adjusted balance will be reached on the other side of the bank reconciliation statement by adding the $45 error and deducting the NSF check of $500 and the bank service charges of $5. Therefore, the unadjusted beginning balance can be obtained by reversing the procedure and adding the last two items and deducting the first. Thus, $2,325 + $500 + $5 − $45 = $2,785.

5. c. A debit is entered in the Petty Cash account only when the fund is established or increased in size. The amount of any check issued to replenish the fund is charged to expense (and possibly other accounts).

6. b. The total of the vouchers in the fund is $154 and this amount must be charged to the proper expense and revenue contra accounts. The fund is also short $6, and this shortage must be charged to an expense account, Cash Short and Over.

7. d. All of the statements are correct.

8. b. A NSF check must be restored to accounts receivable and removed from cash.

9. b. Although technically cash on hand, such receipts are most easily dealt with by treating them as deposits in transit. No real purpose is served by differentiating between cash in bank and cash on hand.

10. b. Bank: $4,649 − $425 = $4,224
    Books: $4,299 − $ 75 = $4,224

11. d. The amount of cash in the fund must be built back up to its $200 amount. The credit must be to Cash.

12. a. Checks that have been processed as described are called cancelled checks.

13. d. The person who signs the checks should have no further access to them.

14. c. $5,613.49 − $50.00 − $15.00 + $500.00 = $6,048.49.

15. d. A credit memorandum would be provided for such a collection.

16. d. Cash of $243.10 is needed to restore the fund's balance to $300.00.

GRANT COMPANY
Bank Reconciliation Statement
June 30, 1990

	Dr.	Cr.
Balance per bank statement, June 30, 1990		
Balance per ledger, June 30, 1990		
ENTRY		

Name _____

_____

FLORES COMPANY
Bank Reconciliation Statement
July 31, 1990

	Dr.	Cr.
Balance per bank statement, July 31, 1990		
Balance per ledger, July 31, 1990		
ENTRY		

Name _____

_____

MASSEY COMPANY

Bank Reconciliation Statement

July 31, 1990

	Dr.	Cr.
Balance per bank statement, July 31, 1990		
Balance per ledger, July 31, 1990		
ENTRY		

Name _____

_____

(a)

HALL COMPANY

Bank Reconciliation Statement

March 31, 1990

Balance per bank statement, March 31, 1990

Balance per ledger account, March 31, 1990

(b)

(c)

Plant Assets: Acquisition and Depreciation

Understanding the Learning Objectives

1. Recognize the characteristics of plant assets and identify the initial costs of acquiring plant assets.

    *   Plant assets include tangible long-lived assets (assets with useful lives that are expected to exceed more than one period) obtained for use in business operations instead of for resale. Examples include land, buildings, machinery, delivery equipment, and office equipment.

    *   Plant assets are usually recorded at cost. Cost includes all normal, reasonable, and necessary outlays to obtain and get the assets ready for use, such as invoice price, installation cost, and transportation.

    *   When plant assets are acquired in an exchange for securities or other assets, they should normally be recorded at the fair market value of the asset acquired or the assets or securities given up, whichever is more clearly evident.

    *   When assets are received as a gift they should be recorded at their fair market value or at an appraised value if a fair market value cannot be determined.

2. Understand the various methods of calculating depreciation expense.

    *   Under the straight-line method, depreciation per period is equal to (cost minus estimated salvage value) divided by the number of accounting periods in the estimated life.

    *   Under the units-of-production method, depreciation per unit of product is equal to (cost minus estimated salvage value) divided by estimated units of production over the life of the assets. Depreciation for the period is equal to depreciation per unit times the number of units produced in the period.

    *   Under the double-declining-balance method, depreciation per period is equal to (cost minus accumulated depreciation) times (100% divided by useful life) times 2.

    *   Under sum-of-the-years'-digits method, depreciation per period is equal to (cost minus estimated salvage value) times (remaining useful life at the beginning of the period divided by the sum-of-the-years' digits).

3. Distinguish between capital and revenue expenditures for plant assets.

    *   Capital expenditures are added to the asset account or charged to the accumulated depreciation account.

    *   Revenue expenditures are recorded as expenses.

    *   An expenditure that increases the quality of services provided by an asset should be debited to an asset account.

    *   An expenditure that increases the quantity of services beyond the original estimated useful life should be debited to the accumulated depreciation account.

    *   An expenditure that neither increases the quality nor quantity of the services should be debited to an expense account.

4. Define and use correctly the new terms in the glossary.

The new terms introduced in the chapter are as follows:

Accelerated depreciation methods—Record higher amounts of depreciation in the early years of an asset's life and lower amounts in later years.

Appraised values—The values assigned to assets by independent, professional appraisers.

Betterments (improvements)—Capital expenditures that are properly charged to asset accounts because they add to the service-rendering ability of the assets; they increase the quality of services that can be obtained from an asset.

Book value—An asset's recorded cost less its accumulated depreciation.

Capital expenditures—Expenditures that are debited to an asset account or to an accumulated depreciation account.

Depreciation—The amount of plant asset cost allocated to each period benefiting from the plant asset's use. The **straight-line depreciation** method charges an equal amount of plant asset cost to each period. The **units-of-production** method assigns an equal amount of depreciation for each unit of product manufactured or service rendered by an asset. The **sum-of-the-years'-digits (SYD)** and the **double-declining-balance (DDB)** depreciation methods assign decreasing amounts of depreciation to successive periods of time.

Depreciation accounting—Distributes in a systematic and rational manner the cost of a depreciable plant asset, less its salvage value, over the asset's estimated useful life.

Extraordinary repairs—Expenditures that are viewed as canceling a part of the existing accumulated depreciation because they increase the quantity of services expected from an asset.

Fair market value—The normal price that would be paid for an item being sold in the normal course of business (not at a forced liquidation sale).

Inadequacy—The inability of a plant to produce enough products or provide enough services to meet current demands.

Obsolescence—Decline in usefulness of an asset brought about by invention and technological progress.

Physical deterioration—Results from use of the asset—wear and tear—and the action of the elements.

Plant assets—Tangible long-lived assets obtained for use in business operations instead of for resale.

Revenue expenditures—Expenditures (on a plant asset) that are immediately expensed.

Salvage (or scrap) value—The amount of money the company expects to recover, less disposal costs, on the date a plant asset is scrapped, sold, or traded in. Also called residual value.

Useful life—The length of time the company holding a depreciable asset intends to use it.

Completion and Exercises

1. To what are accountants referring when they use the term "plant assets"?

_____

_____

_____

_____

2. Plant assets can be broadly classified as _____ and

_____ _____.

3. What is included in the cost of plant assets?

_____

_____

_____

_____

_____

4. The Bell Company acquired land and a building at a lump-sum price of $640,000. The building is to be renovated and used by the company. According to competent appraisers, the land and the building have

   values of $200,000 and $600,000, respectively, on the acquisition date. A cost of _____

   should be assigned to the land, and a cost of _____ should be assigned to the building.

5. The Fox Company purchased a machine for $20,000 less a 2 percent cash discount. Transportation charges were $200, and installation and testing costs totaled $2,000. While being unloaded, the machine was dropped and damaged. It cost $100 to repair the damage. What is the cost of the machine? (Work space is provided below.)

6. What is the *general* rule for determining the valuation to be placed on an exchange of noncash assets?

_____

_____

_____

_____

7. The major causes of depreciation are _____ _____ ,

_____ , and _____ .

8. Is the following statement true or false? _____ Why? Accountants depreciate assets so that the assets will be reported on the balance sheet at their current market values.

_____

_____

_____

_____

_____

9. The _____-_____ method of depreciation allocates the same dollar amount of depreciation to each period in the estimated useful life of the asset.

10. From the following information, what is the yearly depreciation charge under the straight-line method?

Cost of asset	$132,000
Estimated salvage value	6,000
Estimated useful life	9 years

11. From the following information, compute the depreciation for the current year under the units-of-production method.

> Cost of asset $37,500
> Estimated salvage value .... -0-
> Expected production for entire life .... 250,000 units
> Current year's production .... 36,000 units

12. Compute depreciation for each of the first two years of the asset's life under the double-declining-balance method.

> Cost of asset $84,000
> Estimated salvage value 4,000
> Estimated useful life .... 10 years

13. Compute depreciation for the first year of the asset's life under the sum-of-the-years'-digits method.

> Cost of asset $156,000
> Estimated salvage value 12,000
> Estimated useful life .... 7 years

14. A machine was acquired on October 1, 1990, at a cost of $40,000. It has an estimated salvage value of $4,000, and an estimated useful life of eight years. The double-declining-balance method of depreciation is to be used. Compute depreciation for 1990 and 1991.

15. A machine that cost $25,000 has an estimated salvage value of $1,000 and an estimated useful life of five years. The machine is being depreciated on a straight-line basis. At the beginning of the fourth year, it is estimated that the machine will last five more years. The revised annual depreciation charge is

   $_____ .

16. Expenditures for additions to existing assets, such as betterments or improvements, should be charged

   to _____ .

17. If $500 is spent overhauling the engine in a delivery truck, and as a result, the truck will be used an additional two years beyond its original estimated life, what entry is necessary?

DATE	ACCOUNT TITLES AND EXPLANATION	POST. REF.	DEBIT	CREDIT

18. What effect will the engine overhaul in Question 17 have on periodic depreciation of the truck if the overhaul is accounted for as a debit to the accumulated depreciation account, but the original estimated useful life stays the same?

_____

_____

_____

_____

19. Assume the truck in Question 17 at acquisition had an estimated useful life of eight years, a cost of $5,800, and an estimated salvage value of $200. If the overhaul increased the truck's estimated useful life by one year and was made at the beginning of the eighth year, what will be the charge to depreciation expense for each of the last two years of the truck's useful life on a straight-line basis?

20. The main distinction between capital and revenue expenditures is _____

_____

_____.

Multiple-Choice Questions

For each of the following questions, indicate the single best answer by circling the appropriate letter.

1. Which of the following items is properly classifiable as plant and equipment?
    a. Land owned and on which a factory building has been constructed
    b. A factory building owned and used by a manufacturing company
    c. A typewriter purchased by an office supply company to resell to customers
    d. (a) and (b) above are correct

2. The Ace Department Store purchased land and a building from Susan Ling for the purpose of building a parking ramp for its customers. The purchase contract specified that Ace Department Store would pay Ms. Ling $40,000 in cash and would assume the present real estate mortgage note of $8,000. Ace also agreed to assume payment of $200 of property taxes in arrears. The $280 in legal fees incurred by the store in connection with this transaction included: $150 for title search, $50 for drawing up necessary documents, $60 for transfer taxes, and $20 in recording fees. As soon as it gained title to the property, Ace Department Store demolished the existing building and graded the property in preparation for the erection of the parking ramp. The cost of tearing down the old structure and grading was $5,400. On the basis of the above data, at what cost should this land be recorded in Ace's accounts?

   a. $40,280
   b. $48,200
   c. $48,280
   d. $53,880

3. The chief purpose of depreciation accounting is to:

   a.   provide a fund for financing the replacement of depreciable assets.
   b.   provide a deduction for income tax purposes.
   c.   revalue assets whose value has declined.
   d.   systematically allocate the service potential of depreciable assets, usually as measured in terms of cost, against the revenue produced over the estimated useful lives of those assets.

4. On July 1, 1990, the Lind Toy Company purchased a machine invoiced at $12,000 (terms are 2/10, n/30 f.o.b. shipping point). The invoice was paid within the discount period. Freight charges amounted to $250 and installation costs to $590. The estimated useful life of the machine is ten years, after which time it will have an estimated salvage value of $400. It is estimated that this machine will produce a total of 100,000 units during its lifetime. Assume that 6,000 units have been produced by December 31, 1990, the end of the accounting period. Depreciation for 1990 based on usage would be:

   a. $12,440 $\times$ 1/10 $\times$ 1/2 = $622
   b. $0.126 $\times$ 6,000 = $756
   c. $0.1244 $\times$ 6,000 = $746.40
   d. $0.122 $\times$ 6,000 = $732

5. On July 1, 1990, the Jackson Machine Company built and installed a machine for its own use at a total cost of $11,700. The estimated life of the machine was five years; estimated salvage value, $200. It would have cost Jackson Machine Company $12,500 to buy a comparable machine, installed. Which of the following statements is true?

   a.   The charge for depreciation for the year ended June 30, 1991, (first year) would be greater under the double-declining-balance method than under the sum-of-the-years'-digits method.
   b.   The charge for depreciation for the year ended June 30, 1992, (second year) would be greater under the sum-of-the-years'-digits method than under the double-declining-balance method.
   c.   The charge for depreciation for the year ended June 30, 1991, (first year) under the sum-of-the-years'-digits method would be $3,833.
   d.   Statements (a), (b) and (c) are true.

6. The Kent Company acquired a delivery truck for $12,000 on September 1, 1990. The truck has an estimated salvage value of $500 and an estimated useful life of eight years. The company operates on a calendar year accounting period and uses double-declining-balance depreciation. What amounts of depreciation should be recorded for years 1990 and 1991, respectively?

   a. $3,000 and $2,250
   b. $958 and $2,626
   c. $1,000 and $2,250
   d. $1,000 and $2,750

7. A machine has a cost of $18,000, an estimated salvage value of $3,000, and an estimated useful life of five years. The machine is being depreciated on a straight-line basis. At the beginning of the fourth year, it is estimated that the machine will last another four years, with $3,000 of salvage value still expected. What is the revised annual depreciation charge?

    a. $750
    b. $1,500
    c. $1,800
    d. $2,143

8. Which of the following should be expensed immediately?

    a.   Cost of completely overhauling a machine in order to extend its useful life
    b.   Cost of maintaining equipment
    c.   Cost of reconditioning a newly acquired piece of used equipment
    d.   Back taxes on land just acquired

9. The cost of excavating the basement for a new building should be recorded in which of the following accounts?

    a.   Land
    b.   Land improvements
    c.   Building
    d.   Excavating expense

10. The characteristics an asset must possess to be classified as a plant asset include which of the following?

    a.   Tangibility
    b.   An expected life greater than one year
    c.   Held for use rather than sale
    d.   All of the above

11. The cost of land may include all of the following except:

    a.   title insurance premiums.
    b.   unpaid taxes assumed by the purchaser.
    c.   sewer lines.
    d.   paved driveways.

12. Blake Company purchased a used machine for $20,000, paid $2,000 to overhaul it, and $3,000 to install it on a special reinforced base built at a cost of $6,000. In addition, $500 was spent to remove an old fully-depreciated machine to make room for the new machine. The cost to be recorded in the machinery account for this machine is:

    a. $31,000.
    b. $31,500.
    c. $29,000.
    d. $23,000.

13. If the revenues to be produced by a depreciable asset are expected to decline sharply even though output remains fairly constant, depreciation probably should be recorded using which method?

    a.   Straight-line
    b.   Units-of-output
    c.   Double-declining-balance
    d.   Sum-of-the-years'-digits
    e.   Either (c) or (d)

14. An estimate of salvage value is not needed to compute depreciation by which of the following methods?

    a. Straight-line
    b. Double-declining-balance
    c. Sum-of-the-years'-digits
    d. Units-of-output

15. A machine with a cost of $32,000, an estimated life of five years, and an expected salvage value of $2,000 was placed in service on January 5, 1987. It was depreciated using the straight-line method. Early in 1990, the machine was completely overhauled at a cost of $6,000. It is now estimated that the machine will last a total of seven years and that it will have no salvage value at the end of that life. The depreciation to be recorded on the machine in 1991 is:

    a. $3,500.
    b. $5,000.
    c. $2,000.
    d. $3,333.

16. Equipment with an invoice cost of $20,000 was placed in service on January 3, 1990. Installation costs of $8,000 were debited to Repairs Expense. Depreciation for 1990 was computed using the straight-line method, and an estimated useful life of five years, with no salvage value expected. The net income reported for 1990 was:

    a. understated $8,000.
    b. understated $6,400.
    c. overstated $1,600.
    d. overstated $6,400.

17. If depreciation is basically a function of the length of time that an asset is owned, it should be recorded using the:

    a. straight-line method.
    b. units-of-output method.
    c. sum-of-the-years'-digits method.
    d. double-declining-balance method.

18. Which of the following is a capital expenditure?

    a. Cost of painting the offices on the second floor of a 15-story building
    b. Property taxes paid for the first year a building is operated
    c. Insurance premium paid for the period a building was under construction
    d. Cost of repeating construction work on a building due to faulty procedures

Now compare your answers with the correct ones beginning on page 179.

Solutions/Chapter 6

Completion and Exercises

1. Plant assets are the relatively long-lived tangible assets acquired for use in the operations of a business rather than for resale.

2. land; depreciable property

3. The cost of a plant asset consists of all the normal and reasonable expenditures necessary to place the asset in its intended position in a usable condition.

4. $160,000 $\left(\$640,000 \times \dfrac{\$200,000}{\$800,000} \right)$

   $480,000 $\left(\$640,000 \times \dfrac{\$600,000}{\$800,000} \right)$

5.
Invoice price	$20,000
Less: 2 percent cash discount	400
	$19,600
Transportation charges	200
Installation and testing costs	2,000
Cost of machine......................................	$21,800

6. The *general* rule is that of using the fair market value of the assets received or of the assets surrendered or securities issued, whichever is the more clearly evident.

7. physical deterioration; inadequacy; obsolescence

8. False. Depreciation attempts to distribute in a systematic and rational manner the cost (or other basic value) less salvage of the plant asset over the estimated useful life of the asset in order to match the cost of the asset with the revenue produced by the asset.

9. straight-line

10. Depreciation per period = ($132,000 − $6,000) ÷ 9 = $14,000 per year

11. Depreciation per unit = $\dfrac{\$37,500}{250,000}$ = $0.15 per unit; 36,000 × $0.15 per unit = $5,400 depreciation for current year

12. First year:
    Depreciation = $84,000 × 0.20 = $16,800
    Second year:
    Depreciation = ($84,000 − $16,800) × 0.20 = $13,440

13. Sum-of-the-years'-digits = 1 + 2 + 3 + 4 + 5 + 6 + 7 = 28
    Depreciation for first year = 7/28 × $144,000 = $36,000

14. 1990: Depreciation = $40,000 × 0.25 × 3/12 = $2,500
    1991: Depreciation = ($40,000 − $2,500) × 0.25
    = $9,375

15. $1,920, [($25,000 − $1,000)/5 = $4,800; $25,000 − ($4,800 × 3) = $10,600; ($10,600 − $1,000)/5 = $1,920]

16. the asset accounts

17.
Accumulated Depreciation—Delivery Equipment	500	
Cash (or Accounts Payable)		500
Cost of overhauling truck engine.		

18. The truck will still be depreciated over the same number of years, but the yearly charge to depreciation expense will be greater for the remaining years.

19. At the beginning of eighth year:

Cost of truck	$5,800
Less: Estimated salvage value	200
	$5,600
Less: Accumulated depreciation [($5,600/8) × 7]	4,900
Net depreciable book value before overhaul	$ 700
Cost of engine overhaul	500
Net depreciable book value after overhaul	$1,200

$1,200 ÷ 2 remaining years of useful life = $600 of depreciation per year

20. the length of time that the expenditure will be beneficial

Multiple-Choice Questions

1. d. A typewriter purchased by an office supply company to resell to customers is properly classifiable as inventory and not as plant and equipment. Only assets used in the production or sale of another asset or service are properly classifiable as plant and equipment, as in (a) and (b).

2. d. The cost of the land consists of the following items:

Cash payment.............................	$40,000
Mortgage assumed	8,000
Property tax liability assumed	200
Legal fees.................................	280
Removal of old structure and grading	5,400
Total cost...........................	$53,880

3. d. In general, accountants subscribe to the idea of measuring income by matching revenue with the expenses incurred to secure that revenue. Thus, the purpose of depreciation accounting is to allocate the service potential of depreciable assets (measured in terms of cost) used to produce revenue to the period in which the revenue is recorded in the accounts.

4. d. Total cost of the machine is $12,000 − $240 + $250 + $590 = $12,600. The depreciation per unit of production is ($12,600 − $400) ÷ 100,000 = $0.122. The depreciation for the period then is 6,000 times $0.122, or $732.

5. d. The accountant does not subscribe to the idea that a business can produce revenue simply by building a machine for its own use. Therefore, the depreciation charge for the first year under the double-declining-balance method is $11,700 times 40 percent, or $4,680. For the second year, it is ($11,700 − $4,680) × 40 percent, or $2,808. Under the sum-of-the-years'-digits method, the depreciation for the first year is ($11,700 − $200) × 5/15, or $3,833. For the second year, it is ($11,700 − $200) × 4/15, or $3,067. Thus, (a) is true since $4,680 is greater than $3,833; (b) is true because $3,067 is greater than $2,808, and (c) is true—the depreciation for the year ended June 30, 1991, under the sum-of-the-years'-digits method is $3,833. Thus, (a), (b), (c), and (d) are all correct.

6. d. Under the double-declining-balance method, depreciation for 1990 is $1,000 ($12,000 × .25 × 4/12) and depreciation for 1991 is $2,750, .25 ($12,000 − $1,000).

7. b. The revised annual depreciation charge is $1,500, computed as follows:

Cost of machine	$18,000
Depreciation accumulated over three years	
[($18,000 − $3,000) ÷ 5] × 3	9,000
Book value at beginning of fourth year	$ 9,000
Revised annual depreciation charge	
[($9,000 − $3,000) ÷ 4].................	$ 1,500

Name _____

_____

IVY STREET COMPANY
Equipment—Machine C

Name _____

_____

(a)

MORTON COMPANY

Schedule of Building Costs

As of December 31, 1990

(b)   GENERAL JOURNAL

DATE	ACCOUNT TITLES AND EXPLANATION	POST. REF.	DEBIT	CREDIT

Name _____

THE NEAL COMPANY

Depreciation Schedule

May 31, 1990

DESCRIPTION	DATE ACQUIRED	COST	SALVAGE VALUE	NET TO BE DEPRECIATED	LIFE	USAGE 6-1-89 TO 5-31-90	RATE	CURRENT YR. DEPRECIATION

Name _____

(a) _____

DEWEY COMPANY
GENERAL JOURNAL

DATE	ACCOUNT TITLES AND EXPLANATION	POST. REF.	DEBIT	CREDIT

(b)

Name

JARVIS COMPANY

(a)

BLUE COMPANY

Depreciation Schedule

	1990	1991	1992
Building:			
Machinery:			

GREEN COMPANY

Depreciation Schedule

	1990	1991	1992
Building:			
Machinery:			

(b)

BLUE COMPANY

Tax Savings

	1990	1991	1992

(c)

Plant Asset Disposals; Natural Resources and Intangible Assets

Understanding the Learning Objectives

1. Calculate and prepare entries for the sale, retirement, and destruction of plant assets.

    *   When a business disposes of a plant asset by selling it, the asset's book value (cost less accumulated depreciation) is compared with its sales price (or net amount realized if there are selling expenses involved). If the asset is sold for more than the book value, a gain will be realized; conversely, if the sales price is less than the book value, the company will show a loss. Of course, if the asset is sold for its exact book value, there will be no gain or loss resulting from the sale.

    *   In preparing journal entries to record the sale, the asset's accumulated depreciation account is debited for the depreciation taken to date, and cash (or a receivable account) is debited for the sales price. The asset account is then credited for the original cost of the asset, and a gain or loss on disposal of plant assets is credited or debited, as appropriate.

    *   When an asset is retired from productive service, the asset's cost and accumulated depreciation accounts must be removed from the books.

    *   If the asset is to be sold as scrap, a Salvaged Materials account should be set up for the estimated scrap value, and the appropriate gain or loss on disposal should be recorded.

    *   The destruction of a plant asset will normally result in a loss. If the asset was insured, the appropriate amount should be recorded in a Receivable from Insurance Company account with the remainder recorded in a loss account.

2. Describe and record exchanges of dissimilar and similar plant assets.

    *   Similar plant assets are those of the same general type or that perform the same function. Dissimilar plant assets are not of the same general type, such as buildings versus trucks.

    *   An exchange of dissimilar plant assets is accounted for by recording the new asset at the fair market value of the asset received or the asset(s) given up, whichever is more clearly evident. The book value of the old asset is removed from the accounts by debiting accumulated depreciation and crediting the old asset account. After crediting cash (or a payable account), a gain or loss is then recorded to balance the entry.

    *   An exchange of similar plant assets is recorded much the same as dissimilar plant assets, except losses are recognized but gains are not. When a gain has occurred, the new asset is reduced by the amount of the gain.

3. Discuss the differences between accounting principles and tax rules in the treatment of gains and losses from the exchange of plant assets.

   * The Internal Revenue Code does not allow recognition of gains or losses for income tax purposes when similar productive assets are exchanged. Rather, the cost basis of the new asset is the book value of the old asset plus any additional cash paid.

4. Determine the periodic depletion cost of a natural resource and calculate depreciation of plant assets on extractive industry property.

   * Depletion charges are usually computed by using a units-of-production method as follows:

   $$\frac{\text{Total cost}}{\text{Estimated number of units that can be economically extracted}} = \frac{\text{per unit}}{\text{depletion cost}}$$

   * When periodic depreciation charges are computed for plant assets on extractive industry property using the units-of-production method, the following calculation is made:

   $$\frac{\text{Asset cost} - \text{Estimated Salvage Value}}{\text{Total Tons of Ore in Mine}} = \frac{\text{depreciation}}{\text{per unit}}$$

5. Prepare entries for the acquisition and amortization of intangible assets.

   * Intangible assets are recorded initially at the outright purchase costs of the intangible assets. Amortization of intangible assets is similar to plant asset depreciation. Generally, amortization is recorded by debiting Amortization Expense and crediting the intangible asset account. There is, however, a 40-year limitation on amortizing these assets.

6. Define and use correctly the new terms in the glossary.

   The new terms introduced in the chapter are as follows:

   Amortization—The term used to describe the systematic write-off of the cost of an intangible asset to expense.

   Boot—The additional cash outlay made when one asset is traded for a similar asset.

   Capital lease—A lease that transfers to the lessee virtually all of the rewards and the risks that accompany ownership of property.

   Copyright—An exclusive right granted by the federal government giving the owner protection against the illegal reproduction by others of the owner's written works, designs, and literary productions.

   Depletion—The exhaustion of a natural resource; an estimate of the cost of the resource that was removed during the period.

   Franchise—A contract between two parties granting the franchisee (the purchaser of the franchise) certain rights and privileges ranging from name identification to complete monopoly of service.

   Goodwill—An intangible value attached to a company resulting mainly from the company's management skill or know-how and a favorable reputation with customers. Evidenced by the ability to generate an above-average rate of income on each dollar invested in the business.

   Intangible assets—Items that have no physical characteristics but are of value because of the advantages or exclusive privileges and rights they provide to a business.

   Lease—A contract to rent property. Grantor of the lease is the **lessor**; the party obtaining the rights to possess and use property is the **lessee**.

   Leasehold—The rights granted under a lease.

   Leasehold improvement—Any physical alteration to leased property in which benefits are expected beyond the current accounting period.

   "Material" gains or losses—Gains or losses large enough to affect the decisions of an informed user of the financial statements.

Materiality concept—Allows the accountant to deal with immaterial (unimportant) items in a theoretically incorrect manner.

Natural resources—Ore deposits, mineral deposits, oil reserves, gas deposits, and timber stands supplied by nature.

Nonmonetary assets—Items whose price may change over time, such as inventories, property, plant, and equipment.

Operating lease—A lease that does not qualify as a capital lease.

Patent—A right granted by a government giving the owner the exclusive right to manufacture, sell, lease, or otherwise benefit from an invention.

Research and development (R&D) costs—Costs incurred in a planned search for new knowledge and in translating such knowledge into a new product or process.

Trademark—A symbol, design, or logo that is used in conjunction with a particular product or company.

Trade name—A brand name under which a product is sold or a company does business.

Wasting assets—See Natural resources.

Completion and Exercises

1. A gain or loss on the sale of a plant asset is determined by comparing the asset's _____

   _____ with its _____ _____.

2. A machine which cost $55,000 and has an accumulated depreciation account balance of $30,000 is sold

   for $28,000. There is (gain/loss) _____ on the sale of $_____.

3. Prepare the journal entry if the plant asset described below is sold for $6,000 and depreciation has been recorded to the date of sale (omit explanation).

   Cost of asset $25,000
   Accumulated depreciation 18,750

DATE	ACCOUNT TITLES AND EXPLANATION	POST. REF.	DEBIT	CREDIT

4. What entry is required to record the retirement of the machine described below (omit explanation)?

   Cost $10,000
   Accumulated depreciation 9,500
   Estimated salvage value to be realized upon retirement ... 500

   (Use form on next page.)

DATE	ACCOUNT TITLES AND EXPLANATION	POST. REF.	DEBIT	CREDIT

5. Assume that a building costing $140,000 is completely destroyed by fire. Depreciation accumulated to the date of destruction amounts to $65,000. What journal entry is required to record the destruction if $60,000 is expected to be recovered from the insurance company? (Omit explanation.)

DATE	ACCOUNT TITLES AND EXPLANATION	POST. REF.	DEBIT	CREDIT

6. Assume that factory equipment costing $15,000 and having an accumulated depreciation account balance of $10,000 is exchanged for an automobile. In addition to the factory equipment, cash of $9,000 is paid. The automobile has a cash price of $11,000. What journal entry is required to record the exchange? (Omit explanation.)

DATE	ACCOUNT TITLES AND EXPLANATION	POST. REF.	DEBIT	CREDIT

7. Assume that $123,000 cash and an old machine which cost $90,000 and which has an accumulated depreciation account balance of $80,000 are exchanged for a similar new machine that has a cash price of $135,000. What entry is required to record this exchange under generally accepted accounting principles? (Omit explanation.)

DATE	ACCOUNT TITLES AND EXPLANATION	POST. REF.	DEBIT	CREDIT

8. Assume that $42,500 cash and an old delivery truck which cost $28,000 and which has an accumulated depreciation account balance of $25,000 are exchanged for a new delivery truck that has a cash price of $43,000. What entry is required to record this exchange in accordance with generally accepted accounting principles? (Omit explanation.)

DATE	ACCOUNT TITLES AND EXPLANATION	POST. REF.	DEBIT	CREDIT

9. Assume that Machine No. 1, which cost $100,000 and on which $65,000 depreciation has been recorded, is exchanged for Machine No. 2 which has a cash price of $115,000. Machine No. 1 and $75,000 are given in exchange. What entry is needed to record this exchange under the tax method? (Omit explanation.)

DATE	ACCOUNT TITLES AND EXPLANATION	POST. REF.	DEBIT	CREDIT

10. _____ is caused by the physical removal of a quantity of natural resources.

11. What are the forms of the two different possible entries for recording periodic depletion?

DATE	ACCOUNT TITLES AND EXPLANATION	POST. REF.	DEBIT	CREDIT

12. Valley Company paid $330,000 for the mineral rights, estimated at 2,500,000 tons, in a certain tract of land. In its first year of operations, Valley Company extracted 100,000 tons of minerals and sold 90,000 tons. The depletion cost per ton is _____ , and the depletion cost to be charged to expense in the first year of operations is _____ .

13. Specialized machinery was installed at the site of an oil reserve. The machinery has an estimated physical life of 15 years. The oil reserve is expected to be productive for 20 more years. The machinery should be depreciated over _____ years.

14. What are intangible assets?

_____

_____

_____

_____

15. _____ is an estimate, usually expressed in terms of cost, of the services received from an intangible asset in a period.

16. Over what period of time should patents be amortized?

_____

_____

_____

_____

17. _____ is an intangible value attaching to a business because its management is able to produce above-average earnings per dollar of investment.

18. Research and development costs should be _____ as incurred.

Multiple-Choice Questions

For each of the following questions, indicate the single best answer by circling the appropriate letter.

1. On January 2, 1986, Roy's Store purchased office equipment at a cost of $2,700. The equipment had an estimated life of six years with no salvage value. On March 1, 1990 the equipment was sold for $850 cash. At the close of the annual accounting period on December 31, 1989, the Office Equipment account had a balance of $2,700 and the Accumulated Depreciation—Office Equipment account, $1,800. Which of the following entries should be made on March 1, 1990?

a.
Cash	850	
Accumulated Depreciation—Office Equipment	1,800	
Loss on Sale of Plant Assets	50	
Office Equipment		2,700

b.
Depreciation Expense	75	
Accumulated Depreciation—Office Equipment		75
Cash	850	
Accumulated Depreciation—Office Equipment	1,875	
Office Equipment		2,700
Gain on Sale of Plant Assets		25

c.
Depreciation Expense	75	
Accumulated Depreciation—Office Equipment		75
Cash	850	
Accumulated Depreciation—Office Equipment	1,800	
Loss on Sale of Plant Assets	50	
Office Equipment		2,700

d.
Depreciation Expense	100	
Accumulated Depreciation—Office Equipment		100
Cash	850	
Accumulated Depreciation—Office Equipment	1,900	
Office Equipment		2,700
Gain on Sale of Office Equipment		50

2. A building costing $190,000 on which $100,000 of depreciation had been accumulated and a machine costing $60,000 on which $40,000 of depreciation had been accumulated were completely destroyed by fire. Both assets were partially insured, and $90,000 is expected to be recovered from the insurance company. The total amount of the fire loss to be recorded by the company is:

   a. $20,000.
   b. $90,000.
   c. $110,000.
   d. $250,000.

3. Andrews Furniture Company owns one delivery truck, which it purchased on October 1, 1988, at a cost of $19,200. The estimated life of the truck at that time was four years. On June 30, 1991, the close of the fiscal year, the accumulated depreciation account had a balance of $13,200. On July 1, 1991, the company traded this vehicle for a new one. Cash of $16,800 is also paid. The old truck had a fair cash value of $4,500. The journal entry to record the exchange in accordance with accounting principles is:

a.
Delivery Truck (new)	21,300	
Accumulated Depreciation—Delivery Truck	13,200	
Loss on Exchange of Plant Assets	1,500	
Delivery Truck (old)		19,200
Cash		16,800

b.
Delivery Truck (new)	22,800	
Accumulated Depreciation—Delivery Truck	13,200	
Delivery Truck (old)		19,200
Cash		16,800

c.
Delivery Truck (new)	24,000	
Accumulated Depreciation—Delivery Truck	12,000	
Delivery Truck (old)		19,200
Cash		16,800

d.
Delivery Truck (new)	16,800	
Accumulated Depreciation—Delivery Truck	13,200	
Loss on Exchange of Plant Assets	6,000	
Delivery Truck (old)		19,200
Cash		16,800

4. On March 15, 1990, the Strock firm exchanged an old typewriter for a newer model. The cost of the old machine was $400 and its book value (adjusted to March 15, 1990) was $120. The new machine was priced at $1,000 and was acquired for $800 plus the old machine. According to income tax regulations, the cost of the new machine is:

a. $1,000.
b. $1,080.
c. $920.
d. $800.

5. On August 1, 1990, Ryan Metals Company acquired ore deposits estimated at three million tons. 2,600,000 tons are expected to be economically removable. The property on which the ore is situated was acquired at a cost of $1,300,000. In the fiscal year ended July 31, 1991, Ryan mined 300,000 tons of the ore. The correct adjusting entry on July 31, 1991, is:

a.
Depletion	150,000	
Accumulated Depletion		150,000

b.
Depletion	130,000	
Accumulated Depletion		130,000

c.
Depletion	75,000	
Accumulated Depletion		75,000

d.
Depreciation	130,000	
Accumulated Depreciation		130,000

6. Kraft Company purchased a patent on a new drug. The cost of the patent was $180,000. Legal fees in securing the patent amounted to $2,000. It was estimated that the patent would have a useful life of about five years. Shortly after the patent was acquired, Kraft Company became involved in a lawsuit. It successfully defended itself against the claim of patent infringement. The cost of this litigation was $8,000. The correct journal entry to reflect the patent amortization for each fiscal year is:

   a. Patent Amortization Expense 36,000
         Patents 36,000

   b. Patent Amortization Expense 36,400
         Accumulated Amortization—Patents 36,400

   c. Patent Amortization Expense 38,000
         Patents 38,000

   d. Patent Amortization Expense 11,176
         Patents 11,176

7. Which of the following statements is true?

   a. Goodwill is recorded only when purchased.
   b. The goodwill of a business can be purchased separately from the rest of its assets.
   c. Goodwill, once recorded, should not be amortized.
   d. The existence of goodwill can be determined without reference to the earnings of a business.

8. Roxa Company leased a building for ten years. The operating lease contract called for an advance lump-sum payment of $30,000 (20 percent of the total payments due under the lease) plus $12,000 of annual rent payable at the end of each year. The Roxa Company immediately remodeled the building at a cost of $14,000. The building has an estimated useful life of 28 years. Which of the following entries should be made at the end of each year?

   a. Leasehold Improvement Expense 1,400
         Leasehold Improvements 1,400

      Rent Expense 15,000
         Leasehold 3,000
         Cash 12,000

   b. Leasehold Improvement Expense 500
         Leasehold Improvements 500

      Rent Expense 15,000
         Leasehold 3,000
         Cash 12,000

   c. Leasehold Improvement Expense 500
      Rent Expense 15,000
         Leasehold Improvements 3,000
         Cash 12,500

   d. Leasehold Improvement Expense 1,400
      Rent Expense 15,000
         Leasehold 1,400
         Cash 15,000

9. Which of the following statements is true?

   a. Research and development costs can either be expensed as incurred or capitalized and written off over 40 years.
   b. Research and development costs must be capitalized and written off over 40 years.
   c. Research and development costs must be capitalized and written off over the shorter of their useful life or 40 years.
   d. Research and development costs must be expensed as incurred unless they are directly reimbursable by government agencies or others.

10. The cost incurred to acquire a franchise is subject to:

   a. depreciation.
   b. amortization.
   c. depletion.
   d. none of the above.

11. A company paid $480,000 to install machinery at a mine estimated to contain 720,000 recoverable tons of ore. The machinery has an estimated life of 12 years and is capable of exhausting the mine in 10 years. If, in the first year of operations, 120,000 tons of ore were mined, the depreciation to be recorded is:

   a. $180,000.
   b. $80,000.
   c. $120,000.
   d. none of the above.

12. Equipment with a cost of $30,000 and $24,000 of accumulated depreciation is sold for $4,000. Removal costs of $1,000 were incurred to dismantle and remove the machine prior to sale. The loss recorded on the disposition of this equipment is:

   a. $6,000.
   b. $7,000.
   c. $2,000.
   d. $3,000.

13. A company extracted 200,000 tons of ore from a deposit of 2,000,000 tons for which it paid $10,000,000. Mining labor costs amounted to $20,000,000 and other mining costs were $9,000,000. A total of 160,000 tons of ore was sold during the year. The total amount of expense to be recorded from the above data for the year is:

   a. $24,000,000.
   b. $30,000,000.
   c. $29,800,000.
   d. $25,800,000.

14. The balance sheet of Drew Company shows assets of $10,000 and liabilities of $2,000. The market value of these assets is $11,000 and of the liabilities is $2,500. Cox Company now pays Drew Company $8,600 for all of its assets and agrees to assume responsibility for the liabilities. Cox Company should record goodwill on this purchase of:

   a. $600.
   b. $100.
   c. $1,100.
   d. $400.

15. Trask Company leased a tract of land for five years, paying $2,500 immediately in cash and agreeing to make annual payments of $1,000 for five years. It then moved a mobile home (cost, $10,000) on the land at a cost of $2,000. The mobile home is to serve as an office. It has a useful life of 10 years. If depreciation and amortization are recorded under the straight-line method, the total expense recorded in the first year is:

   a. $2,900.
   b. $4,500.
   c. $5,500.
   d. none of the above.

Now compare your answers with the correct ones beginning on page 207.

Solutions/Chapter 7

Completion and Exercises

1. book value (cost less accumulated depreciation); sales price

2. gain; $3,000 [($55,000 − $28,000) − $30,000]

3. Cash 6,000
   Accumulated Depreciation—Plant Assets 18,750
   Loss on Sale of Plant Assets 250
       Plant Assets 25,000

4. Salvaged Materials 500
   Accumulated Depreciation—Machinery 9,500
       Machinery 10,000

5. Receivable from Insurance Company 60,000
   Fire Loss 15,000
   Accumulated Depreciation—Building 65,000
       Building 140,000

6. Automobiles 11,000
   Accumulated Depreciation—Factory Equipment 10,000
   Loss on Exchange of Plant Assets 3,000
       Factory Equipment 15,000
       Cash 9,000

   [Loss on exchange is difference between book value of $5,000 ($15,000 − $10,000) and trade-in allowance of $2,000 ($11,000 − $9,000).]

7. Machinery (new) 133,000
   Accumulated Depreciation—Machinery 80,000
       Machinery (old) 90,000
       Cash 123,000

8. Delivery Trucks (new) 43,000
   Accumulated Depreciation—Delivery Trucks 25,000
   Loss on Exchange of Plant Assets 2,500
       Delivery Trucks (old) 28,000
       Cash 42,500

   [Loss on exchange is difference between book value of $3,000 ($28,000 − $25,000) and trade-in allowance of $500 ($43,000 − $42,500).]

9. Machinery (No. 2) 110,000
   Accumulated Depreciation—Machinery 65,000
       Machinery (No. 1) 100,000
       Cash 75,000

10. Depletion

11. Depletion xxx
        Natural Resource xxx
    Depletion xxx
        Accumulated Depletion xxx

12. $0.132, ($330,000/2,500,000 tons); $11,880 ($0.132 × 90,000 tons sold)

13. 15

14. Intangible assets are noncurrent nonphysical assets acquired for use in business operations rather than for resale. They provide business advantages and exclusive rights or privileges to their owners.

15. Amortization

16. Patents should be amortized over the shorter of their legal life of 17 years or their estimated useful life.

17. Goodwill

18. expensed

Multiple-Choice Questions

1. b. Depreciation should be recorded on the equipment up to the date of sale. The straight-line method is being used, since $2,700/6 = $450 per year and $450 for four years equals $1,800. The amount for the two months in 1990 is 2/12 × $450, or $75. The depreciation accumulated to the date of sale is then $1,800 plus $75, or $1,875. The book value of the equipment at date of sale is $2,700 less $1,875, or $825. Since $850 was received, the equipment was sold at a gain of $25.

2. a. The total amount of the fire loss is $20,000, computed as follows:

Cost of building......................	$190,000
Less accumulated depreciation	100,000
Book value of building	$ 90,000
Cost of machine	$ 60,000
Less accumulated depreciation	40,000
Book value of machine	$ 20,000
Total book value of assets destroyed ($90,000 + $20,000)............	$110,000
Recovery from insurance company...	90,000
Fire loss	$ 20,000

3. a. The new truck should be recorded at the amount of cash paid plus the fair market value of the old truck. The amount of cash paid is $16,800 and the fair market value of the old truck is $4,500. Therefore, the new truck should be recorded at $21,300. The cost of the old truck is $19,200 (which must be removed from the accounts, as must the accumulated depreciation); its accumulated depreciation is $13,200, leaving a net book value of $6,000; and at time of exchange it was worth $4,500, resulting in a loss on exchange of $1,500 which must be recognized.

4. c. According to income tax regulations, the new typewriter will be carried in the accounts at the net book value of the old machine ($120) plus the amount of cash paid ($800).

5. a. Depletion cost per unit is $0.50 ($1,300,000/2,600,000), and since 300,000 tons were mined, the depletion to be recorded is $150,000.

6. c. The cost of a patent should be allocated to the years in which it yields benefits. Thus, the cost of the patent ($180,000 + $2,000 + $8,000) should be charged to the five-year period of useful life at the rate of $38,000 per year.

7. a. Goodwill may only be recorded when purchased. Statement (b) is false; goodwill cannot be purchased separately. Statement (c) is false; goodwill must be amortized. Statement (d) is false; the existence of goodwill can be determined only with reference to the relative earnings of a firm.

8. a. The amount of leasehold improvement expense chargeable to each year is $1,400 ($14,000/10 years.) The annual rent expense is $15,000, consisting of $12,000 payable in cash and $3,000 from amortization of the advance payment ($30,000/10).

9. d. Research and development costs must be expensed as incurred unless they are reimbursable by government agencies or others. Companies no longer have the choice of capitalizing or immediate expense.

10. b. The systematic write off of an intangible asset is called amortization.

11. b.   120,000/720,000 × $480,000 = $80,000.

12. d. $30,000 − $24,000 − $4,000 = $2,000; $2,000 + $1,000 = $3,000.

13. a.   Depletion is .1($10,000,000) or $1,000,000. Other mining costs are $20,000,000 + $9,000,000. Total costs incurred then are $30,000,000—80 percent of which relate to tons sold.

14. b. $8,600 − ($11,000 − $2,500) = $100.

15. a. $2,500/5 + $1,000 + $10,000/10 + $2,000/5 = $2,900. Since the mobile home can be moved, it should be depreciated over its useful life.

Name _____

JACKSON COMPANY
GENERAL JOURNAL

DATE	ACCOUNT TITLES AND EXPLANATION	POST. REF.	DEBIT	CREDIT

Name _____

_____

(a)

WATSON COMPANY
GENERAL JOURNAL

DATE	ACCOUNT TITLES AND EXPLANATION	POST. REF.	DEBIT	CREDIT

(b)

Name _____

_____

SPENGLER COMPANY

(a)

Schedule to Compute Book Value

SPENGLER COMPANY
GENERAL JOURNAL

(b)

DATE	ACCOUNT TITLES AND EXPLANATION	POST. REF.	DEBIT	CREDIT
(c)				

Name _____

_____

(c) (concluded)

SPENGLER COMPANY
GENERAL JOURNAL

DATE	ACCOUNT TITLES AND EXPLANATION	POST. REF.	DEBIT	CREDIT

Name _____

_____

MARTINEZ COMPANY
GENERAL JOURNAL

DATE	ACCOUNT TITLES AND EXPLANATION	POST. REF.	DEBIT	CREDIT

SHELTON COMPANY
GENERAL JOURNAL

DATE	ACCOUNT TITLES AND EXPLANATION	POST. REF.	DEBIT	CREDIT

Name _____

_____

KEN COMPANY

Schedule of Patent Costs

December 31, 1990

Name _____

_____

DANISH COMPANY
GENERAL JOURNAL

DATE	ACCOUNT TITLES AND EXPLANATION	POST. REF.	DEBIT	CREDIT

Name _____

DANISH COMPANY
GENERAL JOURNAL

DATE	ACCOUNT TITLES AND EXPLANATION	POST. REF.	DEBIT	CREDIT

DANISH COMPANY
GENERAL JOURNAL

DATE	ACCOUNT TITLES AND EXPLANATION	POST. REF.	DEBIT	CREDIT

Name _____

_____

WILLOW COMPANY
GENERAL JOURNAL

DATE	ACCOUNT TITLES AND EXPLANATION	POST. REF.	DEBIT	CREDIT

WILLOW COMPANY
GENERAL JOURNAL

DATE	ACCOUNT TITLES AND EXPLANATION	POST. REF.	DEBIT	CREDIT

Name _____

_____

(a)   COWAN COMPANY

(b)

CHENEY COMPANY
GENERAL JOURNAL

(a)

DATE 1990		ACCOUNT TITLES AND EXPLANATION	POST. REF.	DEBIT	CREDIT
(b)					

CHENEY COMPANY
GENERAL JOURNAL

(c)

DATE	ACCOUNT TITLES AND EXPLANATION	POST. REF.	DEBIT	CREDIT

Name

(d)

(e)

Name_____

BETH ANDERSON
GENERAL JOURNAL

(a) (1)

DATE	ACCOUNT TITLES AND EXPLANATION	POST. REF.	DEBIT	CREDIT
(2)				

(b)

Stockholders' Equity

Understanding the Learning Objectives

1. Understand the advantages of a corporation.

    *   Advantages include easy transfer of ownership, limited liability, continuous existence of the entity, professional management, and separation of owners and entity.

2. Describe the various types of capital stock and recognize the differences between the types of stock.

    *   The two classes of stock are common stock and preferred stock.

    *   Common stock represents the residual equity in a corporation, meaning that all other claims rank ahead of the claims of the common stockholders.

    *   Preferred stock is preferred as to dividends and may be preferred as to assets in case of liquidation of the company. Preferred stock may be cumulative, convertible, and/or callable.

3. Record capital stock issued for cash or other assets.

    *   Shares with par value are recorded at par value. Shares without par value are recorded at stated value if such a value has been established by the board of directors. No par shares are recorded at the amount at which they have been issued if no stated value has been set.

    *   When capital stock is issued for other assets, the transaction is recorded at the fair value of (1) the assets received, or (2) the stock issued, whichever is more clearly evident.

    *   When only common stock is outstanding, book value per share is computed by dividing total stockholders' equity by the number of common shares outstanding plus common shares subscribed but not yet issued.

    *   When two or more classes of stock are outstanding, the book value of the preferred stock must first be determined. Normally, the preferred stockholders are entitled to a specified liquidation value per share, plus cumulative dividends in arrears, if any.

4. Record other transactions affecting paid-in capital and retained earnings.

    *   When a company receives a donation of assets the Paid-in Capital—Donations account should be credited.

    *   Dividends are distributions of earnings by a corporation to its stockholders.

    *   The normal dividend is a cash dividend, but additional shares of the corporation's own stock may also be distributed as dividends.

    *   Treasury stock is capital stock that has been issued and has been subsequently reacquired by the issuing corporation.

5. Properly show extraordinary items, changes in accounting principle, and prior period adjustments in the financial statements.

    *   Extraordinary items are defined as those events that are unusual in nature and that occur infrequently.

* Changes in accounting principle include such changes as a change in inventory valuation method or in depreciation method.

* Prior period adjustments consist almost entirely of corrections of errors in previously published financial statements.

* The amount of earnings per share is computed as net income minus preferred stock dividends divided by the number of common shares outstanding.

6. Define and use correctly the new terms in the glossary.

The new terms introduced in the chapter are as follows:

Book value per share—Stockholders' equity per share; computed as the amount per share each stockholder would receive if the corporation were liquidated without incurring any further expenses and if assets were sold and liabilities liquidated at their recorded amounts.

Capital stock—Transferable units of ownership in a corporation.

Capital stock authorized—The number of shares of stock that a corporation is entitled to issue as designated in its charter.

Capital stock outstanding—The number of shares of authorized stock that have been issued and that are currently held by stockholders.

Cash dividends—Cash distributions of net income by a corporation to its stockholders.

Changes in accounting principle—Changes in accounting methods pertaining to such items as inventory and depreciation.

Common stock—Shares of stock representing the residual equity in the corporation. If only one class of stock is issued, it is known as common stock. All other claims rank ahead of common stockholders' claims.

Convertible preferred stock—Preferred stock that is convertible into common stock of the issuing corporation.

Corporation—An entity recognized by law as possessing an existence separate and distinct from its owners; that is, it is a separate legal entity. A corporation is granted many of the rights and placed under many of the obligations of a natural person. In any given state, all corporations organized under the laws of that state are **domestic corporations**; all others are **foreign corporations**.

Cumulative preferred stock—Preferred stock for which the right to receive a basic dividend accumulates if not paid; dividends in arrears must be paid before any dividends can be paid on the common stock.

Date of declaration (of dividends)—The date the board of directors takes action in the form of a motion that dividends be paid.

Date of payment (of dividends)—The date of actual payment of a dividend, or issuance of additional shares in the case of a stock dividend.

Date of record (of dividends)—The date established by the board to determine who will receive a dividend.

Dividend—A distribution of assets (usually cash) that represents a withdrawal of earnings by the owners. Dividends are similar in nature to withdrawals by sole proprietors and partners.

Dividends (cash)—See Cash dividends.

Dividends in arrears—Cumulative unpaid dividends, including passed quarterly dividends for the current year.

Dividends (stock)—See Stock dividends.

Donated capital—Results from donation of assets to the corporation, which increases stockholders' equity.

Earnings per share (EPS)—Earnings to the common stockholders on a per share basis, computed as net income available to common stockholders divided by the number of common shares outstanding.

Extraordinary items—Items that are unusual in nature and that occur infrequently; reported in the income statement net of their tax effects, if any.

Financial leverage—The use of debt or preferred stock to increase (or perhaps decrease) earnings per share to common stockholders.

Income before extraordinary items—Income from operations less applicable income taxes, if any.

Legal capital (stated capital)—An amount prescribed by law (often par value or stated value of shares outstanding) below which a corporation may not reduce stockholders' equity through the declaration of dividends or other payments to stockholders.

Net-of-tax effect—Used for extraordinary items, prior period adjustments, and changes in accounting principle, whereby items are shown at the dollar amounts remaining after deducting the effects of such items on income taxes, if any, payable currently.

Noncumulative preferred stock—Preferred stock on which the right to receive a dividend expires if the dividend is not declared.

No-par stock—Capital stock without par value, to which a stated value may or may not be assigned.

Paid-in (or contributed) capital—Amount of stockholders' equity that normally results from the cash or other assets invested by owners; it may also result from services provided for shares of stock and certain other transactions.

Paid-in Capital—Treasury Stock Transactions—The account credited when treasury stock is reissued for more than its cost; this account is debited to the extent of its credit balance when such shares are reissued at less than cost.

Par value—An arbitrary amount printed on each stock certificate that may be assigned to each share of a given class of stock, usually at the time of incorporation.

Preferred stock—Capital stock that carries certain features or rights not carried by common stock. Preferred stock may be preferred as to dividends, preferred as to assets, or preferred as to both dividends and assets. Preferred stock may be cumulative or noncumulative and participating or nonparticipating.

Prior period adjustments—Consist almost entirely of corrections of errors in previously published financial statements. Prior period adjustments are reported in the statement of retained earnings net of their tax effects, if any.

Retained earnings—The part of stockholders' equity resulting from net income; the account in which the results of corporate activity are reflected and to which dividends are charged.

Shares of stock—Units of ownership in a corporation.

Stated value—An arbitrary amount assigned by the board of directors to each share of a given class of no-par stock.

Statement of retained earnings—A formal statement showing the items causing changes in unappropriated and appropriated retained earnings during a stated period of time.

Stock dividends—Dividends that are payable in additional shares of the declaring corporation's capital stock.

Stock Dividends Distributable—Common account—The stockholders' equity account that is credited for the par or stated value of the shares distributable when recording the declaration of a stock dividend.

Stock preferred as to assets—Means that in liquidation the preferred stockholders are entitled to receive the par value (or a larger stipulated liquidation value) per share before any assets may be distributed to common stockholders.

Stock preferred as to dividends—Means that the preferred stockholders are entitled to receive a specified dividend per share before any dividend on common stock is paid.

Stock split—A distribution of additional shares of the issuing corporation's stock for which the corporation receives no assets. The purpose of a stock split is to cause a large reduction in the market price per share of the outstanding stock.

Stock without par value—See No-par stock.

Treasury stock—Shares of capital stock issued and reacquired by the issuing corporation; they have not been formally canceled and are available for reissuance.

Completion and Exercises

1. What are the advantages of the corporate form of business?

   a. _____

   b. _____

   c. _____

   d. _____

   e. _____

   f. _____

2. What is meant by capital stock authorized?

   _____

   _____

   _____

3. What is meant by capital stock outstanding?

   _____

   _____

4. What are the two ordinary classes of capital stock that may be issued by a corporation?

   a. _____

   b. _____

5. What are the reasons for issuing preferred stock? (a) _____ ,

   (b) _____

   _____ , and

   (c) _____

   _____ .

6. What is the meaning of par value?

_____

_____

_____

7. What is the amount of the credit to the capital stock account for a corporation issuing capital stock without par or stated value?

_____

_____

8. Give the entries if a corporation received subscriptions for 1,000 shares at $20 per share of $5 par value common stock on May 1 and received payment in full on May 27. Omit explanations.

DATE	ACCOUNT TITLES AND EXPLANATION	POST. REF.	DEBIT	CREDIT	

9. When only common stock is outstanding, how is book value per share calculated?

_____

_____

10. From the following information, compute the book value per share of both preferred and common stock.

Preferred stock, 6 percent cumulative par value $50;
   1,000 shares authorized, issued and outstanding .... $ 50,000
Common stock, without par or stated value; 20,000 shares authorized;
   18,000 shares issued and outstanding 126,000
Retained earnings.. 94,000
   Total stockholders' equity $270,000

Note: Two years' dividends are in arrears on the preferred stock, including those for the current year.

11. A separate paid-in capital account is used for each _____ of capital.

12. When a corporation receives assets as donated capital at what amount is the transaction recorded?

_____

13. What are the two major elements of stockholders' equity in a corporation?

_____

14. When the Retained Earnings account has a debit balance it is called a _____.

15. Dividends paid in cash are usually charged against _____ — _____.

16. What effect do stock dividends have on the total amount of stockholders' equity?

_____

_____

17. What was the recommendation of the Committee on Accounting Procedure of the AICPA concerning the amount to be transferred from retained earnings for a small stock dividend?

_____

_____

_____

18. How does an accountant distinguish between small stock dividends and large stock dividends?

_____

_____

_____

_____

_____

_____

19. What is treasury stock?

_____

_____

_____

20. When treasury stock is reissued, the excess of reissue price over cost is credited to _____

_____.

21. From the following information pertaining to Marilyn Corporation prepare the stockholders' equity section of the balance sheet. The information is as of December 31, 1990.

Total retained earnings	$ 505,000
Preferred stock—$50 par; authorized 5,000 shares; issued and outstanding 3,000 shares	$ 150,000
Common stock—$5 par; 1,000,000 shares authorized; 600,000 shares issued	$3,000,000
Cost of treasury stock held—common	$ 90,000
Number of shares of treasury stock held	15,000 shares
Paid-in capital in excess of par value—common	$ 675,000
Paid-in capital from treasury stock transactions	$ 25,000
Paid-in capital from stock dividend	$ 330,000

(Use form supplied on next page.)

MARILYN CORPORATION
Partial Balance Sheet
December 31, 1990

22. An item that has a material effect on net income and is unusual and nonrecurring in called an _____ _____ _____ and is to be reported in the _____ _____ net of its _____ _____ .

23. The correction of a material error in accounting for a prior period's activities is called a _____ _____ _____ . It is reported in the _____ _____ _____ _____ , net of its_____ _____ .

24. Accounting changes consist of changes in principles which give rise to _____ _____ which are reported in a manner similar to _____ _____ .

25. Whether an item is unusual and nonrecurring is to be determined by reference to the _____ in which the firm operates. Thus, a loss on the sale of a plant asset _____ (would/would not) be classified as an extraordinary item.

26. From the following information on the Marilyn Corporation, prepare an income statement for the year 1990:

Expenses (not including federal income taxes)	$32,000,000
Revenues...	37,000,000
Loss from earthquake	675,000

Assume a 50 percent federal income tax rate. The earthquake causing the loss was the first experienced in the area in which the company operates.

(The remaining questions are based on the chapter appendix.)

27. When a corporation invests in common or preferred stocks of other corporations, what constitutes the cost of the securities?

28. If a cash dividend of $6,000 is declared on securities held as investments in one period but paid in the next period, what is the form of the entry required at the end of the first period?

DATE	EXPLANATION	POST. REF.	DEBIT	CREDIT	BALANCE

29. How is a stock dividend treated for securities held as investments?

_____

_____

_____

30. Where is gain or loss on the sale of investments shown in the financial statements?

_____

_____

31. Securities may be written down below cost when their _____ _____ is less than their _____ for current assets taken as a group and for noncurrent assets taken as a group.

32. The account, Net Unrealized Loss on Noncurrent Marketable Equity Securities, would be as shown as

_____ .

Multiple-Choice Questions

For each of the following questions, indicate the single best answer by circling the appropriate letter.

1. Which of the following activities is a characteristic of a corporation?

   a. Full liability of owners to corporate creditors
   b. Difficult transferability of ownership because of widely scattered ownership
   c. Separate legal existence
   d. Shareholders may enter the corporation into a contract

2. The par value of a share of common stock is:

   a. the amount for which the stock can be sold in the market.
   b. the amount at which, according to some state laws, the share must be first issued.
   c. a changing amount which varies according to earnings and losses of the issuing corporation.
   d. generally of little significance, being merely a nominal and arbitrary amount printed on a stock certificate.

3. With regard to common stock without par or stated value, which of the following statements is true?

   a. The Common Stock account will show the total of the amount received for the stock issued plus the subscription price of the stock subscribed but for which payment has not been received.
   b. In the case of a subscription with a cash down payment, the Subscriptions Receivable and the Common Stock Subscribed accounts will show the same dollar amount.
   c. Depending on the price received, a Paid-In Capital in Excess of Stated Value account may be established when the shares are subscribed.
   d. The Common Stock account may be credited for varying amounts if shares are issued at different prices at different times.

4. Ashley Company was incorporated with authorized capital of 200,000 shares of common stock without par value but with a stated value of $40 per share. The company issued 60,000 shares for cash at a price of $50 per share. Which of the following entries should be made?

   a. Cash... 3,000,000
      Common Stock   2,400,000
      Paid-In Capital in Excess of Stated Value   600,000

   b. Cash... 3,000,000
      Common Stock   3,000,000

   c. Cash... 3,000,000
      Common Stock   2,400,000
      Paid-In Capital in Excess of Par Value   600,000

   d. Subscriptions Receivable—Common................. 3,000,000
      Common Stock   2,400,000
      Paid-In Capital in Excess of Stated Value   600,000

5. The Southland Corporation issued 160 shares of common stock (par value $100 per share) for real estate having a fair market value of $18,000 at the date of transfer. Which of the following is the required entry?

   a. Land.. 16,000
      Common Stock   16,000

   b. Land.. 18,000
      Common Stock   18,000

   c. Land.. 18,000
      Common Stock   16,000
      Paid-In Capital in Excess of Par Value   2,000

   d. Land.. 18,000
      Common Stock   16,000
      Paid-In Capital in Excess of Stated Value   2,000

6. In accounting for stockholders' equity, the accountant is primarily concerned with which of the following?

   a. Determining the total amount of stockholders' equity
   b. Distinguishing between realized and unrealized revenues
   c. Recording the source of each of the various elements of stockholders' equity
   d. Making sure that the board of directors does not declare dividends in excess of retained earnings

7. Favorable financial leverage means that the:

   a. preferred shareholders receive more earnings per share than otherwise.
   b. company has more accounts receivable than accounts payable.
   c. company is able to meet its short-run cash flows.
   d. common shareholders receive higher earnings per share than otherwise.

8. If a corporation issued 4,000 shares of 6 percent, $20 par value preferred stock for the first time in exchange for land valued at $120,000, what would be the appropriate amounts entered into the Land account and the Preferred Stock account?

   a. $80,000; $40,000
   b. $120,000; $80,000
   c. $80,000; $120,000
   d. $120,000; $120,000

9. The Caron Company received real estate having a fair market value of $40,000 from its principal stockholder. No stock was issued or other consideration given in exchange for this land, even though the company has $80,000 of authorized but unissued par value stock. What entry should be made to record the receipt of the land?

   a. Land 40,000
            Paid-In Capital—from Recapitalization   40,000

   b. Land 40,000
            Paid-In Capital—Donations   40,000

   c. Land 40,000
            Retained Earnings   40,000

   d. Land 40,000
            Revenue from Gift of Land   40,000

10. On a balance sheet, paid-in capital could include:

    a. capital contributed to the extent of the stated value of the common shares outstanding.
    b. capital contributed to the extent of the premium on outstanding preferred shares.
    c. retained earnings capitalized as a result of the issuance of a stock dividend.
    d. all of the above.
    e. only (a) and (b) of the above.

11. On July 7, 1990, the board of directors of the Jakes Corporation declared a cash dividend of $6 per share on 10,000 shares of outstanding common stock, payable September 2, 1990, to stockholders of record on August 23, 1990. The entry to record the declaration of this dividend is:

    a. Retained Earnings 60,000
            Cash   60,000

    b. Retained Earnings 60,000
            Dividends Payable   60,000

    c. Dividends 60,000
            Dividends Payable   60,000

    d. Either (b) or (c)

12. Which of the following statements regarding a dividend in common stock to common stockholders is true?

    a. A stock dividend reduces paid-in capital.
    b. A stock dividend reduces the individual stockholder's percentage of ownership in the corporation.
    c. A stock dividend reduces the book value per share of that class of stock.
    d. Stock Dividends Payable is a current liability account.

13. Rex Corporation has outstanding 20,000 shares of common stock, $50 per share. The board of directors declares a 5 percent stock dividend on the common stock. The market price of the stock on the date the dividend is declared is $55 per share. The entry to record the declaration of the stock dividend is:

a.

Retained Earnings	55,000	
Stock Dividends Distributable—Common		55,000

b.

Retained Earnings	50,000	
Stock Dividends Distributable—Common		50,000

c.

Retained Earnings	55,000	
Stock Dividends Distributable—Common		50,000
Paid-In Capital—Stock Dividend		5,000

d.

Retained Earnings	50,000	
Cash		50,000

14. The ABC Corporation acquired 100 shares of its own $20 par value common stock, all of which had been previously issued at par, for $2,200 ($22 per share). Three weeks later it reissued all 100 of these treasury shares at $21 per share. The entry to record reissuance of these shares, assuming no previous transactions in treasury stock, is:

a.

Cash	2,100	
Treasury Stock—Common		2,100

b.

Cash	2,100	
Treasury Stock—Common		2,000
Paid-In Capital—Treasury Stock Transactions		100

c.

Cash	2,100	
Paid-In Capital—Treasury Stock Transactions	300	
Treasury Stock—Common		2,400

d. None of the above.

15. In the preparation of a balance sheet, which of the following statements is true?

a. No reference need be made to treasury stock, since the acquisition of such stock does not restrict retained earnings.

b. Treasury shares and unissued shares can be reported as a total of shares not outstanding with no distinguishing comments.

c. Treasury shares should be shown as a deduction, at cost, from total stockholders' equity and a restriction on retained earnings occasioned by their acquisition must also be stated.

d. Treasury shares should be shown as a deduction, at cost, from the total paid-in capital of the company.

16. The following is the stockholders' equity section of a balance sheet dated June 30, 1990.

Stockholders' Equity

Paid-in capital:
    Capital stock—preferred, 5 percent, $100 par value; authorized and
      issued 1,000 shares of which 100 are held in treasury $100,000
    Capital stock—common, $10 par value; authorized, 100,000 shares,
      issued, 50,000 shares of which 900 are held in treasury 500,000
        Total paid-in capital.. $600,000
Retained earnings (restricted to the extent of cost of 100 shares of preferred
    treasury stock, $10,500, and 900 shares of common treasury stock $18,000) 200,000
        Total... $800,000
Less: Cost of treasury stock: preferred (100 shares), $10,500;
    common (900 shares) $18,000 28,500
        Total stockholders' equity $771,500

Which of the following statements is true?

a.   A dividend declared on June 30, 1990, of $1 per share on the common stock would involve a total amount to be paid out of $50,000.

b.   The cost of the common treasury stock is $18 per share.

c.   The corporation has 50,900 shares of common stock (50,000 shares unissued and 900 shares in treasury) available for issuance, and it is free to issue these shares to whomever it wishes, since 900 of the shares have previously been outstanding and the stockholders have authorized the issuance of the other 50,000 shares.

d.   The restriction upon retained earnings by the acquisition of common stock is limited to the cost of the 900 shares acquired by purchase.

17. A company wrote down a substantial amount of excess inventory to its scrap value. This loss is to be reported in the year it was recognized in the:

a.   income statement, net of its tax effect, as an extraordinary item.

b.   income statement, net of its tax effect, as part of the expenses related to regular operations.

c.   income statement at full amount, as part of the expenses related to regular operations.

d.   income statement, net of tax effect, as a cumulative adjustment from an accounting change.

18. In 1990 a corporation had revenues of $50 million; total expenses related to the above revenues, exclusive of federal income taxes, of $40 million; and was subject to federal income taxation at a 50 percent rate. It also suffered a tax-deductible earthquake loss (its first such loss) of $2 million, sold investment securities (a recurring event) at a gain of $3 million (subject to income taxation at a 30 percent rate), paid additional federal income taxes for 1987 of $500,000 and settled for $800,000 (tax deductible) litigation brought against it for failure to comply in 1986 with the provisions of a contract to install a battery of missiles. The corporation discontinued this line activity in 1989. Which of the following statements is *true?*

a.   Net income before extraordinary items is $5.85 million.

b.   The earthquake loss should be reported at $1 million ($2 million less tax effect) as an extraordinary item in the income statement.

c.   The gain on sale of securities should be reported in the income statement, not net of tax effects, as an element of income from normal operations.

d.   All of the above.

19. Bell Corporation had authorized and issued 10,000 shares of $100 par value common stock. On January 15, 1990, the Board of Directors declared a $4 per share dividend to be paid on February 28, 1990, to stockholders of record on February 1, 1990. Which of the following entries is correct?

a. Feb. 28   Dividends Payable 40,000
            Cash   40,000

b. Jan. 15   Retained Earnings 40,000
            Cash   40,000

c. Feb. 1   Retained Earnings 40,000
            Dividends Payable...................   40,000

d. Feb. 1   Dividends Payable 40,000
            Cash   40,000

20. A distribution of a 30 percent stock dividend is:

a. charged against retained earnings at fair market value.
b. charged against retained earnings at par or stated value.
c. treated like a cash dividend.
d. called a treasury stock transaction.

21. An example of an extraordinary item is a:

a. loss in selling obsolete inventory.
b. gain in the increased value of treasury stock.
c. loss from litigation in a medical practice.
d. loss from confiscation by the government of Brazil of the company's only overseas plant.

22. The correction of the effects of the improper use of an accounting method is called a(n):

a. prior period adjustment.
b. change in accounting estimate.
c. extraordinary item.
d. stock dividend.

23. Earnings per share should be disclosed for:

a. net income before extraordinary items and after taxes.
b. extraordinary items.
c. cumulative effect of accounting changes.
d. all of the above.

Now compare your answers with the correct ones beginning on page 242.

Solutions/Chapter 8

Completion and Exercises

1. (a) Transferable shares; (b) Limited liability; (c) Continuous existence; (d) Opportunity to employ professional management; (e) Centralized authority and responsibility; (f) Stockholders are not agents of a corporation

2. The number of shares and par value, if any, per share of each class of stock that the corporate charter will permit to be issued

3. The shares authorized, issued, and currently held by stockholders

4. (a) Preferred stock; (b) Common stock

5. (a) To attract investors with differing investment objectives; (b) It does not dilute control of the corporation by the common stockholder; (c) It permits use of financial leverage through fixed dividend rates

6. Par value is an arbitrarily assigned dollar amount appearing on stock certificates which serves as the basis for the credit to the stock account.

7. The entire amount received for the stock.

8.
May 1	Subscriptions Receivable—Common	20,000	
	Common Stock Subscribed		5,000
	Paid-In Capital in Excess of Par Value—Common		15,000
May 27	Cash	20,000	
	Subscriptions Receivable—Common		20,000
	Common Stock Subscribed	5,000	
	Common Stock		5,000

9. Book value per share is calculated by dividing stockholders' equity by the number of shares outstanding.

10.

		Total	Per share
Total stockholders' equity		$270,000	
Book value of preferred stock (1,000 shares):			
Par value	$50,000		
Dividends (two years at $3,000)	6,000	56,000	$56.00
Book value of common stock (18,000 shares)		$214,000	$11.89

11. source

12. The fair market value of the asset received

13. Paid-in capital and retained earnings

14. deficit

15. retained earnings

16. Stock dividends have no effect. They merely increase paid-in capital and decrease retained earnings by the same amount.

17. The Committee recommended capitalizing retained earnings equal to the current market value of the shares previously outstanding.

18. Stock issuances of less than 20 to 25 percent would not materially affect the market price of the stock and are classified as stock dividends. Issuances of greater than 20 to 25 percent are classified as large stock dividends.

19. Treasury stock is stock that has been issued and then reacquired by the issuing corporation.

20. Paid-In Capital—Treasury Stock Transactions

21.

MARILYN CORPORATION
Partial Balance Sheet
December 31, 1990

Stockholders' Equity
  Paid-in capital:
    Preferred stock—$50 par value; 5,000 shares authorized,
      3,000 shares issued and outstanding .... $ 150,000
    Common stock—$5 par value; 1,000,000 shares authorized,
      600,000 shares issued and outstanding of which 15,000 shares
      are held in treasury   3,000,000
    Paid-in capital in excess of par value:
      From common stock issuances $675,000
      From capitalization of retained earnings through stock dividends.. 330,000
      From treasury stock transactions 25,000   1,030,000
        Total paid-in capital $4,180,000
  Retained earnings:
    Unappropriated (restricted to the extent of $90,000, the cost
      of treasury shares held)   505,000
       $4,685,000
  Less: Treasury stock common, 15,000 shares at cost 90,000
    Total stockholders' equity $4,595,000

22. extraordinary item; income statement; tax effects

23. prior period adjustment; statement of retained earnings; tax effects

24. cumulative effects; extraordinary items

25. environment; would not

26.

MARILYN CORPORATION
Income Statement
For Year Ended December 31, 1990

Revenues $37,000,000
Expenses $32,000,000
Federal income taxes 2,500,000   34,500,000
Net income before extraordinary items .... $ 2,500,000
Loss from earthquake (net of tax effect of $337,500) 337,500
Net income .... $ 2,162,500

27. The cost of securities is the actual price of the securities plus any brokerage fee.

28. Dividends Receivable 6,000
     Dividend Revenue   6,000

29. A notation is made of the larger number of shares held and the smaller per share cost.

30. Such gains or losses are shown in the nonoperating portion of the income statement.

31. market value; cost

32. a deduction from stockholders' equity

Multiple-Choice Questions

1. c.   None of the other answers is a characteristic of a corporation. But a corporation does become a separate legal entity upon formation.

2. d.   Par value is a nominal and arbitrary amount printed on a stock certificate and has very little significance except possibly as an indicator of the amount of capital which must be legally maintained.

3. d.   Because the stock is without par or stated value, there is no alternative but to credit the common stock account with the entire proceeds received through issuance of the shares.

4. a.   Since the stock has a stated value of $40 per share, this amount should be carried in the Common Stock account for each share issued, a total of $2.4 million. The amount received in excess of stated value, $600,000, should be recorded in a Paid-In Capital in Excess of Stated Value account. The $3.0 million of cash received must, of course, be recorded in the Cash account.

5. c.   The land should be recorded at its fair market value of $18,000. The assets received had a fair market value of $2,000 more than the par value of the shares issued, so Paid-In Capital in Excess of Par is recognized.

6. c.   By affixing the source of each of the various elements of the stockholders' equity, the accountant not only distinguishes between capital and earnings but also describes the source of each of the various elements of capital. The accountant is concerned with all of the elements listed in the other answers; but in accounting for stockholders' equity, he or she is primarily concerned with accounting for its sources.

7. d.   Financial leverage is favorable if it results in higher earnings per share for common shareholders than without financial leverage.

8. b.   The proper entry would have been:

Land	120,000	
Preferred Stock		80,000
Paid-In Capital in Excess of Par—Preferred		40,000

Since no market value was available for the stock, the fair market value of the land is used.

9. b.   An asset has been received and must be recorded in the accounts. Since no liability arose out of its receipt and no asset was surrendered, it must be a part of stockholders' equity. Since it was not earned, it cannot be a part of retained earnings; therefore, it must be capital. The capital arose from a donation, and (b) clearly describes this fact as well as the fact that land was received.

10. d.   All of the items mentioned are paid-in capital.

11. d.   The act of declaring a cash dividend creates a liability on the part of the corporation to pay. Thus, the credit must be to Dividends Payable. The debit must be charged to Retained Earnings since, by the act of distributing assets as dividends, the amount of earnings retained is reduced. The use of a temporary Dividends account to accumulate all of the dividend charges during the year is proper accounting if the account is closed to Retained Earnings. Thus, either (b) or (c) is correct.

12. c.   Since a stock dividend merely transfers retained earnings to paid-in capital, it does not increase total stockholders' equity. But it does increase the number of shares outstanding. Thus, the book value per share is reduced.

13. c.   The amount of the dividend is $55,000 (5 percent of 20,000 shares equals 1,000; 1,000 times $55 equals $55,000). This is the amount to be charged to Retained Earnings. Since the shares to be issued have a par value, it is customary to set up the Stock Dividends Distributable account at the par value of the shares to be issued, in this case, $50,000. The difference represents the amount above par value to be capitalized, for which the source must be indicated—stock dividends.

14. d. The correct entry is:

Cash...	2,100	
Retained Earnings	100	
Treasury Stock.............................		2,200

Reissued 100 treasury shares at $21; cost, $22.

15. c. Treasury stock is shown in both of these places on the balance sheet.

16. d. The only correct answer is (d). Answer (a) is incorrect because the amount of the dividend is $49,100, since 900 of the 50,000 common shares are in the treasury. The common treasury stock acquired by purchase cost $20 per share ($18,000/900). The corporation is free to issue 900 shares of common treasury stock to whomever it wishes, but the other 50,000 shares must be offered to the existing stockholders (common) on a pro rata basis unless these stockholders have waived their preemptive rights.

17. c. The loss is so closely related to regular or normal operations that it cannot be considered a prior period adjustment or an extraordinary item. The tax effects of regular revenues and expenses are not determined for each individual item; therefore, the amount should be reported gross (without deducting its tax effect).

18. d. The earthquake loss is unusual in nature and infrequent in occurrence and thus is an extraordinary item reported not of tax because it is tax deductible. Transactions involving securities are everyday business occurrences and thus are a part of normal business operations.

19. a. Not only must the entry be correct, but the date must also be correct. The only correctly dated entry is the payment entry.

20. b. A stock dividend greater than 20-25 percent is charged against retained earnings at par or stated value.

21. d. All other gains and losses are part of everyday business practices. Only the confiscation by the Brazilian government is *unusual* in nature and *infrequent*.

22. a. A prior period adjustment is an adjustment resulting from accounting errors made in prior accounting periods. An improper use of an accounting method is an accounting error.

23. d. All of these items should have earnings per share amounts disclosed on the income statement.

Name _____

_____

PALL COMPANY

(a)

JENNIE COMPANY
Partial Balance Sheet
June 30, 1991

(b)

Name _____

ZELLER BROTHERS, INC.

Computation of Book Values—Preferred and Common

As of June 30, 1991

Name _____

RICARDO CORPORATION
Statement of Retained Earnings
For the Year Ended December 31, 1990

Name _____

_____

(a)

ALDEN COMPANY
Book Value Computations

(b)

(c)

Name _____

(a)

LORENZO COMPANY

Partial Balance Sheet

July 1, 1990

(b)

Name _____

_____

COLORADO COMPANY
GENERAL JOURNAL

(a)

DATE	ACCOUNT TITLES AND EXPLANATION	POST. REF.	DEBIT	CREDIT

(b)

COLORADO COMPANY

Partial Balance Sheet

December 31, 1991

(c)

Name _____

_____

ATWOOD CORPORATION

Partial Balance Sheet

December 31, 1990

Name _____

_____

CLAUDE COMPANY

Income Statement

For the Year Ended December 31, 1991

Name _____

CLAUDE COMPANY
Statement of Retained Earnings
For the Year Ended December 31, 1991

(a)

GLENN CORPORATION
Income Statement

For the Year Ended December 31, 1990

GLENN CORPORATION
Statement of Retained Earnings
For the Year Ended December 31, 1990

(b)

Name _____

_____

(a)

KIZER COMPANY

July 15

August 1

November 3

December 1

(b)

NOBLE CORPORATION

(a)

(b)

(c)

(d)

9

Debt Financing and Bond Investments

Understanding the Learning Objectives

1. Account for notes receivable and payable, including calculation of interest.

   * A promissory note is an unconditional promise in writing made and signed by the borrower (the maker) obligating the borrower to pay the lender (the payee) or someone else who legally acquired the note a certain sum of money on demand or at a definite time.

   * Interest is the fee charged for the use of money through time. Interest equals principal times rate of interest times time.

2. Record the discounting of a customer's note at the bank.

   * The cash proceeds are computed by determining the maturity value of the note, the discount period, and the amount of the discount charged by the bank. The bank discount is deducted from the maturity value to find the cash proceeds.

3. Describe the features of bonds and tell how bonds differ from shares of stock.

   * A bond is a liability (with a maturity date) that bears interest which is deductible in computing both net income and taxable income.

   * A share of stock is a unit of ownership that remains outstanding indefinitely on which a dividend is paid only if declared, and dividends are not deductible in determining net income or taxable income.

   * Bonds may be secured, registered, callable, and/or convertible.

4. List the advantages and disadvantages of financing with long-term debt and prepare examples showing how financial leverage is employed.

   * Advantages include stockholders retaining control of the company, tax deductibility of interest, and possible creation of favorable financial leverage.

   * Disadvantages include having to make a fixed interest payment each period, reduction in a company's ability to sustain a major loss, possible limitations on dividends and future borrowings, and possible suffering caused by unfavorable financial leverage.

5. Explain how interest rates affect bond prices and what causes a bond to sell at a premium or discount.

   * If the contract rate is higher than the market value, the bonds will sell for more than face value, and a premium will be recorded.

   * If the contract rate is lower than the market rate, the bonds will sell for less than face value, and a discount will be recorded.

6. Apply the concept of present value to compute the price of a bond.

   * The present value of the principal plus the present value of the interest payment is equal to the price of the bond.

   * The contract rate of interest is used to determine the amount of future cash interest payments.

   * The effective rate of interest is used to discount the future payment of principal and of interest back to the present value.

7. Prepare journal entries to account for bonds payable.

   * Any premium or discount must be amortized over the period the bonds are outstanding.

   * Under the effective interest rate method, interest expense for any period is equal to the effective (market) rate of interest at date of issuance times the carrying value of the bond at the beginning of that interest period.

   * Under the straight-line method of amortization, an equal amount of discount or premium is allocated to each month the bonds are outstanding.

   * When bonds are redeemed before they mature, a loss or gain on bond redemption may occur.

8. Prepare journal entries to account for bond investments.

   * Premiums and discounts on short-term bond investments are not amortized because the length of time the bonds will be held is not known.

   * Premiums or discounts on bond investments are not recorded in a separate account. Instead, they affect the amount recorded in the bond investments account.

   * Premiums and discounts on long-term bond investments are amortized in a manner similar to that used for bonds payable.

9. Define and use correctly the new terms in the glossary.

   The new terms introduced in the chapter are as follows:

   Annuity—A series of equal cash flows spaced equally in time.

   Bearer bond—See Unregistered bond.

   Bond—A long-term debt owed by its issuer. A **bond certificate** is a negotiable instrument and is the formal, physical evidence of the debt owed.

   Bond certificate—A negotiable instrument that represents physical evidence of the debt.

   Bond indenture—The contract or loan agreement under which bonds are issued.

   Call premium—The price paid in excess of face value that the issuer of bonds may be required to pay to redeem (call) bonds before their maturity date.

   Callable bond—A bond that gives the issuer the right to call (buy back) the bond before its maturity date.

   Carrying value (of bonds)—The face value of bonds minus any unamortized discount or plus any unamortized premium. Sometimes referred to as **net liability** on the bonds when used for bonds payable.

   Compound interest—Interest calculated on the principal and on interest of prior periods.

   Contract rate of interest—The interest rate printed on the bond certificates and specified on the bond indenture; also called the **stated**, **coupon**, or **nominal rate**.

   Convertible bond—A bond that may be exchanged, at the bondholder's option, for shares of stock of the issuing corporation.

   Coupon bond—A bond not registered as to interest; it carries detachable coupons that are to be clipped and presented for payment of interest due.

   Debenture bond—An unsecured bond backed only by the general credit worthiness of its issuer.

   Discount (on bonds)—Excess of face value over issue or selling price.

   Discount on Notes Payable—A contra account used to reduce notes payable from face value to the net amount shown in the balance sheet.

   Discount period—The exact number of days from the date of sale of a note to the date of maturity.

   Discount rate—Rate of interest the bank charges on a discounted note receivable.

Discounting a note receivable—The act of selling a note receivable with recourse to a bank. With recourse means that the bank can collect from the company that sold the note to the bank if the maker does not pay at maturity.

Dishonored note—A note that the maker failed to pay at maturity.

Effective interest rate method (interest method)—A procedure for calculating periodic interest expense (or revenue) in which the first period's interest is computed by multiplying the carrying value of bonds payable (bond investments) by the market rate at the issue date. The difference between computed interest expense (revenue) and the interest paid (received), based on nominal rate times face value, is the discount or premium amortized for the period. Computations for subsequent periods are based on carrying value at the beginning of the period.

Face value—Principal amount of a bond.

Favorable financial leverage—An increase in EPS and rate of return on owners' equity resulting from earning a higher rate of return on borrowed funds than the fixed cost of such funds. **Unfavorable financial leverage** results when the cost of borrowed funds exceeds the income they generate, resulting in decreased income to owners.

Future value or worth—The amount to which a sum of money invested today will grow in a stated time period at a specified interest rate.

Interest—The fee charged for use of money through time.

Interest method—See Effective interest rate method.

Maker (of a note)—The party who prepares a note and is responsible for paying the note at maturity.

Market interest rate—The interest rate that an investor will earn on a bond investment by paying a specified price for it and the rate of interest expense a borrower will incur by issuing bonds at that price. Also called **effective interest** or **yield rate**.

Maturity date—The date on which a note becomes due and must be paid.

Maturity value—The amount that the maker must pay on a note on its maturity date.

Mortgage—A legal claim (lien) on a specific property that gives the bondholder the right to sell the pledged property if the company fails to make required payments. A bond secured by a mortgage is called a **mortgage bond**.

Mortgage Note Payable—A note that is secured by a pledge of certain property.

Payee (of a note)—The party who receives a note and will be paid cash at maturity.

Premium (on bonds)—Excess of selling or issue price over face value.

Present value—The current worth of a future cash receipt(s); computed by discounting future receipts at a stipulated interest rate.

Promissory note—An unconditional written promise by a borrower (maker) to pay a definite sum of money to the lender (payee) on demand or at a specific date.

Registered bond—A bond for which the owner's name appears on both the bond certificate and in the record of bond owners kept by the bond issuer or its agent, the registrar.

Secured bond—A bond for which specific property has been pledged to ensure its payment.

Serial bonds—Bonds in a given bond issue with maturities spread over several dates.

Simple interest—Interest on principal only.

Stock warrant—A right that allows the bondholder to purchase shares of common stock at a fixed price for a stated period of time. Warrants may be detachable or nondetachable.

Straight-line method of amortization—A procedure that, when applied to bond discount or premium, allocates an equal amount of discount or premium to each period in the life of a bond.

Term bond—A bond that matures on the same date as all other bonds in a given bond issue.

Trustee—Usually a bank or trust company appointed to represent the bondholders in a bond issue and to enforce the provisions of the bond indenture against the issuer.

Underwriter—An investment company that performs many tasks for the bond issuer in issuing bonds; may also guarantee the issuer a fixed price for the bonds.

Unfavorable financial leverage—Results when the cost of borrowed funds exceeds the revenue they generate; it is the opposite of **favorable financial leverage**.

Unregistered (bearer) bond—Ownership transfers by physical delivery.

Unsecured bond—A **debenture bond**, or simply a *debenture*; it is backed only by the general credit worthiness of the issuer, not by a lien on any specific property.

Completion and Exercises

1. If a 120-day note is dated July 25, what is the due date?

2. In commercial transactions, interest is commonly calculated on the basis of _____ days per year.

3. What is the interest on $300,000 for 120 days at 6 percent? _____

4. What is a dishonored note? _____

    _____

    _____

5. Assume that on December 1, 1990, a company presented its own $100,000 noninterest-bearing 90-day note to the bank. The discount rate is 12 percent. Give the entries required on December 1, December 31 (the end of the accounting period), and on the maturity date.

DATE	ACCOUNT TITLES AND EXPLANATION	POST. REF.	DEBIT	CREDIT	

6. Assume Jones received a 12 percent, 120-day, $20,000 note. What would be the proceeds if on the same day Jones sold the note to the bank and the bank discounted it at 8 percent?

$$18 \qquad \frac{300}{.06} \times \frac{120}{360}$$

7. What would the cash proceeds have been in Question 6 if Jones had held the note for 30 days before selling it?

8. What entry would Jones make when he sells the note in Question 7 to the bank?

DATE	ACCOUNT TITLES AND EXPLANATION	POST. REF.	DEBIT	CREDIT

9. When a note has been discounted, the _____ usually presents the note to the maker for payment.

10. What entries would Jones make if the note in Question 7 were dishonored? (Assume a $5 protest fee was incurred.)

DATE	ACCOUNT TITLES AND EXPLANATION	POST. REF.	DEBIT	CREDIT

11. Long-term notes are to be recorded at their _____ _____ .

12. Company A issued $1,000,000, 20 year, 10 percent bonds, on January 1, 1990, and received cash of $825,300.

Required:

a. What is the entry to record the sale of the bonds on January 1, 1990?
b. Give the entry for the first semiannual interest payment. (Use straight-line amortization.)
c. When may the straight-line method be used?

a.

b.

c.

13. Present entries, in general journal form, to record the following selected transactions:

    a. Issued $100,000 of 10-year, 8 percent bonds at 98½.
    b. The amortization of bond discount for one semiannual period was $46.
    c. Redemption of bonds at 96. The bonds were carried at $99,000 at the time of the redemption.

14. If the interest rate on the bonds is higher than the market rate of interest for bonds of that risk category, the bonds will be issued at a _____ .

15. On August 1, 1990, Issuer Company issued for cash to Purchaser Company, at 100 plus accrued interest, $1,000,000 of ten-year, 9-percent bonds, dated January 1, 1990, which call for semiannual interest payments on January 1 and July 1. What entries are necessary at issuance, and at December 31, 1990 (the accounting year-end for both companies)?

Issuer

Purchaser

16. Assume the bonds in Question 15 were issued on January 1, 1990, for cash of $1,067,952—a price that yields 8 percent. Give the entries for 1990, including the December 31 adjusting entries for both the Issuer Company and the Purchaser Company.

Issuer

16. (concluded)

Purchaser

17. The total cost of borrowing is the sum of the periodic interest payments _____ (plus/minus) the discount at issuance or _____ (plus/minus) the premium.

18. Discount and premium on bonds should be amortized using the _____ method.

19. When bonds are issued between interest dates, _____ must be recorded on both the issuer's and purchaser's books.

20. The issue price of a bond is the total of the present values of the promises to pay the _____ at maturity and the _____ periodically throughout the life of the bonds.

21. Prove that a $1,000 face value bond, bearing interest at 8 percent, payable semiannually, and maturing in 10 years, will sell for $1,000 if sold to yield eight percent.

22. If a $1,000 face value, 10-year, 6 percent, bond is issued to yield 8 percent, what price will it bring? Interest is paid semiannually.

23. Give the entry to record the issuance of the bond in Question 22 and the entry to record the first six months' interest expense.

24. Compute the present value of the bond in Question 22 to yield 8 percent with 19 periods (9½ years) life remaining.

25. The difference between the present value computed in Question 24 and the present value (price) computed in Question 22 is $ _____ . This difference is equal (except for rounding difference) to an amount in one of the entries in Question 23 and is described as the amount of _____ _____ .

(The remaining questions are based on the chapter Appendix.)

26. Interest is compounded whenever the amount of _____ for a period is computed and is added to the _____ to serve as the basis for computing interest for the next period.

27. The future value of $10,000 five years from now if invested at 6 percent compounded annually is _____ .

28. If the interest in Question 27 had been compounded semiannually, what would the future value have been? _____

29. Present value is the _____ of future value.

30. Prove that Question 29 is true by showing that the present value of $13,382.30 (the answer to Question 24) to be received five years from now at 6 percent is $10,000. (Hint: Multiply $13,382.30 by the reciprocal of the factor used to answer Question 28.)

31. What is the present value of an annuity of $1,000 to be received at the end of each of the next ten years at 8 percent interest?

Multiple-Choice Questions

For each of the following questions, indicate the single best answer by circling the appropriate letter.

1. D. C. Ebel arranged a loan at the bank. He gave the bank a 90-day note on which both the face value and the maturity value are $28,000. The bank discounted the note at 10 percent. Which of the following statements is correct?

   a. Mr. Ebel received $28,800 in cash.
   b. This type of note is often called an interest-bearing note.
   c. The effective rate of interest on the loan is greater than 10 percent.
   d. The effective rate of interest on the loan is less than 10 percent.

2. On April 1, Goodenuf Brothers received an $800, 45-day, 8 percent note from P. C. Barnum. On May 10, it sold the note to the bank, which discounted it at 10 percent. Which of the following statements regarding this set of transactions is *true*?

   a. Face value of the note is $800.
   b. Maturity value of the note is $864.00.
   c. The discount period is 39 days.
   d. The discount is $800 × .10 × 39/360.

3. On June 10, Barnett Shops received a $5,000, 60-day, 12 percent note from Mrs. P. J. Hubel. This note was sold to the bank, which discounted it at 15 percent on the day it was received. The journal entry to record the discounting transaction is:

   a. Cash 4,972.50
      Interest Expense 27.50
          Notes Receivable 5,000.00

   b. Cash 5,000.00
      Interest Expense 100.00
          Notes Receivable 5,100.00

   c. Cash 4,872.50
      Interest Revenue 127.50
          Notes Receivable 5,000.00

   d. Cash 5,000.00
      Interest Expense 100.00
          Notes Receivable 5,000.00
          Interest Revenue 100.00

4. At the date of discounting a note receivable from R. J. Johns, the Charter Company made the following entry:

   Cash 7,850
   Interest Expense 150
       Notes Receivable 8,000

4. (concluded)

The maturity value of the note is $8,150. R. T. Johns did not pay the note. The bank deducted the amount due from Charter Company's account. Which of the following correctly records the default transaction on Charter Company's books?

a. Uncollectible Accounts Expense 8,150
       Cash   8,250

b. Dishonored Notes Receivable 8,150
       Cash   8,150

c. Accounts Receivable 8,150
       Cash   8,150

d. Accounts Receivable 8,340
       Cash   8,300

5. A $50,000, 90-day, 12 percent note receivable has been dishonored. The entry to record this event by the payee would include a:

a. debit to Notes Receivable of $50,000.
b. credit to Notes Receivable Dishonored of $50,000.
c. credit to Notes Receivable of $51,500.
d. debit to Accounts Receivable of $51,500.

6. The maker of a $60,000, 120-day, 14 percent note failed to pay the note at maturity. To record this fact, the maker of the note should prepare a journal entry that includes a:

a. debit to Interest Receivable of $2,800.
b. credit to Interest Revenue of $2,800.
c. debit to Interest Payable of $3,000.
d. debit to Interest Expense of $2,800.

7. The Clark Company presented its own $15,000, 60-day noninterest-bearing note to its bank, which discounted it at 12 percent. Clark should prepare an entry that includes a:

a. debit to Cash of $15,300.
b. debit to Cash of $14,700.
c. credit to Notes Payable of $15,300.
d. credit to Notes Payable of $14,700.

8. The Discount on Notes Payable account is a(n):

a. asset account.
b. expense account.
c. contra liability account.
d. liability account.

9. The Green Company has a fiscal year ending on March 31. On January 31, it borrowed $60,000 by giving a 6-month, 15 percent note. The company's March 31 balance sheet should report accrued interest payable of:

a. $9,000.
b. $4,500.
c. $3,000.
d. $1,500.

10. A bond issued at a discount indicates that at the date of issue:

a. its contract rate was lower than the prevailing market rate of interest on similar bonds.
b. its contract rate was higher than the prevailing market rate of interest on similar bonds.
c. the bonds were issued at a price greater than their face value.
d. the bonds are noninterest bearing.

11. On the day the bonds are dated, the Stanhope Corporation issued 12 percent, first-mortgage bonds having a face value of $500,000 for $575,000. What entry is required?

a.
| Cash | 575,000 | |
| Bonds Payable | | 575,000 |

b.
Cash	575,000	
Bond Interest Payable		75,000
Bonds Payable		500,000

c.
Cash	575,000	
Bonds Payable—Discount		75,000
Bonds Payable		500,000

d.
Cash	575,000	
Bonds Payable—Premium		75,000
Bonds Payable		500,000

12. On December 31, 1990, GK Company issued $100,000 face value of 8 percent, 10-year, bonds for cash of $87,538—a price that yields 10 percent. Interest is payable semiannually on the bonds, which mature on December 31, 2000. Using the interest rate method, interest expense for the first six months of the life of the bonds is:

a. $4,000.
b. $4,377.
c. $4,623.
d. $5,246.

13. On September 30, 1990, Ball Company issued $200,000 face value of 8 percent, 10-year bonds for cash of $175,076—a price that yields 10 percent. Interest is payable semiannually on the bonds, which mature on September 30, 2000. Using the interest method, the adjusting entry on December 31, 1990, to record the accrued interest would read:

a.
| Interest Expense | 4,000 | |
| Interest Payable | | 4,000 |

b.
Interest expense	4,353	
Discount on Bonds Payable		353
Interest Payable		4,000

c.
Interest Expense	4,377	
Discount on Bonds Payable		377
Interest Payable		4,000

d.
Interest Expense	4,000	
Discount on Bonds Payable	353	
Interest Payable		4,353

14. On July 1 James Company purchased $100,000 face value of Carol Corporation bonds which have an interest rate of 9 percent, payable semiannually on January 1 and July 1. James Company paid $102,000 in the transaction. The journal entry to record the purchase is:

a. Investment in Bonds 102,000
   Cash 102,000

b. Investment in Bonds 97,500
   Interest Receivable 4,500
   Cash 102,000

c. Investment in Bonds 100,000
   Premium on Investment in Bonds 2,000
   Cash 102,000

d. Investment in Bonds 100,000
   Bond Purchase Costs 2,000
   Cash 102,000

15. The present value of $1 due in 40 periods at 2 percent is .45289. The present value of $1 due in 20 periods at 4 percent is .45639. The present value of $1 due at the end of each of 40 periods at 2 percent is 27.35548. The present value of $1 due at the end of each of 20 periods at 4 percent is 13.59033. If $100,000 of 20-year, 5 percent bonds issued and dated on July 1, 1990, and calling for semiannual interest payments on January 1 and July 1, are issued to yield 4 percent, their issue price is:

a. $114,927.70.
b. $ 79,614.82.
c. $113,677.70.
d. $ 79,264.82.

16. On July 1, 1990, Carrilson Corporation issued $100,000 face value of 10-year, 6 percent bonds and received $86,400 which reflects a yield of 8 percent. The bonds are dated July 1, 1990, and call for semiannual interest payments on January 1 and July 1. Using the effective rate method, the interest expense on these bonds for the six months ending December 31, 1990, is:

a. $4,000.
b. $3,456.
c. $2,592.
d. $3,680.

Now compare your answers with the correct ones beginning on page 276.

Solutions/Chapter 9

Completion and Exercises

1. Total note days......................... 120
   - July—days............................ 31
   - Date of note 25
                                           ──
                                            6
   - August—days 31
   - September—days 30
   - October—days 31   98
                                              ── ──
   - Due date, November 22

2. 360

3. $6,000

4. A note is dishonored if its maker fails to pay at maturity.

5. Dec. 1   Cash 97,000
   - Notes Payable—Discount 3,000
   -     Notes Payable 100,000
   - To record discounting of own note at the bank.

   Dec. 31   Interest Expense 1,000
   -     Notes Payable—Discount........................ 1,000
   - To record interest incurred on note.

   $$\left(\$100,000 \times \frac{12}{100} \times \frac{30}{360} \right).$$

   Mar. 1   Interest Expense 2,000
   -     Notes Payable—Discount........................ 2,000
   - To record interest on note to maturity date.

   Notes Payable.. 100,000
   -     Cash 100,000
   - To record payment of note payable.

6. Face value of note $20,000.00
   - Add: Interest at 12 percent for 120 days 800.00
   - Maturity value.. $20,800.00
   - Bank discount for 120 days at 8 percent............... 554.67
   - Cash Proceeds $20,245.33

7. Maturity value of note $20,800.00
   - Less: Bank discount for 90 days at 8 percent 416.00
   - Cash Proceeds $20,384.00

8. Cash 20,384
   - Notes Receivable 20,000
   - Interest Revenue 384
   - To record discounting of note at the bank at 8 percent.

9. holder

10. Accounts Receivable 20,805
      Cash 20,805
     To record payment of note which was discounted at the bank
     and dishonored when due. Protest fee is $5.00.

11. present value

12. a.   Cash 825,300.00
      Discount on Bonds Payable 174,700.00
        Bonds Payable 1,000,000.00

    b.   Bond Interest Expense 54,367.50
        Discount on Bonds Payable ($174,700/40) 4,367.50
        Cash 50,000.00

    c.   The straight-line method may be used only when it does not differ materially from the interest method. The interest method is theoretically correct.

13. a.   Cash 98,500
      Discount on Bonds Payable 1,500
        Bonds Payable 100,000

    b.   Interest Expense 446
        Discount on Bonds Payable 46
        Cash 400

    c.   Bonds Payable 100,000
        Discount on Bonds Payable 1,000
        Gain on Bond Redemption 3,000
        Cash 96,000

14. premium

Issuer

15. Aug. 1, 1990   Cash 1,007,500
                Bonds Payable 1,000,000
                Interest Payable 7,500

    Dec. 31, 1990   Interest Expense 37,500
                Interest Payable 37,500

Purchaser

    Aug. 1, 1990   Bond Investments 1,000,000
                Interest Receivable 7,500
                Cash 1,007,500

    Dec. 31, 1990   Interest Receivable 37,500
                Interest Revenue 37,500

16. **Jan. 1, 1990**

Cash	1,067,952	
Bonds Payable		1,000,000
Premium on Bonds Payable		67,952

July 1, 1990

Interest Expense ($1,067,952 × .04)	42,718	
Premium on Bonds Payable	2,282	
Cash		45,000

Dec. 31, 1990

Interest Expense [($1,067,952 − $2,282) × .04)]	42,627	
Premium on Bonds Payable	2,373	
Interest Payable		45,000

Purchaser

Jan. 1, 1990

Bond Investments	1,067,952	
Cash		1,067,952

July 1, 1990

Cash	45,000	
Bond Investments		2,282
Interest Revenue		42,718

Dec. 31, 1990

Interest Receivable	45,000	
Bond Investments		2,373
Interest Revenue		42,627

17. plus, minus

18. effective rate of interest

19. accrued interest

20. principal; interest

21.
Present value of principal: $1,000 × .45639	$ 456.39
Present value of interest: $40 × 13.59033	543.61
Total present value	$1,000.00

22.
Present value of principal: $1,000 × .45639	$ 456.39
Present value of interest: $30 × 13.59033	407.71
Total price (present value)	$ 864.10

23.
Cash	864.10	
Discount on Bonds Payable	135.90	
Bonds Payable		1,000.00

Interest Expense ($864.10 × .04)	34.56	
Discount on Bonds Payable		4.56
Cash		30.00

24.
Present value of principal: $1,000 × .47464	$ 474.64
Present value of interest: $30 × 13.13393	394.02
Total present value	$ 868.66

25. $4.56; discount amortized

26. interest; principal

27. $13,382.30. This can be found by looking at Table I at the factor in the 5 periods row and 6 percent column (which is 1.33823). Multiply this factor times $10,000 and the answer is $13,382.30.

28. $13,439.16. This is found by looking at the factor in Table I in the 10 periods row and 3 percent column (since there are 10 semiannual periods and the interest rate is 3 percent per period). 1.34392 × $10,000 = $13,439.20.

29. reciprocal or reverse

30. $13,382.30 \times \dfrac{1}{1.33823} = \$10,000$

Of course, this could also be found by using:

$13,382.30 \times 0.74726 = \$10,000$. This is so because $1/1.33823 = 0.74726$.

31. $1,000 \times 6.71008 = \$6,710.08$. The factor of 6.71008 is found in the 10 periods row and 8 percent column.

Multiple-Choice Questions

1. c. The effective rate of interest may be computed as follows:

$$\frac{\text{Discount}}{\text{Cash proceeds}} \times \frac{360}{90} = \text{Rate of interest}$$

$$\frac{\$700}{\$27,300} \times \frac{360}{90} = .1026$$

Thus, the effective rate is 10.26 percent.

2. a. The discount period is 6 days, and the discount is computed on the maturity value of $808.00, not on the face value of $800. Thus, (d) should read: $808.00 \times .10 \times 6/360$. Therefore, (b), (c), and (d) are false.

3. a. The cash proceeds are computed as follows:

Face amount	$5,000.00
Interest, 12 percent for 60 days	100.00
Maturity value	$5,100.00
Discount of bank	
$\left(\$5,100 \times \dfrac{15}{100} \times \dfrac{60}{360} \right)$	127.50
Cash proceeds.	$4,972.50

The difference between the cash proceeds and the face value plus accrued interest is the amount of the financing expense. In practice, this would be debited to Interest Expense ($5,000.00 − $4,972.50 = $27.50). There was no accrued interest at the date of discount.

4. c. The amount receivable from R. T. Johns includes the $150 of interest and $8,000 face value and is debited to Accounts Receivable. The bank would deduct the maturity amount from the company's Cash account.

5. d. The payee would record the maturity value of the note—$50,000 + [.12 ($50,000) × 1/4] = $51,500—in an account receivable from the defaulting maker.

6. d. Upon dishonor of its note, the payee should accrue interest on the note to maturity date as an expense.

7. b. Proceeds equal ($15,000 − ($15,000 × 60/360) × .12) = $14,700.

8. c. The treatment as a contra account reports a net liability that is equal to the amount borrowed, plus the interest expense recognized to the date of the balance sheet.

9. d. Interest must be accrued for two months: $60,000 × 2/12 × .15 = $1,500.

10. a. A bond sells in the market at a price less than face value when the rate of interest offered by the bonds is considered by investors to be inadequate relative to the face value of the bonds (the amount paid if there is no premium or discount). Changing the price at which a bond sells is the market's way of changing the rate of interest actually earned on a bond, since an investor cannot change the rate in the face of the bond.

11. d. Cash must be debited for the $575,000 received. It is customary to carry bonds (notes, stock, etc.) at their face value in a separate account. Thus, the bonds should be recorded in a separate account for their face value of $500,000. The remaining $75,000 is credited to a premium account, which in reality is an adjunct account to Bonds Payable. Together, these accounts show the liability to the bondholders.

12. b. Computed as effective rate per period (.05) times carrying value of bonds on issue date ($87,538).

13. c. Computed as follows: interest expense is equal to $175,076 × .05 × 1/2; interest payable is equal to $200,000 × .04 × 1/2; amortization of the discount is equal to the difference between the two previous computations.

14. a. Since the bonds were purchased on their issue date, there is no accrued interest. Thus, the bonds were purchased at a premium. It is customary in accounting to carry investments at cost in a single account. Hence, the answer (a).

15. c. The present value of the promise to pay $100,000 in 40 periods at 2 percent is $100,000 times .45289, or $45,289. The present value of the promise to pay $2,500 at the end of each of the next 40 periods at 2 percent is $2,500 times 27.35548, or $68,388.70. These sums added together equal $113,677.70.

16. b. The interest is computed as $86,400 × .04. The rate of .04 is used because the bonds call for semiannual interest payments.

Name _____

_____

November 1, 1990   CHAPMAN COMPANY

December 31, 1990

March 1, 1991

Name _____

CRANWOOD COMPANY
GENERAL JOURNAL

DATE	ACCOUNT TITLES AND EXPLANATION	POST. REF.	DEBIT	CREDIT

Name _____

_____

(a) _____ HUNTER COMPANY _____

(b)

Name _____

GREEN CORPORATION
GENERAL JOURNAL

DATE	ACCOUNT TITLES AND EXPLANATION	POST. REF.	DEBIT	CREDIT

Name _____

_____

ALLIED COMPANY

(a)

Price received:

(b) _____ Amortization Schedule _____

(A) Interest Payment Date	(B) Interest Expense Debit	(C) Cash Credit	(D) Discount on Bonds Payable Credit	(E) Carrying Value of Bonds Payable

(c) GENERAL JOURNAL

DATE	ACCOUNT TITLES AND EXPLANATION	POST. REF.	DEBIT	CREDIT

Name _____

BOWEN COMPANY
GENERAL JOURNAL

(a)

DATE	ACCOUNT TITLES AND EXPLANATION	POST. REF.	DEBIT	CREDIT
(b)				

Name _____

_____

(a)   COOK COMPANY

Price received:

(b) _____ *Amortization Schedule*

(A)	(B)	(C)	(D)	(E)
Interest Payment Date	Interest Expense Debit	Cash Credit	Premium on Bonds Payable Debit	Carrying Value of Bonds Payable

COOK COMPANY
GENERAL JOURNAL

(c)

DATE	ACCOUNT TITLES AND EXPLANATION	POST. REF.	DEBIT	CREDIT

Name _____

_____

(a)

KENT CORPORATION
GENERAL JOURNAL

DATE	ACCOUNT TITLES AND EXPLANATION	POST. REF.	DEBIT	CREDIT

(b)

Name_____

_____

	Alternative (1)	Alternative (2)
Expected Net Operating Income	$2,200,000	$2,200,000

Statement of Cash Flows

Understanding the Learning Objectives

1. Understand the uses of the statement of cash flows.

    *   The statement of cash flows summarizes the effects on cash of the operating, financing, and investing activities of a company for a period.

    *   Management can see the effects of its past major policy decisions in quantitative form by reviewing the statement.

    *   Investors and creditors can assess the entity's ability to generate positive future net cash flows, to pay its debts, to pay dividends, and can assess the need for external financing.

2. Conceptually understand the statement of cash flows.

    *   Operating activities generally include the cash effects of transactions and other events that enter into the determination of net income. The net cash flow from operating activities can be measured in two ways. The direct method deducts from cash sales only those operating expenses that consumed cash. The indirect method starts with net income and adjusts net income for items that affected reported net income but did not involve cash.

    *   Investment activities include lending money and collecting the principal on those loans; acquiring and selling or disposing of securities of other companies or entities; and acquiring and selling or disposing of property, plant, and equipment.

    *   Financing activities include obtaining resources from owners and providing them with a return on their investment and of their investment and obtaining resources from creditors and repaying or otherwise settling the debt.

3. Prepare the statement of cash flows.

    *   The first step is to determine the cash flows from operating activities. Either the direct or indirect method may be used.

    *   The second step is to analyze all the noncurrent accounts for changes resulting from investing and financing activities.

    *   The third step is to arrange the information gathered in steps 1 and 2 into the format required for the statement of cash flows.

4. Understand the historical development from the statement of changes in financial position to a statement of cash flows.

    *   Through mid 1988, a statement of changes in financial position was required to report on funds flows. This statement showed the sources and uses of funds as the two main categories. Funds generally meant working capital (current assets minus current liabilities).

    *   In late 1987, the Financial Accounting Standards Board issued a standard requiring the substitution of a statement of cash flows for the statement of changes in financial position.

5. Understand how to prepare a schedule of changes in working capital.

   * A schedule of changes in working capital lists all current assets and current liabilities, their beginning and ending balances, and the changes in these balances summarized into a single amount—the net change in working capital.

6. Define and use correctly the new terms in the glossary.

   The new terms introduced in the chapter are as follows:

   Cash flows from operating activities—The net amount of cash received or disbursed for a given period on items that normally appear on the income statement. Usually obtained by converting accrual basis net income to a cash basis amount.

   Direct method—Deducts from cash sales only those operating expenses that consumed cash.

   Financing activities—Include obtaining resources from owners and providing them with a return on their investment and of their investment and obtaining resources from creditors and repaying or otherwise settling the debt.

   Indirect method—A way of determining cash flows from operations that starts with net income and adjusts for expenses and revenues that do not affect cash or working capital. Also called the **addback** method.

   Investing activities—Include lending money and collecting the principal on those loans; acquiring and selling or disposing of securities of other companies or entities; and acquiring and selling or disposing of property, plant, and equipment.

   Noncash charges or expenses—Expenses and losses that are added back to net income because they do not actually use cash of the company. The items added back include amounts of depletion that were expensed, amortization of intangible assets such as patents and goodwill, amortization of discount on bonds payable, and losses from disposals of noncurrent assets.

   Noncash credits or revenues—Revenues and gains included in arriving at net income that do not provide cash; an example is a gain on the disposal of a noncurrent asset.

   Operating activities—Generally include the cash effects of transactions and other events that enter into the determination of net income.

   Schedule of changes in working capital—A schedule listing all current assets and current liabilities, their beginning and ending balances, and the changes in these balances summarized into a single amount—the net change in working capital.

   Statement of cash flows—A statement that summarizes the effects on cash of the operating, investing, and financing activities of a company for a period. Both inflows and outflows are included in each category. The statement of cash flows must be prepared each time an income statement is prepared.

   Statement of changes in financial position—A statement that reports the flows of cash or working capital into and out of a business in a given time period; it also shows significant financing and investing activities that do not involve cash or working capital flows.

   Working capital—Equal to current assets minus current liabilities.

Completion and Exercises

1. The increases and decreases in the individual current asset and current liability accounts are reflected in the aggregate as a change in the firm's _____.

2. A statement of cash flows shows the _____ of net change in cash between two dates.

3. The old statement of changes in financial position showed the _____ and _____ of financial resources.

4. Deterioration in the firm's _____ position due to inadequate planning by management leads to a company's inability to meet short-run financial requirements.

5. The main source of cash of a business enterprise is _____

    _____ .

6. In addition to Question 5, what are three other sources of cash that result from financing or investing activities?

    (a) _____

    (b) _____

    (c) _____

7. What are four uses of cash that result from operating, financing, or investing activities?

    (a) _____ ,

    (b) _____ ,

    (c) _____ , and

    (d) _____ .

8. What is a "noncash financing or investing activity"?

    _____

    _____

    _____

9. From the following condensed income statement show how the items shown would be presented in a statement of cash flows.

Sales		$162,500
Expenses (except depreciation and amortization)		113,750
		$ 48,750
Depreciation	$16,250	
Amortization of patent	6,500	22,750
Net income		$ 26,000

10. From the following current assets and current liabilities sections prepare a schedule of changes in working capital for the Pretend Corporation as of December 31, 1990 and 1991.

	December 31	
	1991	1990
Current assets:		
Cash	$11,000	$ 8,250
Accounts receivable (net)	23,100	20,625
Inventories	28,160	26,180
Prepaid expenses	1,210	1,375
Total current assets	$63,470	$56,430
Current liabilities:		
Accounts payable	$14,300	$12,650
Notes payable	17,050	19,250
Accrued liabilities	13,750	12,650
Total current liabilities	$45,100	$44,550

11. Using the schedule of changes in working capital in Question 10 and the following information, prepare a statement of cash flows for the Pretend Corporation for 1991.

Net income for 1991	$44,000
Depreciation expense	16,500

An analysis of changes in noncurrent accounts revealed the following:

a. Sold equipment for $2,750; original cost, $11,000, accumulated depreciation, $8,800.
b. Purchased equipment for $13,750.
c. Sold capital stock; 55 shares at $50 per share.
d. Purchased land and building for $34,210.
e. Paid cash dividends, $11,000.

12. An adequate working capital position does not ensure an adequate _____ position for meeting payments.

13. The income statement does not measure cash flow from operating activities because it is prepared on a(n) _____ basis.

14. Assume an income statement shows sales of $243,750. The accounts receivable balance was $21,000 on January 1 and $16,500 on December 31. Given only this information, determine how much cash was collected from customers.

15. The income statement shows that purchases for the year amounted to $187,500. Accounts payable on January 1 were $27,000, and on December 31 they were $31,500. Given only this information, determine how much cash was paid to vendors for merchandise during the year.

16. To derive the cash flows from operating activities for the period, net income on an accrual basis must be converted to net income on a _____ basis.

17. Cash flows from operating activities equal net income on an accrual basis plus (a) _____ _____ , minus (b) _____ , plus (c) decreases in _____ _____ , plus (d) increases in _____ , minus (e) decreases in _____ _____ for operating expense items and minus (f) increases in _____ _____ .

Multiple-Choice Questions

For each of the following questions, indicate the single best answer by circling the appropriate letter.

Using the following information, answer questions 1-3 concerning a statement of cash flows.

1. The company reported a $35,000 net income for 1990.
2. The company recorded $7,000 depreciation on its store equipment.
3. Store equipment that cost $2,800 and had depreciated $1,400 was sold for $700.
4. Fully depreciated store equipment that cost $4,900 was discarded.
5. $5,600 of new store equipment was purchased during the year.
6. $6,720 of cash dividends were declared and paid during the year.
7. A 1,000-share stock dividend was declared and distributed at a time when the stock was selling for $15 per share.

1. Which of the above data will be used to determine cash flows from operating activities?

   a. 1, 5, 6
   b. 1, 2, 3
   c. 5, 3, 2
   d. 1, 2, 7
   e. 2, 3

2. Which of the above data will be used to determine cash flows from investing activities?

   a. 7
   b. 1, 2, 3
   c. 6
   d. 3, 5
   e. 4, 5

3. Which of the above data will be used to determine cash flows from financing activities?

   a. 4, 5
   b. 1, 2, 3
   c. 6
   d. 6, 7
   e. 7

Questions 4-6. How would the following transactions be shown on a statement of cash flows?

4. Treasury stock was purchased for $6,500 cash during this year.

   a. Shown as a positive cash flow from investing activities
   b. Shown as a negative cash flow from investing activities
   c. Shown as a negative cash flow from financing activities
   d. Not shown on the statement
   e. Shown as an operating activity item

5. Equipment was purchased for $41,250 during the year.

   a. Shown as a negative cash flow from investing activities
   b. Shown as a negative cash flow from financing activities
   c. Shown as a negative cash flow from operating activities
   d. Shown as a positive cash flow from financing activities
   e. Not shown on the statement

6. A five-year, 6 percent mortgage note payable for $87,500 was signed and given to the bank for cash so the company could acquire additional land and a building.

   a. Shown on the statement of cash flows or in a separate schedule
   b. Not shown at all since cash was not affected
   c. Shown as a cash flow from operating activities
   d. A and C are both correct
   e. None of the above statements is correct

7. Which of the following is true concerning depreciation, amortization of patents, amortization of bond discount, interest expense, and salary expense?

   a. All are added to income to determine cash flows from operating activities.
   b. Only interest and salary expense are added to income to determine cash flows from operating activities.
   c. Depreciation, amortization of patents, and bond discounts are added to income to determine cash flows from operating activities.
   d. Only depreciation and interest expense are added to income to determine cash flows from operating activities.

8. Indicate the effect on the statement of cash flows if fully depreciated office equipment costing $4,800 was discarded and its cost and accumulated depreciation were removed from the books.

   a. The transaction would be shown as an investing activity.
   b. The transaction would be shown as a financing activity.
   c. The transaction would be shown in determining cash flows from operating activities.
   d. The transaction would not be shown on a statement of cash flows.

9. Machinery with a cost of $13,500 and accumulated depreciation of $11,970 was sold for $1,800 cash. How would the proceeds of sale be reported in the statement of cash flows?

   a. Cash flows from investing activities; sale of machinery of $270
   b. Cash flows from financing activities; $1,800
   c. Would be shown as a decrease in a current asset
   d. Cash flows from investing activities; sale of machinery of $1,800
   e. Not shown on statement of cash flows

10. A corporation issued $2,000,000 of 10-year bonds for cash at 95. How would the transaction be shown on the statement of cash flows?

    a. Positive cash inflow from financing activities, $1,900,000.
    b. Positive cash inflow from financing activities, $2,000,000.
    c. Negative cash flow from investing activities, $1,900,000.
    d. Negative cash flow from investing activities, $2,000,000.
    e. Not shown on the statement of cash flows.

11. A company paid the following dividends during the year:

    Cash Dividends $ 6,000
    Stock Dividends   15,000

    The correct statement concerning a statement of cash flows is:

    a. Neither dividend is shown on the statement.
    b. Both dividends are shown on the statement.
    c. Cash dividends are shown, while stock dividends are not shown.
    d. Stock dividends are shown while cash dividends are not.
    e. None of the above statements is true.

12. On a statement of cash flows, the correct statement concerning a gain of $1,440 from the sale of a patent is:

    a.   The gain appears as an investing activity of $1,440.
    b.   The gain is used to adjust the income reported.
    c.   The gain does not appear on the statement.
    d.   None of the above statements is true.

13. You are given the following data concerning the Land account:

Land

Date		Debit	Credit	Balance
July 1	Balance			$337,500
Aug. 8	Sold for $75,000 cash		$45,000	292,500
Sept. 1	Purchased for cash	$ 37,500		330,000
Oct. 31	Purchased for cash	112,500		442,500

The above data would be shown on the statement of cash flows as:

    a.   cash flows from investing activities; sale of land, $75,000.
    b.   cash flows from investing activities; sale of land, $45,000.
    c.   cash flows from financing activities; purchase of land, $37,500.
    d.   cash flows from financing activities; purchase of land, $112,500.
    e.   none of the above is correct.

Now compare your answers with the correct ones beginning on page 302.

Solutions/Chapter 10

Completion and Exercises

1. working capital

2. causes

3. sources; uses (or disposition)

4. cash

5. profitable operations (net income)

6. (a) Capital stock issues; (b) Bond or other long-term debt issues, (c) Sales of noncurrent assets

7. (a) Net loss existing after adjustment for noncash items; (b) Dividends paid; (c) Debt repayment; (d) Purchase of noncurrent assets

8. A noncash financing activity is one that neither provides nor consumes cash.

9. *Cash flows from operating activities:*

Net income	$26,000
Adjustments to reconcile net income to net cash provided by operating activities:	
Depreciation	$16,250
Amortization of patent	6,500

10.

PRETEND CORPORATION
Schedule of Changes in Working Capital
December 31, 1990 and 1991

	December 31 1991	December 31 1990	Working Capital Increase	Working Capital Decrease
Current assets:				
Cash...	$11,000	$ 8,250	$2,750	
Accounts receivable (net)	23,100	20,625	2,475	
Inventories	28,160	26,180	1,980	
Prepaid expenses................................	1,210	1,375		$ 165
Total current assets	$63,470	$56,430		
Current liabilities:				
Accounts payable	$14,300	$12,650		1,650
Notes payable..................................	17,050	19,250	2,200	
Accrued liabilities	13,750	12,650		1,100
Total current liabilities	$45,100	$44,550		
Working capital..................................	$18,370	$11,880		
Net increase in working capital				6,490
			$9,405	$9,405

11.

PRETEND CORPORATION
Statement of Cash Flows
For the Year Ended December 31, 1991

Cash flows from operating activities:

Net income	$ 44,000	
Adjustments to reconcile net income to net cash provided by operations:		
Depreciation	16,500	
Gain on sale of equipment.................................	(550)	
Increase in accounts receivable...........................	(2,475)	
Increase in inventories	(1,980)	
Decrease in prepaid expenses	165	
Increase in accounts payable	1,650	
Decrease in notes payable.................................	(2,200)	
Increase in accrued liabilities	1,100	
Net cash provided by operating activities..............		$56,210
Cash flows from investing activities:		
Sale of equipment	$ 2,750	
Purchase of equipment....................................	(13,750)	
Purchase of land and building	(34,210)	
Net cash used by investing activities		(45,210)
Cash flows from financing activities:		
Sale of capital stock	$ 2,750	
Payment of dividends	(11,000)	
Net cash used by financing activities..................		(8,250)
Increase in cash		$ 2,750

12. cash

13. accrual

14.

Accounts receivable, beginning	$ 21,000
Additions to accounts receivable resulting from sales......................	243,750
	$264,750
Accounts receivable, ending	16,500
Amount of cash collected from customers	$248,250

15.

Accounts payable, beginning	$ 27,000
Additions to accounts payable resulting from purchases	187,500
	$214,500
Accounts payable, ending	31,500
Cash payments to vendors for merchandise................................	$183,000

16. cash

17. (a) noncash expenses and losses; (b) noncash revenues and gains; (c) current assets; (d) current liabilities; (e) current liabilities; (f) current assets.

Multiple-Choice Questions

1. b.

2. d.

3. c.

4. c.

5. a. Equipment is purchased with a current asset, cash, and there is a decrease in cash.

6. a.

7. c. Interest expense and salaries expense, unlike the other expenses listed, involve an outflow of cash.

8. d. There would be no effect on cash because Accumulated Depreciation would be debited for the same amount that Office Equipment would be credited.

9. d.

10. a.

11. c.

12. b.

13. a.

Name _____

_____

ROCK CORPORATION

Statement of Cash Flows—Indirect Method

For the Year Ended _____ 31, 1991

Cash flows from operating activities:

Cash flows from investing activities:

Cash flows from financing activities:

Name _____

_____

D & J INC.

Statement of Cash Flows—Indirect Method

For the Year Ended _____ 31, 1991

Cash flows from operating activities:

  Net income:

Cash flows from investing activities:

Cash flows from financing activities:

Name _____

_____

(a)

BOW CORPORATION

Working Paper for Statement of Cash Flows

For the Year Ended _____ 31, 1991

	ACCOUNT BALANCE ___ ___, 1990	DEBIT	CREDIT	ACCOUNT BALANCE ___ ___, 1991
Debits				
Cash				
Accounts receivable				
Credits				

Name _____

(a) _____

	ACCOUNT BALANCE _____ ____, 1990	DEBIT	CREDIT	ACCOUNT BALANCE _____ ____, 1991

Name _____

(b)

BOW COMPANY

Statement of Cash Flows—Indirect Method

For the Year Ended _____ 31, 1991

Cash flows from operating activities:

Cash flows from investing activities:

Cash flows from financing activities:

Name _____

(c)

BOW COMPANY

Income Statement

For the Year Ended December 31, 1991

ACCRUAL BASIS	ADD	DEDUCT	CASH BASIS

Name _____

(d)   BOW COMPANY

Statement of Cash Flows—Direct Method

For the Year Ended December 31, 1991

Cash flows from operating activities:							
Cash flows from investing activities:							
Cash flows from financing activites:							

Name _____

_____

(a)

BRIGHT CORPORATION
Working Paper for Statement of Cash Flows
For the Year Ended December 31, 1991

	ACCOUNT BALANCE	DEBIT	CREDIT	ACCOUNT BALANCE
Debits				
Cash				
Credits				

(a)

	ACCOUNT BALANCE	DEBIT	CREDIT	ACCOUNT BALANCE

(b)   BRIGHT CORPORATION
                   Statement of Cash Flows—Indirect Method
                    For the Year Ended December 31, 1991

Cash flows from operating activities:

Cash flows from investing activities:

Cash flows from financing activities:

Schedule of noncash financing and investing activities:

Name _____

(c)

BRIGHT CORPORATION

Income Statement

For the Year Ended December 31, 1991

	ACCRUAL BASIS	ADD	DEDUCT	CASH BASIS

(d)

BRIGHT CORPORATION

Statement of Cash Flows—Direct Method

For the Year Ended December 31, 1991

Cash flows from operating activities:

Cash flows from investing activities:

Cash flows from financing activities:

Name _____

BOW COMPANY
Schedule of Changes in Working Capital
For the Year Ended December 31, 1991

	December 31		Working Capital	
	1991	1990	Increase	Decrease

Name

BRIGHT CORPORATION

Schedule of Changes in Working Capital

For the Year Ended December 31, 1991

	December 31		Working Capital	
	1991	1990	Increase	Decrease

SMITH COMPANY

Schedule of Cash Flows from Operating Activities—Indirect Method

For the Year Ended December 31, 1991

Net income	

Financial Statement Analysis

Understanding the Learning Objectives

1. Describe and explain the objectives of financial statement analysis.

   * This analysis displays significant relationships between data and trends for assessing the company's past performance and current financial position.

   * The analysis is also used to make predictions that may have a direct effect on decisions made by many users of financial statements.

2. Calculate and explain changes in financial statements using horizontal analysis, vertical analysis, and trend analysis.

   * Comparative financial statements present a company's financial statements for two or more successive periods side-by-side. The calculation of dollar or percentage changes for each account on the financial statement is known as horizontal analysis.

   * Vertical analysis shows a single financial statement and expresses each account as a percentage of a significant total. Financial statements recast as only percentage amounts are known as common-size statements.

   * Trend analysis compares the percentage differences using one year as a base. It is helpful for disclosing changes and trends occurring through time.

3. Perform ratio analysis on financial statements using liquidity ratios, long-term solvency ratios, profitability tests, and market tests.

   * Liquidity ratios indicate a company's short-term debt-paying ability. Such ratios include:

     current, or working capital, ratio
     acid test, or quick, ratio
     accounts receivable turnover
     number of days' sales in accounts receivable
     inventory turnover
     total assets turnover

   * Long-term solvency ratios, or equity ratios, show the relationship between debt and equity financing in a company. Such ratios include:

     equity (or stockholders' equity) ratio
     stockholders' equity to debt ratio

   * Profitability tests measure:

     (1) relationships on the income statement that indicate a company's ability to recover costs and expenses, and

     (2) relationships of income to various balance sheet measures that indicate the company's relative ability to earn income on assets employed.

Such tests include:

rate of return on operating assets
[operating margin and turnover of operating assets]
net income to average stockholders' equity
earnings per share
times interest earned ratio
times preferred dividends earned ratio

* Market tests are computed using information from the financial statements and information about market price for the company's stock. These tests help investors and potential investors assess the relative merits of the various stocks in the marketplace. Such tests include:

earnings yield on common stock
dividend yield on common stock
dividend yield on preferred stock

4. Understand the considerations used in financial statement analysis.

* Such comparisons must use comparable data—especially for different periods or different companies.

* Facts and conditions not disclosed by the financial statements may affect their interpretation.

* Financial statements fail to reveal the impact of inflation on the reporting entity.

* Comparisons with standards provide a starting point for the analyst's thinking and may include the analyst's experience and observations, the company's past performance, and information about other companies.

5. Define and correctly use the new terms in the glossary.

The new terms introduced in the chapter are as follows:

Accounts receivable turnover—Net sales divided by average net accounts receivable.

Acid-test (quick) ratio—Ratio of quick assets (cash, marketable securities, net receivables) to current liabilities.

Common-size statements—Show only percentages and no absolute dollar amounts.

Comparative financial statements—Present the same company's financial statements for two or more successive periods in side-by-side columns.

Current (working capital) ratio—The ratio that relates current assets to current liabilities.

Debt to equity ratio—Total debt divided by owners' equity.

Dividend yield on common stock—Dividend per share divided by current market price per share of common stock.

Dividend yield on preferred stock—Dividend per share divided by current market price per share of preferred stock.

Earnings per share (EPS)—Usually computed for common stock; earnings available to common stockholders (which equals net income less preferred dividends) divided by weighted-average number of shares of common stock outstanding.

Earnings yield on common stock—Ratio of current EPS to current market price per share.

Equity ratio—The ratio of stockholders' equity to total assets (or total equities).

Horizontal analysis—Analysis of a company's financial statements for two or more successive periods showing percentage and/or absolute changes from prior year. This type of analysis helps detect changes in a company's performance and highlights trends.

Inventory turnover—Cost of goods sold divided by average inventory.

Liquidity—State of possessing liquid assets, such as cash and other assets, that will soon be converted into cash.

Net income to average stockholders' equity--Net income divided by average stockholders' equity; often called **rate of return on stockholders' equity**, or simply **return on equity (ROE)**.

Net income to net sales—Net income divided by net sales.

Nonoperating assets—Assets owned but not used in producing operating revenues.

Nonoperating income elements—Elements that are excluded from net operating income because they are not directly related to operations; includes such elements as extraordinary items, interest revenue, interest expense, and income taxes.

Number of days' sales in accounts receivable—The number of days in a year (365) divided by the accounts receivable turnover. Also called the **average collection period for accounts receivable**.

Operating assets—All assets actively used in producing operating revenues.

Operating margin—Net operating income divided by net sales.

Payout ratio (on common stock)—The ratio of dividends per share divided by EPS.

Price-earnings ratio—The ratio of current market price per share divided by the EPS of the stock.

Quick ratio—Same as acid-test ratio.

Rate of return on operating assets—(Net operating income ÷ Net sales) × (Net sales ÷ Operating assets). Result is equal to net operating income divided by operating assets.

Ratios—They express the logical relationship between certain items in the financial statements.

Return on equity (ROE)—Net income divided by average stockholders' equity.

Stockholders' equity to debt ratio—Stockholders' equity divided by total debt; often used in inverted form and called the **debt to equity ratio**.

Times interest earned ratio—A ratio computed by dividing income before interest expense and income taxes by interest expense (also called **interest coverage ratio**).

Times preferred dividends earned ratio—Net income divided by annual preferred dividends.

Total assets turnover—Net sales divided by average total assets.

Trend percentages—Similar to horizontal analysis except that a base year is selected and comparisons are made to the base year.

Turnover—The relationship between the amount of an asset and some measure of its use. See accounts receivable turnover, inventory turnover, and total assets turnover.

Turnover of operating assets—Net sales divided by operating assets.

Vertical analysis—The study of a single financial statement in which each item is expressed as a percentage of a significant total; for example, percentages of sales calculations.

Working capital ratio—Same as current ratio.

Yield (on stock)—The yield on a stock investment refers to either an earnings yield or a dividend yield. Also see Earnings yield on common stock and Dividend yield on common stock and on preferred stock.

Completion and Exercises

1. Statement analysis is the selection and use of data presented in the financial statements to establish significant _____ and _____ .

2. What are comparative financial statements? _____
   _____

3. What are net assets? _____ – _____ =
   _____ _____ .

323

4. What is the definition of working capital? _____ – _____
_____.

5. How is the current ratio computed? _____ _____ _____ ÷ _____
_____.

6. What is the purpose of the current ratio? _____
_____
_____
_____

7. What is the definition of current assets? _____
_____
_____
_____
_____

8. Does the payment of a current liability leave the current ratio unchanged? _____
Why? _____
_____
_____
_____

9. If a company borrows money from a bank on a one-year note, what effect does this have on the working capital of the company? _____ Why? _____
_____
_____

10. What items are included in "quick assets" for the purpose of computing the acid-test or quick ratio?
_____
_____

11. _____ and _____ are the two sources of assets for a business enterprise.

12. How is the equity ratio computed? _____ ÷ _____
_____.

13. Fill in the blank spaces below:

| | December 31 | | Increase or Decrease* 1991 over 1990 | |
	1991	1990	Dollars	Percentage
Current assets:				
Cash	$ 54,000	$ 48,000	_____	_____
Accounts receivable, net	106,000	80,000	_____	_____
Inventories	92,000	84,000	_____	_____
Prepaid expenses	26,000	36,000	_____	_____
	$278,000	$248,000	_____	_____

14. What do turnovers express and what do they measure? _____

_____

_____

_____

_____

15. What can be interpreted from the accounts receivable turnover ratio?

_____

_____

_____

_____

16. What does the inventory turnover ratio show? _____

_____

_____

_____

_____

17. What does the turnover of total assets show? _____

_____

_____

_____

_____

_____

18. The price-earnings ratio is computed by dividing _____ _____ per share by

_____ per share.

19. The dividend yield on stock is computed by dividing _____ per share by the

_____ _____ per share.

20. The payout ratio is equal to _____ _____ _____ ÷

_____ _____ _____ .

325

21. Compute the requested figures for 1991 from the financial statements of the Dale Company presented on the following pages. (Assume all assets are operating assets.)

a. Accounts receivable turnover = _____ ÷ _____ .

b. Average life of accounts receivable = _____ ÷ _____ = _____ .

c. Inventory turnover = _____ ÷ _____ .

d. Total assets turnover = _____ ÷ _____ .

e. Percentage of net income to net sales = _____ ÷ _____ .

f. Rate of return on operating assets = _____ × _____ = _____ .

g. Percentage of net income to stockholders' equity = _____ ÷ _____ .

h. Earnings per share of common stock = _____ ÷ _____ .

i. Number of times interest is earned = _____ ÷ _____ .

DALE COMPANY
Comparative Balance Sheets
December 31, 1990 and 1991

	December 31 1991	December 31 1990
Assets		
Current assets:		
Cash	$ 35,000	$ 30,000
Accounts receivable	48,000	42,000
Merchandise inventory	51,000	47,000
Prepaid expenses	5,000	4,000
Total current assets	$139,000	$123,000
Plant and equipment (net)	278,000	250,000
Intangible assets	13,000	15,000
Total assets	$430,000	$388,000
Liabilities and Stockholders' Equity		
Liabilities:		
Current liabilities	$ 72,000	$ 70,000
9 percent first-mortgage bonds	90,000	90,000
Total liabilities	$162,000	$160,000
Stockholders' equity:		
6 percent preferred stock, par $100, 500 shares authorized and outstanding	$ 50,000	$ 50,000
Common stock, par $10	90,000	90,000
Paid-in capital in excess of par value	17,000	17,000
Retained earnings	111,000	71,000
Total stockholders' equity	$268,000	$228,000
Total liabilities and stockholders' equity	$430,000	$388,000

DALE COMPANY
Income Statement
For the Year Ended December 31, 1991

Sales	$615,000	
Less: Sales returns and allowances	15,000	
Net sales		$600,000
Cost of goods sold:		
Beginning inventory	$ 47,000	
Purchases	380,000	
Goods available for sale	$427,000	
Less: Ending inventory	51,000	
Cost of goods sold		376,000
Gross margin		$224,000
Operating expenses		153,900
Net operating income		$ 70,100
Interest expense		8,100
Net income before income taxes		$ 62,000
Income taxes		20,000
Net income after income taxes		$ 42,000

Multiple-Choice Questions

For each of the following questions, indicate the single best answer by circling the appropriate letter.

1-3 Consider each of the following transactions separately and state the effect of each transaction on working capital, current ratio and acid-test ratio. Assume the current ratio is 1:1 before these transactions occurred.

1. Purchased merchandise on account, $70,000.

   a. No effect on working capital, decrease both current ratio and acid-test ratio
   b. No effect on working capital or current ratio, decrease acid-test ratio
   c. No effect on all three financial analysis techniques
   d. Decrease all three financial analysis techniques

2. Paid cash for office supplies, $3,000.

   a. Increase working capital and current ratio, decrease acid-test ratio
   b. No effect on all three financial analysis techniques
   c. No effect on working capital and current ratio, decrease acid-test ratio
   d. Decrease all three financial analysis techniques

3. Paid short-term portion of notes payable, $100,000.

   a. Decrease working capital, current ratio, and acid-test ratios
   b. Increase working capital, no effect on current and acid-test ratios
   c. Increase working capital, decrease current and acid-test ratios
   d. No effect on all three financial analysis techniques

4. A firm's current ratio at the end of any given accounting period:

   a. is generally larger than the acid-test ratio of that firm for the same period.
   b. is never smaller than the acid-test ratio for the same period.
   c. is always equal to the working capital ratio for that date.
   d. all of the above are true.

5. Which of the following transactions would result in an increase in the current ratio if the ratio presently is 3:1?

   a. Repaid a 120-day loan
   b. Purchased merchandise on account
   c. Liquidated a long-term liability
   d. Received payment of an account receivable

6. Business enterprises obtain their assets from which of the following sources?

   a. Common and preferred stockholders
   b. Stockholders and bondholders
   c. Trade creditors
   d. All of the above are correct

7. The Waysafe Food Company accounts show the following for the fiscal year ended September 30, 1991:

Gross sales	$1,869,300
Sales returns and allowances	49,300
Net sales	$1,820,000

   Accounts receivable (net):
On 9/30/89	$ 170,000
On 9/30/90	260,000

   The turnover of accounts receivable is:

   a. 10.7 times per year.
   b. 7 times per year.
   c. 8.5 times per year.
   d. 8.7 times per year.

8. Assuming relatively stable business conditions, a decline in the average number of days an account receivable is outstanding from one year to the next might indicate:

   a. a stiffening of the company's credit policies.
   b. that the second year's sales were made at lower prices than the first year's sales.
   c. a longer discount period and a more distant due date were extended to customers in the second year.
   d. a significant decrease in sales in the second year.

9. The R, B, & D Company accounts show the following:

Net sales	$1,200,000	Net accounts receivable (1/1)	$130,000
Net income	60,000	Net accounts receivable (12/31)	240,000

   The average collection period is:

   a. 40 days.
   b. 56 days.
   c. 73 days.
   d. 54 days.

10. Given the following data:

Net sales	$1,600,000	Inventory (1/1/90)	$440,000
Cost of goods sold	1,080,000	Inventory (12/31/90)	540,000

    The inventory turnover is:

    a. 2.20.
    b. 3.27.
    c. 2.00.
    d. 2.45.

11. The following selected data are taken from the Green Manufacturing Company balance sheet dated May 31, 1990:

Accounts payable	$ 222,000
Accrued liabilities	78,000
Bonds payable	1,200,000
Common stock (par $100)	1,800,000
Paid-in capital in excess of par—common	300,000
Retained earnings	900,000
Total liabilities and stockholders' equity	$4,500,000

The owners' equity ratio is:

a.   2.0 to 1.
b.   1.75 to 1.
c.   1.2 to 1.
d.   66-2/3 percent.

12. The Watkins Company had 1,000 shares of $100 par value, 6 percent cumulative preferred stock outstanding during all of 1990. It started 1990 with 100,000 shares of $25 par value common stock outstanding. During 1990, the company issued 44,000 shares on March 31 for cash, and purchased 6,000 shares of treasury stock (common) on October 31. Net income for 1990 was $270,000; no dividends were declared during 1990. Earnings per share of common stock for 1990 are:

a. $2.00.
b. $2.05.
c. $2.36.
d. $2.41.

13. Johnson Company had earnings available to common stockholders of $300,000 in 1990 and $450,000 in 1991. It had 300,000 shares of common stock outstanding as of January 1, 1990 and this remained unchanged until a 50 percent stock dividend was distributed on December 31, 1991. In its 1991 annual report, earnings per share of common stock would be:

a. $1.00 for 1991 and $1.00 for 1990.
b. $1.50 for 1991 and $0.67 for 1990.
c. $1.00 for 1991 and $0.67 for 1990.
d. $1.50 for 1991 and $1.00 for 1990.

14. Given the following data:

Income before interest expense and income taxes	$1,800,000
Interest expense	270,000
Income before income taxes	$1,530,000
Income taxes (40% rate)	612,000
Net income	$ 918,000
Preferred dividends	102,000
Earnings available to common stockholders	$ 816,000

The number of times preferred dividends were earned was:

a.   17.6 times.
b.   8.0 times.
c.   9.0 times.
d.   15.0 times.

15. Given the following data:

Income before interest expense and income taxes..	$1,800,000
Interest expense	270,000
Income before income taxes	$1,530,000
Income taxes (40% rate)	612,000
Net income	$ 918,000
Preferred dividends	102,000
Earnings available to common stockholders	$ 816,000

The number of times interest was earned was:

a. 3.4 times.
b. 6.67 times.
c. 5.67 times.
d. 3.0 times.

16. From the following data, compute the earnings yield on the common stock:

Common stock ($40 par value)	$1,200,000	Net sales	$6,000,000
Cash dividends	600,000	Net income	1,600,000

The stock is currently selling for $64 per share.

a. 50%
b. 3.125%
c. 83.3%
d. 37.5%

17. The Lever Corporation stockholders earned a return of 16 percent on stock which had a market price of $192 per share. What was the price-earnings ratio?

a. 16 to 1
b. 6 to 1
c. 6.25 to 1
d. .17 to 1

18. Given the following data, what was the payout ratio on the common stock, assuming no shares were issued during the year?

Net income before interest		Net sales	$3,000,000
and income taxes...............	$1,200,000	Common stock ($25 par)	2,000,000
Net income......................	800,000	Cash dividends—common	280,000
Preferred stock, 6 percent ($100 par)	800,000	Cash dividends—preferred......	48,000

The market price of the common stock at year-end was $30 per share.

a. 23.3%
b. 35%
c. 24.3%
d. 37.2%

Now compare your answers with the correct ones beginning on page 331.

Solutions/Chapter 11

Completion and Exercises

1. relationships; trends

2. Comparative financial statements are those which present the statements of the same firm for each of two or more accounting periods.

3. Total assets − Total liabilities = Net assets

4. Current assets − Current liabilities

5. Current assets ÷ Current liabilities

6. The purpose of the current ratio is to measure the immediate debt-paying ability and the strength of the working capital position of a company.

7. Current assets are cash or other assets reasonably expected to be realized in cash, or sold or consumed, in the course of normal operations during the normal operating cycle of the business or one year, whichever is longer.

8. Not usually. If the current ratio is greater than one, the payment of a current liability will increase the current ratio. If the current ratio is less than one, the payment of a current liability will reduce the current ratio. Only if the ratio is equal to one will it remain unchanged.

9. None. The borrowing increases Cash (current asset) and Notes Payable (current liability) by the same amount.

10. The "quick assets" consist of cash, net receivables, and marketable securities.

11. Owners; creditors

12. Owners' equity ÷ Total equities (or Total assets)

13.

Increase or Decrease*
1991 over 1990

Dollars		Percentage
$ 6,000	....	13
26,000	....	33
8,000	....	10
10,000*	....	28*
$30,000	....	12

14. Turnovers express the number of times during a period that an asset or group of assets is disposed of or converted into another asset or group of assets. Turnovers measure the efficiency with which the asset or assets are used.

15. The accounts receivable turnover ratio shows the average age of accounts receivable. A high turnover rate means that funds are freed quickly for investment elsewhere. A low turnover rate means that funds are "tied up" in accounts receivable.

16. The inventory turnover ratio indicates the rapidity with which inventories are sold and replenished. The higher the turnover, the smaller the amount of capital needed to produce a given amount of sales.

17. The turnover of total assets shows the relationship between dollar volume of sales and total assets as a measure of the efficiency of the use of capital invested in the assets.

18. market price; earnings

19. dividends; market price

20. Dividends per share ÷ Earnings per share

21.

a. $\dfrac{\$600,000}{\$45,000}$ = 13.3 times

b. 365 ÷ 13.3 = 27.44 (if 360 days were used in the calculation the answer would be 27.07)

c. $\dfrac{\$376,000}{\$49,000}$ = 7.67

d. $\dfrac{\$600,000}{\$430,000}$ = 1.4 or $\dfrac{\$600,000}{\$409,000}$ = 1.47

e. $\dfrac{\$42,000}{\$600,000}$ = 7 percent

f. $\dfrac{\$70,100}{\$600,000} \times \dfrac{\$600,000}{\$430,000}$ = 16.3 percent or $\dfrac{\$70,100}{\$600,000} \times \dfrac{\$600,000}{\$409,000}$ = 17.1 percent

g. $\dfrac{\$42,000}{\$268,000}$ = 15.67 percent or $\dfrac{\$42,000}{\$248,000}$ = 16.9 percent

h. $\dfrac{\$39,000}{9,000}$ = \$4.33*

i. $\dfrac{\$70,100}{8,100}$ = 8.65 times

---

*Dividend on preferred stock must be deducted from earnings after taxes to arrive at the numerator of \$39,000.

Multiple-Choice Questions

1. b. Current assets and current liabilities are both increased equally.

2. c. Prepaid expenses are not included in the numerator for the acid-test ratio.

3. d. Current assets and current liabilities.

4. d. The denominators of the two ratios are the same. The numerator of the current ratio is larger than the numerator of the acid-test ratio unless there are no prepaid expenses or inventory. The current ratio, therefore, can be equal to, but not smaller than, the acid-test ratio.

5. a. For questions of this type, it is advisable to set up the ratio as follows:

   A ratio of 3:1 would be the same as having

   $\dfrac{\text{Current assets}}{\text{Current liabilities}} = \dfrac{\$12}{\$4}$

   If you use \$3 of cash in the numerator to pay a short-term note payable of \$3, the ratio becomes

   $\dfrac{\$12 - \$3}{\$4 - \$3} = \dfrac{\$9}{\$1}$ = 9:1

6. d. All of the items shown on the equities half of the balance sheet can be viewed as sources of assets.

7. c. $\dfrac{\text{Net sales}}{\text{Average accounts receivable}} = \dfrac{\$1,820,000}{\$200,000}$ = 8.5

Name _____

_____

WALLY COMPANY

DECEMBER 31

	1991	1990
(a)		
(b)		
(c)		
(d)		

Name _____

TIME COMPANY

		INCREASED	DECREASED	UNAFFECTED
(a) (1)				
(2)				
(3)				
(4)				
(5)				
(6)				
(7)				
(8)				
(b) (1)				
(2)				
(3)				
(4)				
(5)				
(6)				
(7)				
(8)				

(a)

DAVIS CORPORATION
Comparative Income Statements
For the Years Ended December 31, 1990 and 1991

	1991		1990	
	AMOUNT	PERCENT	AMOUNT	PERCENT
Sales				
Cost of goods sold				
Gross margin				
Selling and admin. exp.				
Net operating income				
Interest expense				
Net income				

Name _____

_____

(b)

DAVIS CORPORATION
Comparative Balance Sheets
December 31, 1990 and 1991

Assets	Dec. 31, 1991		Dec 31, 1990	
	AMOUNT	PERCENT	AMOUNT	PERCENT
Current assets:				
Cash				
Accts. receivable, net				
Merchandise inventory				
Total current assets				
Plant assets, net				
Total assets				
Liabilities and				
Stockholders' Equity				
Current liabilities:				
Accounts payable				
Notes payable				
Total current liabilities				
Notes payable, due in 2001				
Total liabilities				
Stockholders' equity:				
Common stock				
Retained earnings				
Total stockholders' equity				
Total liabilities and stockholders' equity				

DAILEY COMPANY

(a)

(b)

SPECTER CORPORATION

(a)

(b)

(c)

(d)

(a)   LYLE MANUFACTURING COMPANY

(b)

(a)

ANALYSIS OF INVESTMENT ALTERNATIVES

	Co. A	Co. B	Co. C
(1) Using First Advisor's Estimate			
Using Second Advisor's Estimate			
(2) Using First Advisor's Estimate			
Using Second Advisor's Estimate			

(a)

		Co. A	Co. B	Co. C
(3)	Using First Advisor's Estimate			
	Using Second Advisor's Estimate			

(b)

(c)

12

Accounting Theory and International Accounting

Understanding the Learning Objectives

1. Identify and discuss the basic assumptions, principles, and modifying conventions of accounting.

    *   The major underlying assumptions of accounting are (1) entity, (2) going concern (continuity), (3) money measurement, and (4) periodicity.

    *   Other basic accounting concepts that affect the accounting for entities are (1) general-purpose financial statements, (2) substance over form, (3) consistency, (4) double-entry, and (5) articulation.

    *   The major principles include exchange-price (or cost), matching, revenue recognition, expense and loss recognition, and full disclosure. Major exceptions to the realization principle include cash collection as point of revenue recognition, installment basis of revenue recognition, the percentage-of-completion method of recognizing revenue on long-term construction projects, and revenue recognition at completion of production.

    *   Modifying conventions include cost-benefit, materiality, and conservatism.

2. Describe the Conceptual Framework Project of the Financial Accounting Standards Board.

    *   The FASB has defined the objectives of financial reporting, qualitative characteristics of accounting information, and elements of financial statements.

    *   Financial reporting objectives are the broad overriding goals sought by accountants engaged in financial reporting.

    *   Qualitative characteristics are those characteristics that accounting information should possess to be useful in decision making. The two primary qualitative characteristics are relevance and reliability. Another qualitative characteristic is comparability.

    *   Pervasive constraints include cost-benefit analysis and materiality.

    *   The basic elements of financial statements have been identified and defined by the FASB.

    *   The FASB has also described revenue recognition criteria and provided guidance as to the timing and nature of information to be included in financial statements.

3. Discuss the differences of international accounting among nations. (Appendix).

    *   Accounting principles differ among nations because they were developed independently.

    *   There have been attempts at harmonizing accounting principles throughout the world.

    *   Various differences in accounting principles that exist between nations are described.

4. Define and use correctly the new terms in the glossary.

    The new terms introduced in the chapter are as follows:

    Accounting theory—"A set of basic concepts and assumptions and related principles that explain and guide the accountant's actions in identifying, measuring, and communicating economic information."

Comparability—A qualitative characteristic of accounting information; when information is comparable, it reveals differences and similarities that are real and are not the result of differing accounting treatments.

Completed-contract method—A method of recognizing revenue on long-term projects in which no revenue is recognized until the period in which the project is completed; similar to recognizing revenue upon the completion of a sale.

Completeness—A qualitative characteristic of accounting information; requires disclosure of all significant information in a way that aids understanding and does not mislead; sometimes called the full-disclosure principle.

Conservatism—Being cautious or prudent and making sure that any errors in estimates tend to understate rather than overstate net assets and net income.

Consistency—Requires a company to use the same accounting principles and reporting practices through time.

Cost-benefit consideration—Determining whether benefits exceed costs.

Cost principle—See Exchange-price principle.

Current/historical-rates approach—Regards the parent company and its foreign subsidiaries as a single business undertaking.

Current-noncurrent method—Translates current assets and current liabilities at the current rate and noncurrent items at the historical rate.

Current rate—Exchange rate in effect on the balance sheet date.

Current rate approach—The current or closing rate method translates all assets and liabilities at the exchange rate in effect on the balance sheet date.

Earning principle—The requirement that revenue be substantially earned before it is recognized (recorded).

Entity—The specific unit, such as a business, for which accounting information is gathered. Entities have a separate existence from owners, creditors, employees, customers, other interest parties, and other businesses.

Exchange gain or loss (Time of transaction method)—The difference between the amount recorded in Accounts Payable on the purchase date and decrease in Cash on the settlement date.

Exchange-price (or cost) principle—Transfers of resources are recorded at prices agreed on by the parties to the exchange at the time of the exchange.

Feedback value—A qualitative characteristic that information has when it reveals the relative success of users in predicting outcomes.

Financial reporting objectives—The broad overriding goals sought by accountants engaging in financial reporting.

Going-concern (continuity) assumption—The assumption that an entity will continue to operate indefinitely unless there is strong evidence that the entity will terminate.

Historical cost—The amount paid, or the fair value of a liability incurred or other resource surrendered, to acquire an asset.

Historical rate—The rate in effect when items were originally recorded.

Installment basis—A revenue recognition procedure in which the percentage of total gross margin recognized in a period on an installment sale is equal to the percentage of total cash from the sale that is received in that period.

Liquidation—Terminating a business by ceasing business operations and selling off the assets.

Losses—Asset expirations that are usually involuntary and do not create revenues.

Matching principle—The principle that net income of a period is determined by associating or relating revenues earned in a period with expenses incurred to generate the revenues.

Materiality—A modifying convention that allows the accountant to deal with immaterial (unimportant) items in a theoretically incorrect, expedient manner; also a qualitative characteristic specifying that financial accounting report only information significant enough to influence decisions or evaluations.

Modifying conventions—Customs emerging from accounting practice that alter the results that would be obtained from a strict application of accounting principles; conservatism is an example.

Monetary-nonmonetary method—The current rate is used for monetary assets and liabilities, while historical rate is applied to nonmonetary items.

Money measurement—Use of a monetary unit of measurement, such as the dollar, instead of physical or other units of measurement—feet, inches, grams, and so on.

Neutrality—A qualitative characteristic that requires accounting information to be free of measurement method bias.

Percentage-of-completion method—A method of recognizing revenue based on the estimated stage of completion of a long-term project. The stage of completion is measured by comparing actual costs incurred in a period with total estimated costs to be incurred in all periods.

Period costs—Costs that cannot be traced to specific revenue and are expensed in the period in which incurred.

Periodicity (time periods)—An assumption of the accountant that an entity's life can be subdivided into time periods for purposes of reporting its economic activities.

Predictive value—A qualitative characteristic that information has when it improves users' abilities to predict outcomes of events.

Product costs—Costs incurred in the acquisition or manufacture of goods. Product costs are accounted for as if they were attached to the goods, with the result that they are charged to expense when the goods are sold.

Production basis—A method of revenue recognition used in limited circumstances that recognizes revenue at the time of completion of production or extraction.

Qualitative characteristics—Characteristics that accounting information should possess to be useful in decision making.

Realization principle—A principle directing that revenue is recognized only after the seller acquires the right to receive payment from the buyer.

Relevance—A qualitative characteristic requiring that information be pertinent to or bear upon a decision.

Reliability—A qualitative characteristic requiring that information faithfully depict for users what it purports to represent.

Representational faithfulness—A qualitative characteristic requiring that accounting statements on economic activity correspond to the actual underlying activity.

Revenue recognition principle—The principle that revenue should be earned and realized before it is recognized (recorded).

Stable dollar—An assumption that the dollar is a reasonably stable unit of measurement.

Timeliness—A qualitative characteristic requiring that accounting information be provided at a time when it may be considered in reaching a decision.

Verifiability—A qualitative characteristic of accounting information; information is verifiable when it can be substantially duplicated by independent measurers using the same measurement methods.

Completion and Exercises

1. Give three advantages of recognizing revenue at the time of sale.

   a. _____
   _____

   b. _____
   _____

   c. _____
   _____

2. A disadvantage of recognizing revenue at the time of sale is _____
   _____
   _____

3. Give two arguments in support of use of the production basis for recognizing revenue.

   a. _____
   _____

   b. _____
   _____

4. In financial accounting, substance is to be emphasized over form. This means that _____
   _____
   _____

5. An item is to be considered material if _____
   _____

6. The basic ideas that made the accounting practices followed by different accountants fairly similar are

   called _____ _____ _____ _____ .

7. An underlying assumption of accounting that has not been true in recent years is the assumption that the

   _____ _____ _____ _____ unit of measure.

8. Accounting measurements are characterized by approximation and judgment from application of the

   _____ basis of accounting which is required if the activities of an enterprise are to be

   reflected in _____ _____ _____ .

9. The primary data entered in the accounting system are _____ _____ .

10. In general, in accounting, net income is determined through a process of _____

    revenues and expenses by _____ _____ .

11. In general, revenue must be _____ and _____ before it is recorded in the accounts. Revenue is considered realized at the _____ _____ _____ for merchandise transactions and when _____ _____ for service transactions.

12. In specified, limited circumstances, it is considered acceptable to recognize revenue—

    a. _____ c. _____

    b. _____

13. In accounting for expenses, a line of distinction is usually drawn between _____ costs and _____ costs. The former are expensed when the _____ _____ _____, the latter are expensed in the _____ _____ _____ _____.

14. For measurement purposes, assets are classified as _____ or _____. Cash and accounts receivable are examples of _____ assets, and these assets are measured at their _____ _____ _____. Plant and equipment are examples of _____ assets, and these assets are measured at their _____ _____. Liabilities are generally measured at the amount of _____ _____ _____ _____ or the value of the _____ _____ _____ _____ for their satisfaction. Changes in net assets are of great concern to the accountant because they may lead to the recognition of _____ _____ _____ _____ _____.

15. The existence of inflation shows that the accounting assumption of a _____ _____ _____ _____ is not true. Inflation can be defined as a period of _____ prices or of _____ purchasing power of the dollar.

16. Neutrality essentially means that accounting information should not be _____.

17. Financial reporting is, according to the FASB, intended primarily for informed _____ and _____ to aid them in making _____ and _____ _____. It also seeks to help these parties assess the prospects of receiving _____ from their investments or loans to an enterprise. Because they affect cash inflows and outflows, financial statements should provide information about the _____ _____ , _____ _____ , and _____ of an enterprise.

18. Relevance and verifiability are examples of _____ _____ which accounting information should possess to be useful.

19. (Based on the appendix) Accounting must reflect the national _____ and _____ environment in which it is practiced.

20. (Based on the appendix) Other accounting differences among nations stem from the legal or _____ system.

21. (Based on the appendix) Commonwealth nations tend to adopt _____ accounting standards.

22. (Based on the appendix) Several organizations are working to achieve greater understanding and _____ of accounting principles.

23. (Based on the appendix) Ultimately, the success of international pronouncements depends on the willingness of the nations to _____ them.

24. (Based on the appendix) _____ _____ translation is probably the most common problem in an international business environment.

Multiple-Choice Questions

For each of the following questions, indicate the single best answer by circling the appropriate letter.

1. The practice of overstating expenses in the current period to avoid handicapping future periods is:

   a. acceptable because it is conservative.
   b. acceptable if done consistently.
   c. acceptable if fully disclosed.
   d. acceptable only if the amounts are immaterial.

2. Materiality is:

   a. unimportant in determining whether or not there is adequate disclosure.
   b. measured strictly by the dollar amounts of the individual items—for example, a $100,000 amount is always material.
   c. measured by whether or not the manner in which the item is treated might influence decisions or evaluations.
   d. always an aggregate consideration.

3. If the accountant were to attempt to arrive at an absolutely correct figure for period net income, which of the following would be most useful?

   a. Comparability
   b. Matching
   c. Materiality
   d. Disclosure

4. Revenue may, under proper circumstances, be recognized at all of the following moments in time except:

   a. after the earning process has been completed and an exchange has taken place.
   b. upon the receipt of cash from the customer.
   c. when manufactured goods are acquired for resale.
   d. upon the completion of the production process but before a sale has taken place.

5. Advertising costs incurred are typically treated as expenses of the period in which incurred under the expense recognition principle of:

   a. associating cause and effect.
   b. systematic and rational allocation.
   c. immediate recognition of a period cost.
   d. matching.

6. Which of the following is considered a major principle of accounting?

   a. Entity
   b. Matching
   c. Going concern (continuity)
   d. Periodicity (time periods)

7. Which of the following statements is *true*?

   a. The incurring of expense generally means that an exchange has taken place in which another asset has been received for merchandise delivered or services rendered.
   b. Accounting is often said to deal with costs, expired costs, and lost costs, and these costs, rather than service potentials, expire over time.
   c. Revenue is earned throughout the entire range of activities of an enterprise and usually is recorded prior to sale.
   d. A loss is an involuntary expiration of an asset without any expectation of receiving benefits from the expiration.

8. Which of the following statements is *true*?

   a. The economic substance of a transaction cannot conflict with its legal form.
   b. Consistency requires that all companies use the same accounting principles and reporting practices to record similar transactions.
   c. Financial statements are fundamentally related and articulate with each other.
   d. The cash basis is superior to the accrual basis for financial reporting purposes.

9. Company Z uses the installment basis of accounting. On September 1, 1990, it sold a refrigerator for $400. Cost of the refrigerator was $240. Payments from the customer were to be received over a ten-month period beginning September 30. The amount of gross margin realized in *1991* is:

   a. $ 96.
   b. $ 64.
   c. $160.
   d. $ 80.

10. Company R uses the percentage-of-completion method. The company agreed to build a bridge at a price of $20 million. Estimated costs to construct the bridge are $16 million. Costs incurred in the first year of construction (1990) were $4 million. The amount of *gross margin* to recognize in 1990 is:

   a. -0-.
   b. $1 million.
   c. $5 million.
   d. $3 million.

11. In the conceptual framework, how many financial reporting objectives were identified by the FASB?

   a. One
   b. Two
   c. Three
   d. Four

12. The two primary qualitative characteristics are:

   a. predictive value and feedback value.
   b. timeliness and verifiability.
   c. comparability and neutrality.
   d. relevance and reliability.

13. A pervasive constraint of accounting information is that:

 a. benefits must exceed costs.
 b. the information must be timely.
 c. the information must be neutral.
 d. the information must be verifiable.

14. To be reliable, information must (identify the incorrect quality):

 a. be verifiable.
 b. be timely.
 c. have representational faithfulness.
 d. be neutral.

15. The *basic elements* of financial statements consist of:

 a. terms and their definitions.
 b. the objectives of financial reporting.
 c. the qualitative characteristics.
 d. the new income statement format.

16. (Based on the appendix) Methods that are used to account for transactions between companies in different nations when goods are received on one date and the invoice is paid on another date include:

 a. Time-of-transaction method.
 b. Time-of-settlement method.
 c. Current-rate method.
 d. (a) and (b) are correct.

17. (Based on the appendix) Which of the following statements is *false* regarding translating financial statements of foreign subsidiaries?

 a. Under the *current-rate approach*, all assets and liabilities are translated at the exchange rate in effect on the balance sheet date.
 b. Under the *current-noncurrent method*, current assets and current liabilities are translated at the current rate, and noncurrent items are translated at their historical rates.
 c. Under the *monetary-nonmonetary method*, monetary assets and liabilities are translated at their historical rate, while nonmonetary items are translated at their historical rates.
 d. The nations of the world now have settled on the current-rate method.

18. (Based on the appendix) Variations between nations in accounting for inventories include all *except* which of the following?

 a. The basis for determining cost
 b. Whether "cost" should be increased or decreased to reflect changes in market value
 c. Whether direct or absorption costing should be used
 d. Whether standard costs should be used

19. (Based on the appendix) In accounting for the effects of inflation, the approach that seems to be favored by most nations that have adopted an approach is:

 a. current-cost.
 b. constant dollar (general price-level) adjusted statements.
 c. a combination of (a) and (b) in one set of financial statements.
 d. both (a) and (b) as two sets of financial statements.

 Now compare your answers with the correct ones beginning on page 361.

Solutions/Chapter 12

Completion and Exercises

1. The following are advantages of recognizing revenue at the time of sale. Any three of the following could be given.

    a. Delivery of goods is an observable event.
    b. Revenue is measurable.
    c. Risk of loss due to price decline or destruction of goods has passed to the buyer.
    d. Revenue has been earned or substantially so.
    e. Expenses and net income can be determined because the revenue has been earned.

2. revenue might not be recorded in the period in which most of the activity creating it occurred.

3. Arguments for the production basis could include any two of the following:

    a. homogeneous nature of the products.
    b. products can usually be sold at their market prices.
    c. difficulties are sometimes encountered in determining unit production costs.

4. where economic substance and legal form conflict, economic substance is to be entered in the accounting system and reported.

5. knowledge of it would make a difference in the decision of an informed investor or creditor.

6. generally accepted accounting principles

7. dollar is a stable

8. accrual; periodic financial statements

9. exchange prices (cost)

10. matching; time periods

11. earned; realized; time of sale; services are rendered

12. (a) at completion of production; (b) when cash is received (installment method); (c) as production progresses

13. product; period; product is sold; period in which incurred

14. monetary; nonmonetary; monetary; expected cash inflow; nonmonetary; acquisition cost; cash to be paid; services to be performed; net income or net loss

15. stable unit of measure; rising; declining

16. biased

17. investors; creditors; investment; credit decisions; cash; economic resources; economic obligations; earnings.

18. qualitative characteristics

19. economic; social

20. political

21. British

22. harmonization

23. support

24. Foreign currency

1. d. If the amounts are immaterial, no real damage can be done. If the amounts are material, it is simply incorrect accounting.

2. c. An amount is material only if it would make a difference to an informed reader in his or her evaluations and decisions.

3. b. Presumably, the accountant would try to perfectly match revenues and expenses. If attained, this would provide comparability. Disclosure would become less meaningful because of the absolute consistency followed in the matching process. And materiality would not be involved, since all items would be handled in the theoretically correct manner.

4. c. No accounting principle permits revenue recognition at this point.

5. c. Such costs are typically treated as period costs because of the difficulties encountered in measuring the amounts to be deferred or the benefits to be received in future periods.

6. b. The others are all considered underlying assumptions or concepts.

7. d. A loss is involuntary with no expectation of receiving benefits.

8. c. The financial statements do articulate with each other. The net income for a period is carried to the statement of owner's equity. The final owner's equity balance is carried to the balance sheet.

9. a. Total gross margin is $400 - $240 = $160. Four payments would be received in 1990 and six in 1991. 40×6 payments $\times 40$ percent gross margin $= $96.

10. b. Total gross margin is $4 million. Since one-fourth of the estimated costs have been incurred, one-fourth of the total estimated gross margin should be recognized.

11. c.

12. d. Relevance and reliability were identified as the primary decision-specific qualities.

13. a. The benefits of accounting information must exceed the costs of obtaining the information.

14. b. Timeliness is an ingredient of relevance, not of reliability.

15. a. Various terms and their definitions are described as the basic elements of financial statements.

16. d. Both the time-of-transaction and time-of-settlement methods have been used.

17. d. The nations of the world have been unable to agree on one common method.

18. d. No mention was made about disagreements regarding the use of standard costing.

19. a. The current trend appears to be toward current-cost accounting and away from general price-level accounting.

Accounting for Manufacturing Companies

Understanding the Learning Objectives

1. Describe the three basic components of manufacturing costs incurred in the production of a product.

    *   The three basic components of manufacturing costs incurred to produce a product are:

        —*Direct Materials* that have three characteristics: (1) they are included in the finished product, (2) they are used only in the manufacture of the product, and (3) they are clearly and easily traceable to the product.

        —*Direct Labor* that include labor costs of all employees actually working on materials to convert them into finished goods.

        —*Manufacturing Overhead* that is a "catchall" classification since it includes all manufacturing costs except for those costs accounted for as direct materials and direct labor.

2. Describe the difference between product costs and period costs and the importance of proper classification.

    *   The difference between product costs and period costs is as follows:

        —*Product Costs* are costs incurred to manufacture a product which are assignable to units of a product produced.

        —*Period Costs* are related more closely to time periods rather than products produced and are not assignable to units of a product produced.

    *   The proper classification of costs as product costs or period costs is important for income determination purposes.

3. Describe the flow of costs of a manufacturing company under periodic inventory procedure and prepare journal entries.

    *   The flow of costs through the inventory accounts begins when the company incurs costs for materials, direct labor, and factory overhead. The material costs flow first into the Materials Inventory account. All the manufacturing costs such as materials, direct labor, and factory overhead are recorded in the Work in Process Inventory account as they are placed into the production process. As the products are completed, their costs are transferred from the Work in Process Inventory account to the Finished Goods Inventory account. The costs remain in the Finished Goods Inventory account until the products are sold, then the costs are transferred to the Cost of Goods Sold account.

4. Describe the difference in financial reporting by a merchandiser and a manufacturer and prepare a statement of cost of goods manufactured, an income statement, and a balance sheet for a manufacturer.

    *   The major difference between a merchandiser and a manufacturer is in the types of inventories carried. Because inventories are reported on the balance sheet and also affect income (through cost of goods sold) on the income statement, the balance sheet and income statement of a merchandiser will differ from the balance sheet and income statement of a manufacturer.

5. Describe the general pattern of the flow of costs of a manufacturing company under perpetual inventory procedure and prepare journal entries.

   * The flow of costs under perpetual inventory procedure is the same as under periodic inventory procedure. The difference in perpetual inventory procedure is in the preparation of journal entries. For example, under periodic inventory procedure, materials purchased would be recorded in a Materials Purchases account. However, under perpetual inventory procedure, the materials would be recorded as Materials Inventory.

6. Define and use correctly the new terms in the glossary.

   The new terms introduced in the chapter are as follows:

   Administrative costs—Nonmanufacturing costs that include the costs of top administrative functions and various staff departments such as accounting, data processing, and personnel.

   Conversion cost—The sum of direct labor and manufacturing overhead costs.

   Cost—A financial measure of the resources used or given up to achieve a stated purpose.

   Cost of goods manufactured—Consists of the costs of all goods completed during the period; total manufacturing cost plus beginning work in process inventory minus ending work in process inventory.

   Cost to manufacture—Includes the costs of all resources put into production during the period.

   Direct labor—Labor costs of all employees actually working on materials to convert them into finished goods.

   Direct materials—Materials that are (1) included in the finished product, (2) used only in the manufacture of the product, and (3) clearly and easily traceable to the product.

   Factory cost—See Manufacturing cost.

   Finished goods—Completed manufactured products ready to be sold; also, Finished Goods Inventory is the title of an inventory account maintained for such products.

   Fixed costs—Costs that remain constant in total amount over wide variations in the level of manufacturing activity.

   Indirect labor—The services of factory employees that cannot or will not, for practical reasons, be traced to the products being manufactured.

   Indirect materials—Materials used in the manufacture of a product that cannot or will not, for practical reasons, be traced directly to the products being manufactured.

   Manufacturing cost—The cost incurred to produce or create a product. It includes direct materials, direct labor, and manufacturing overhead costs.

   Manufacturing overhead—All manufacturing costs except for those costs accounted for as direct materials and direct labor.

   Manufacturing overhead rate—Expresses manufacturing overhead costs in relation to some measure of manufacturing activity.

   Materials—Unprocessed items that will be used in the manufacturing process.

   Period costs—Costs related more closely to periods of time than to products produced. Period costs cannot be traced directly to the manufacture of a specific product; they are expensed in the period in which they are incurred.

   Prime cost—The sum of the direct materials costs and direct labor costs incurred to manufacture a product.

   Product costs—(See also Manufacturing cost.) Costs incurred in the manufacture of products and assigned to units of the product produced by the manufacturing company. These costs include costs of direct materials, direct labor, and manufacturing overhead.

Selling costs—Costs incurred to obtain customer orders and get the finished product into the customer's possession.

Statement of cost of goods manufactured—An accounting report showing the cost to manufacture and the cost of goods manufactured.

Variable costs—Costs that directly vary in total amount with changes in the volume of production activity or output.

Work in process—Partially manufactured products; also, Work in Process Inventory is the title of an inventory account maintained for such products.

Completion and Exercises

1. When classified according to their behavior as volume changes, costs are either _____ or _____ . _____ _____ are those costs that change in total amount directly with changes in output. _____ _____ decrease per unit as volume expands.

2. A manufacturing firm's costs can be classified broadly as _____ , _____ , and _____ . Its costs to manufacture a product are classifed as _____ _____ , _____ _____ , and _____ _____ .

3. Classify each of the following costs of a mobile home manufacturer using these symbols: DM = Direct Material, DL = Direct Labor, MO = Manufacturing Overhead, and O = Other.

   _DM_ a. Sheet aluminum.
   _MO_ b. Wages of drill press operators.
   _MO_ c. Oil for factory machines.
   _O_ d. Salary of company president.
   _MO_ e. Factory supervisor's salary.
   _O_ f. Sales salaries.
   _MO_ g. Factory building insurance.

   _DL_ h. Wages of assemblers.
   _MO_ i. Salaries of inspectors.
   _DM_ j. Lumber.
   _MO_ k. Cost accountant's salary.
   _O_ l. Executive office rent.
   _MO_ m. Nails and staples.
   _MO_ n. Purchasing agent's salary.

4. Identify by letters the costs in Question 3 that would be classified as product costs _____ _a, b, c, h, i, j, k_ , as period costs _d, e, f, g, l,_ _m, n._ . Why? _____
   _____
   _____
   _____
   _____
   _____
   _____
   _____

5. The sum of direct materials costs and direct labor costs is referred to as _____ cost.

   The sum of direct labor costs and manufacturing overhead costs is called _____ cost.

6. Selling costs are usually classifed as _____ _____ and _____ _____

   costs. Selling and administrative costs are often called _____ costs and are

   _____ as incurred.

7. Give the entries required to record the purchase of $20,000 of raw materials on account and the issuance of $12,000 of these materials as direct materials and $2,000 as indirect materials and supplies.

8. Give the entry to record the preparation of the factory payroll for a given week of $25,000, less withheld amounts for federal income taxes of $1,500, social security taxes of $1,000, and union dues of $100. Then give the entry to record the distribution of the payroll costs if 90 percent of them are direct labor costs and the balance consists of indirect labor.

9. The entry to record $25,000 depreciation on factory equipment and the expiration of $7,000 of prepaid factory rent would read:

10. The entry to assign manufacturing overhead to production includes a debit to _____ _____ _____ _____ and a credit to _____ _____ .

11. Give the entries required to record the completion of goods costing $100,000 and the sale of one half of these goods at a price equal to 120 percent of cost.

12. At the end of the accounting year, the Cost of Goods Sold account would be _____ to the _____ _____ _____ .

13. What is included in "Cost to manufacture" in a statement of cost of goods manufactured and sold? Show the relationship between "Cost to manufacture" and "Cost of goods sold."

_____

_____

_____

_____

_____

_____

14. Give three reasons why the actual overhead costs incurred in a period are not the overhead costs assigned to the goods produced in that period.

    a. _____
    _____
    _____

    b. _____
    _____
    _____

    c. _____
    _____
    _____

15. Generally speaking, manufacturing overhead is applied to production by means of a _____
    _____ _____ which is computed under the general formula of dividing
    _____ _____ _____ by some measure of the
    _____ _____ _____ .

16. Give the entry to assign overhead to production for a given period assuming the overhead rate is 150 percent of direct labor cost and that $30,000 of direct labor cost was incurred in that period.

17. Give two reasons why overhead is usually assigned to production through use of a predetermined rate.

    a. _____
    _____
    _____

    b. _____
    _____
    _____

18. Common bases or levels of activity upon which overhead rates are often based include _____
    _____ _____ _____ _____ , _____
    _____-_____ , and _____-_____ .

19. Manufacturing overhead is _____ when the amount of overhead applied to production exceeds the amount of overhead incurred in a period. When the reverse is true, overhead is
    _____ .

20. Assume that budgeted total overhead is $200,000 and that budgeted direct labor-hours are 25,000 for the coming period. Actual overhead was $202,000 and actual direct labor-hours were 26,000. Overhead for the period is _____ by $_____ , and the most probable cause of this is _____

_____

_____

Multiple-Choice Questions

For each of the following questions, indicate the single best answer by circling the appropriate letter.

1. Which of the following would be classified as manufacturing overhead? (1) marketing research; (2) depreciation on president's office facilities; (3) advertising; (4) factory taxes; (5) indirect material; (6) machinery maintenance.

    a. 1, 3, 4 are manufacturing overhead costs.
    b. 4, 5, 6 are manufacturing overhead costs.
    c. 4, 6 are manufacturing overhead costs.
    d. 1, 2, 3, 4, 5, 6, are manufacturing overhead costs.
    e. None of the above.

2. In reference to the six items listed in question 1 above, which of these would be classified as administrative expenses?

    a. None, they are all manufacturing overhead costs.
    b. 2, 4 are administrative costs.
    c. 1, 2, 3 are administrative costs.
    d. 2 is the only administrative cost.
    e. 4, 5, 6 are administrative costs.

3. In reference to the six items listed in question 1, which of these would be classified as selling expenses?

    a. 1, 3 are selling costs.
    b. 1, 2, 3 are selling costs.
    c. 3, 5 are selling costs.
    d. 3, 6 are selling costs.
    e. 1, 2, 3, 4, 5, 6 are selling costs.

4. Which of the following probably would be accounted for as indirect materials in the manufacture of furniture?

    a. Lumber for frames
    b. Foam rubber padding
    c. Nylon thread
    d. Nylon upholstery fabric

5. A company employing a perpetual inventory system sells for $120,000 cash finished goods costing $76,000. The entry is:

    a. Dr. Cost of Goods Sold, 76,000
       Cr. Finished Goods Inventory, 76,000
    b. Dr. Cash, 120,000
       Cr. Sales, 120,000
    c. Dr. Cost of Goods Sold, 76,000
       Cr. Work in Process Inventory, 76,000
    d. Both a and c are necessary.
    e. Both a and b are necessary.

6. Which of the four elements listed below would *not* be considered a product cost?

    a. Repairs and maintenance on factory equipment
    b. Salary of the president of the company
    c. Salary of toolroom personnel
    d. Salary of factory supervisors

7. If factory rent is $3,000 and Miscellaneous Factory Expense is $700 incurred on account, the required entry is:

    a. Dr. Factory Rent Expense, 3,000
        Dr. Miscellaneous Factory Expense, 700
        Cr. Vouchers Payable, 3,700
    b. Dr. Factory Rent Expense, 3,000
        Dr. Miscellaneous Factory Expense, 700
        Cr. Accounts Payable, 3,700
    c. both a and b are correct
    d. Dr. Manufacturing Overhead, 3,700
        Cr. Accounts Payable, 3,700
    e. Dr. Work in Process Inventory, 3,700
        Cr. Accounts Payable, 3,700

8. Assume that goods are finished during the month. Under a perpetual inventory system, the entry is:

    a. Dr. Work in Process Inventory
        Cr. Finished Goods Inventory
    b. Dr. Work in Process Inventory
        Cr. Factory Overhead Costs
    c. Dr. Finished Goods Inventory
        Cr. Work in Process Inventory
    d. Dr. Cost of Goods Sold
        Cr. Finished Goods Inventory

Use the following information for the next three questions.

Assume a company has the following accounts in its trial balance at year-end:

Materials inventory, January 1	$228,050
Materials purchases	524,000
Direct labor	900,000
Work in Process, January 1	480,000
Selling expense	144,000
Materials inventory, December 31	240,000
Manufacturing Overhead	600,000
Work in Process, December 31	250,000
Transportation-In	14,500

9. The cost of the materials available for use was:

    a. $230,000.
    b. $766,550.
    c. $228,050.
    d. $752,050.
    e. none of the above.

10. Total cost to manufacture was:

    a. $ 526,540.
    b. $1,426,550.
    c. $2,026,550.
    d. $2,516,550.

11. Cost of goods manufactured was:

    a. $2,026,550.
    b. $2,256,550.
    c. $1,786,550.
    d. $1,426,550.
    e. $1,570,550.

12. A company uses the relation between manufacturing overhead and direct labor costs to apply overhead to its work in process and finished goods inventories. If direct materials of $320,000, direct labor of $200,000, and factory overhead costs applied of $400,000 were incurred during a period, what is the company's overhead rate?

    a. 100%
    b.   80%
    c. 200%
    d. 130%
    e. None of the above

Use the following information for the next two questions.

    Russell, Inc. estimates that its manufacturing overhead costs for 1990 will be $178,500. The following levels of activity are also estimated:

    Production .... 357,000 units
    Direct labor hours 120,000
    Direct labor costs $1,500,000
    Machine hours 100,000

13. What is the predetermined manufacturing overhead rate based on machine hours?

    a. $1.4875
    b. $0.50
    c. $0.119
    d. $1.785
    e. None of the above

14. If the predetermined overhead rate is based on direct labor hours and the total direct labor hours for February are 9,500, what is the applied overhead for Russell in February?

    a. $14,131.25
    b. $ 4,750.00
    c. $ 1,130.50
    d. $16,957.50
    e. Cannot be determined

15. The following data pertain to the Baldwin Company:

Direct materials used (100,000 units)	$800,000
Direct labor (70,000 hours).................	$700,000
Manufacturing overhead	$700,000
Ending inventory	$700,000
Work in process	6,000 units
Finished goods	4,000 units

Baldwin manufactures only one product. Each finished product contains two units of direct materials (added at the beginning of production), and requires one-half hour of direct labor. It is estimated that the units still in production each contain one-quarter hour of direct labor. What is the cost of the ending work in process inventory if overhead is assigned on the basis of direct labor cost?

a. $ 84,000
b. $156,000
c. $126,000
d. $140,000

Now compare your answers with the correct ones beginning on page 379.

Solutions/Chapter 13

Completion and Exercises

1. fixed; variable; Variable costs; Fixed costs

2. manufacturing; selling; administrative; direct materials; direct labor; manufacturing overhead

3. (a) DM; (b) DL; (c) MO; (d) O; (e) MO; (f) O; (g) MO; (h) DL; (i) MO; (j) DM; (k) MO; (l) O; (m) MO (or possibly DM); (n) MO

4. product costs: a, b, c, e, g, h, i, j, k, m, n
   period costs: d, f, l
   Product costs are incurred to help create the product; period costs are incurred either to dispose of the product or to facilitate the general administration of the entire firm's operations.

5. prime; conversion

6. order getting, order filling; period; expensed

7.
Materials Inventory	20,000	
Accounts Payable		20,000
Work in Process	12,000	
Manufacturing Overhead	2,000	
Materials Inventory		14,000

8.
Payroll Summary	25,000	
Federal Income Taxes Withheld		1,500
Social Security Taxes Payable		1,000
Union Dues Withheld		100
Payroll Payable		22,400
Work in Process Inventory	22,500	
Manufacturing Overhead	2,500	
Payroll Summary		25,000

9.
Manufacturing Overhead	32,000	
Accumulated Depreciation—Equipment		25,000
Prepaid Rent		7,000

10. Work in Process Inventory; Manufacturing Overhead

11.
Finished Goods Inventory	100,000	
Work in Process Inventory		100,000
Accounts Receivable	120,000	
Sales		120,000
Cost of Goods Sold	50,000	
Finished Goods Inventory		50,000

12. closed; Income Summary account

13. Cost to manufacture includes the cost of direct materials, direct labor, and manufacturing overhead incurred in a period. Cost to manufacture + Beginning work in process inventory − Ending work in process inventory = Cost of goods manufactured; Cost of goods manufactured + Beginning finished goods inventory − Ending finished goods inventory = Cost of goods sold.

14. (a) Per unit costs may vary sharply from month to month when actual fixed overhead costs are spread over varying amounts of monthly production; (b) Overhead costs may not be uniformly incurred on a monthly basis and if production volume is stable this leads to fluctuating unit costs; (c) Actual cost data can be computed only at month end and this may be too late to be useful.

15. predetermined overhead rate; total budgeted overhead; level of activity

16. Work in Process Inventory.. 45,000
    Manufacturing Overhead... 45,000

17. (a) In order to calculate a cost for the units of product completed as production proceeds rather than waiting until the end of the period; (b) To assign more uniform amounts to production than would be assigned if an attempt was made to assign actual costs and these actual costs varied substantially through time, such as seasonally incurred heating and air-conditioning costs.

18. dollars of direct labor cost; direct labor-hours; machine-hours

19. overabsorbed; underabsorbed

20. overabsorbed; $2,000; fixed overhead is overabsorbed because the firm operated at a higher level of activity than the 25,000 hours used in setting the overhead rate

Multiple-Choice Questions

1. b. 4, 5, and 6 all relate to manufacturing activities.

2. d. 2 is the only administrative expense.

3. a. 1 and 3 both relate to selling activities.

4. c. Nylon thread may be so small a cost element that it is not worthwhile to trace it directly to production. The others are all direct materials.

5. e. An entry is needed to remove the cost from finished goods inventory and also an entry is required to record the increase in cash and revenue increase.

6. b. The salary of the president of the company is not related to production and is therefore a period cost. The other choices are elements of manufacturing overhead, which is a product cost.

7. d. Actual manufacturing overhead is debited to Manufacturing Overhead.

8. c. Finished goods leave Work in Process Inventory, the inventory account containing the cost of goods being worked on, when they are completed and their cost is carried in the Finished Goods Inventory account.

9. b. $228,050 + $524,000 + $14,500 = $766,550

10. c. $ 526,550
        900,000
        600,000
    $2,026,550

11. b. $2,026,550
          480,000
      $2,506,550
       − 250,000
      $2,256,550

12. c. $\dfrac{\$400,000 \text{ factory overhead applied}}{\$200,000 \text{ direct labor}} = 200\%$

13. d. $\dfrac{\$178,500}{100,000} = \$1.785$

14.   a.   ($178,500 ÷ 120,000) × 9,500 = $14,131.25

15.   c.

$$\underset{\$16.00}{\underset{\text{Materials}}{\text{Direct}}} + \underset{\$2.50^1}{\underset{\text{Labor}}{\text{Direct}}} + \underset{\$2.50^2}{\underset{\text{Overhead}}{\underset{\text{Manufacturing}}{}}} = \underset{\$21.00}{\underset{}{\text{Total}}} \times \underset{6,000}{\underset{\text{Units}}{\text{No.}}} = \underset{\$126,000}{\underset{\text{Inventory Cost}}{\text{Total}}}$$

^{1}Direct Labor $= \dfrac{\$700,000}{70,000 \text{ hrs.}} \times 1/4 = \$2.50$

^{2}Manufacturing overhead $=$ 100 percent of direct labor cost.

Name _____

_____

(a)

1.   8.

2.   9.

3.   10.

4.   11.

5.   12.

6.   13.

7.

(b)

(a)

CLAXTON COMPANY
Statement of Cost of Goods Manufactured and Sold
For the Year Ended December 31, 1990

(b)

CLAXTON COMPANY

Income Statement

For the Year Ended December 31, 1990

(c)

(a)   SINGLETARY COMPANY
                            Statement of Cost of Goods Manufactured
                            For the Year Ended December 31, 1990

(b)

SINGLETARY COMPANY

Income Statement

For the Year Ended December 31, 1990

Name_____

SINGLETARY COMPANY
GENERAL JOURNAL

DATE	ACCOUNT TITLES AND EXPLANATION	POST. REF.	DEBIT	CREDIT

Name_____

GENERAL JOURNAL

DATE	ACCOUNT TITLES AND EXPLANATION	POST. REF.	DEBIT	CREDIT

Name_____

(a) _____ WHIRL COMPANY

(b)

(c)   WHIRL COMPANY
                        Statement of Cost of Goods Manufactured and Sold
                             For the Quarter Ended March 31, 1990

Name_____

(a)

MATTHEWS COMPANY
GENERAL JOURNAL

DATE	ACCOUNT TITLES AND EXPLANATION	POST. REF.	DEBIT	CREDIT

(a) (concluded)   GENERAL JOURNAL

DATE	ACCOUNT TITLES AND EXPLANATION	POST. REF.	DEBIT	CREDIT

Name _____

_____

(b)

Materials Inventory

Work in Process Inventory

Finished Goods Inventory

Name_____

COURTNEY MANUFACTURING COMPANY
GENERAL JOURNAL

(a)

DATE	ACCOUNT TITLES AND EXPLANATION	POST. REF.	DEBIT	CREDIT

(a) (concluded)

GENERAL JOURNAL

DATE	ACCOUNT TITLES AND EXPLANATION	POST. REF.	DEBIT	CREDIT

(b)   COURTNEY MANUFACTURING COMPANY
                              Income Statement
                         For the Month of May, 1990

Name

(a)

FURMAN COMPANY

(b)

PAT COMPANY

Materials Inventory	Work in Process Inventory

Payroll Summary	Finished Goods Inventory

Manufacturing Overhead	Cost of Goods Sold

Selling Expenses	Sales

Administrative Expenses

COURTNEY MANUFACTURING COMPANY
GENERAL JOURNAL

(c)

DATE		ACCOUNT TITLES AND EXPLANATION	POST. REF.	DEBIT	CREDIT

(a)   (b)

(c)

(a)

NO.
1.
2.
3.
4.
5.
6.
7.
8.
9.
10.
11.
12.
13.
14.

(b)

Job Order Cost Systems

Understanding the Learning Objectives

1. Define Job Order Costing.

   * Job Order Costing is defined as the accumulating of costs incurred to produce a product for each individual job.

2. Describe where job order cost systems can be used.

   * Job order cost systems are used where the products being manufactured are separately identified or where goods are produced to meet a customer's particular needs.

3. Describe the documents used to accumulate product costs in a job order cost system.

   * The *job order cost sheet* summarizes all costs—direct materials, direct labor, and applied manufacturing overhead—of producing a given batch of products. A sheet is maintained for each job order.

   * A *store (or materials) card* is kept for each type of direct and indirect material maintained in inventory. The stores card shows the quantities (and costs) or each type of material received, issued, and on hand.

   * The *work ticket* shows what employees worked on what job for how many hours and at what wage rate.

     The *manufacturing overhead costs sheet* summarizes the various factory indirect costs incurred.

   * A *finished goods card* is a running record of units and costs of products completed, sold, and on hand.

4. Describe job order cost flows and record the proper journal entries beginning with initial materials requisition and ending with the sale of the final product.

   * The costs of a job flow through three inventory accounts and one expense account. The costs of materials purchased are accumulated in a Materials Inventory account. As the materials are used, the costs flow through to the Work in Process Inventory account. The costs of direct labor and manufacturing overhead flow into the Work in Process Inventory account. The cost of the goods completed flows from the Work in Process Inventory account to the Finished Goods Inventory. The costs remain in this account until the goods are sold. Upon sale of the goods, the costs are transferred to the Cost of Goods Sold account.

   * The journal entries to record the cost flows are presented in the chapter and in Chapter 13.

5. Show how a predetermined overhead rate is computed and how it is used to assign overhead to production.

   * $$\frac{\text{Estimated manufacturing overhead costs}}{\text{Estimated level of activity (such as machine-hours)}} = \text{Predetermined overhead rate}$$

   * The predetermined overhead rate is multiplied times the actual level of activity to get the overhead assigned to production.

6. Transfer any overapplied or underapplied overhead to Cost of Goods Sold.

   * If overhead is applied, the journal entry required to dispose of it is:

     Cost of Goods Sold
         Manufacturing Overhead

   * If overhead is overapplied, the journal entry required to dispose of it is:

     Manufacturing Overhead
         Cost of Goods Sold

7. Define and use correctly the new terms in the glossary.

   The new terms introduced in the chapter are as follows:

   Actual overhead rate—Total manufacturing overhead divided by total manufacturing activity.

   Average cost per unit—Total manufacturing cost of a job divided by the total number of good finished units in the job.

   Bill of materials—A control sheet that shows the type and quantity of each item of material going into a completed unit.

   Cost driver—A measure of activity, such as machine-hours and computer time, that is a causal factor in the incurrence of costs in an organization.

   Finished goods card—A running record of units and costs of products completed, sold, and on hand.

   Job order cost sheet—A form used to summarize the costs of direct materials, direct labor, and manufacturing overhead incurred for a job. The job order cost sheets for all partially completed jobs form the subsidiary ledger for the Work in Process Inventory account.

   Job order cost system (job costing)—A cost accounting system in which the costs incurred to produce a product are accumulated according to the individual job, such as a building, dam, 1,000 chairs, or 10 desks.

   Manufacturing overhead cost sheet—A record that summarizes the various manufacturing overhead costs incurred.

   Materials requisition—A written order directing the stores clerk to issue certain materials to a production center.

   Overapplied (overabsorbed) overhead—The amount by which the overhead applied to production exceeds the actual overhead costs incurred in that same period.

   Predetermined overhead rate—Calculated by dividing estimated total overhead costs for a period by the expected level of activity, such as machine-hours or direct labor costs for the period.

   Process cost system (process costing)—A manufacturing cost system in which costs incurred to produce a product are accumulated according to the processes or departments a product goes through on its way to completion.

   Stores (or materials) card—A record that shows the quantities and costs of each type of material received, issued to a job, and left on hand.

   Underapplied (underabsorbed) overhead—The amount by which actual overhead costs incurred in a period exceeds the overhead applied to production in that period.

   Work (labor time) ticket—A form used to record labor costs. Information recorded on the work ticket includes employee number, job number, number of hours worked, and any other important information; may be prepared for both direct and indirect labor.

Completion and Exercises

1. What is a job order cost system and when is it generally used?

_____

_____

_____

_____

2. When costs are accumulated by jobs, the three elements of manufacturing cost, _____ _____, _____, and _____ _____ related to each job, are recorded on a key record called the _____ _____, which also serves as a subsidiary record underlying the _____ _____ _____ inventory account.

3. The basic document authorizing the transfer of direct materials from the storeroom to the producing departments is called a _____. Direct labor-hours worked on a given job are first recorded on _____ _____. Manufacturing overhead is usually assiged to a job through use of a _____ _____.

4. What use is made in the accounting system of the unit costs that are shown or can be computed from the information contained on a job order sheet? _____

_____

_____

5. How is a predetermined overhead rate calculated? _____

_____

_____

6. The goal of a cost accumulation system is _____

_____

7. Explain in a general way how unit costs are determined in a job order cost system. _____

_____

8. Assume the following information relates to the A Company for the month of June:

	Job No. 505	Job No. 506	Job No. 507
In process—June 1:			
Materials	$20,000	$10,000	-0-
Labor	30,000	20,000	-0-
Overhead	45,000	30,000	-0-
Costs added in June:			
Materials	5,000	20,000	$20,000
Labor	20,000	20,000	40,000
Overhead	?	?	?

Actual overhead costs incurred in June amounted to $115,000. Job Nos. 505 and 506 were completed and transferred out in June.

405

8. (continued)

From the given data compute:

a. The cost of the June 1 work in process inventory $_____.

b. The total amount of overhead assigned to production in June assuming no change in the overhead rate employed $_____.

c. The cost of Job No. 505 when completed $_____.

d. The cost of the goods completed and transferred $_____.

e. The cost of the June 30 work in process inventory $_____.

f. Present three journal entries, one to record each of the following in total for the month of June: direct materials used in production, direct labor costs incurred on jobs during the month, and the overhead assigned to production. Also, give one entry to record the total cost of the goods completed and transferred in June.

9. _____ _____ is the amount by which the overhead applied to production exceeds the actual overhead costs incurred in that same period.

10. _____ _____ is the amount by which actual overhead costs incurred in a period exceed the overhead applied to production in that period.

11. Underapplied or overapplied overhead is usually transferred to _____ _____.

12. A practical disposition of underapplied overhead, if most of the goods manufactured in the period have been sold or if its amount is nominal, is to _____

_____ . An alternative—allocating underapplied overhead to Work in Process Inventory, Finished Goods Inventory, and Cost of Goods Sold—is theoretically preferred when the underapplied overhead is not due to _____ _____ or

_____ .

13. Fixed overhead rates may be based upon different levels of capacity or activity, of which the three most commonly used are _____ _____ , _____

_____ , and _____ _____ .

14. Assume that the fixed overhead for a given department is $120,000 and that its capacity levels are (a) practical capacity, 120,000 hours; (b) normal capacity, 100,000 hours; (c) expected activity, 60,000 hours. Assume that actual activity was at the 50,000-hour level. What three differing amounts of fixed overhead could be assigned to production depending upon the level of activity (capacity) used in establishing the fixed overhead rate?

_____

_____

_____

_____

_____

_____

_____

15. The long-run average annual demand for a product is 40,000 units. But the firm producing these units expects to manufacture 50,000 units in Year 1 and only 30,000 units in Year 2, because of an expected temporary shortage of materials in Year 2. Fixed overhead costs are $150,000 annually. Compute the fixed overhead cost per unit for Years 1 & 2, assuming overhead rates are based on expected activity and that actual activity was as planned.

_____

_____

_____

_____

16. A _____ _____ is a cost center in whch work indirectly related to the units produced is performed.

17. The costs incurred by factory service centers are applied to production finally through use of a _____ _____ _____ _____ for the production centers.

Multiple-Choice Questions

For each of the following questions, indicate the single best answer by circling the appropriate letter.

Use the following information for the first three questions:

In December 1989 the cost accountants of the Amos Company established the following base for allocating manufacturing overhead to all jobs worked on in 1990.

$$\frac{\$200,000 \text{ Estimated manufacturing overhead}}{25,000 \text{ machine-hours}} = \$8 \text{ per machine-hour}$$

During 1990, the machine-hours totalled 30,000 and the actual manufacturing overhead was:

Cash expenses:	
Factory supplies	$14,000
Rent..............................	72,000
Heat, light and power	24,000
Indirect labor	18,000
Indirect materials..................	30,000
Non-cash expenses:	
Depreciation on machinery	50,000
Factory insurance	6,000

1. The entry to record the actual overhead costs is:

   a.   Manufacturing Overhead..   214,000
          Cash   214,000

   b.   Manufacturing Overhead..   214,000
          Cash   158,000
          Accumulated Depreciation   50,000
          Prepaid Insurance   6,000

   c.   Work in Process...   240,000
          Manufacturing Overhead...   240,000

   d.   Manufacturing Overhead..   240,000
          Cash   184,000
          Prepaid Insurance   6,000
          Accumulated Depreciation   50,000

2. The entry to record the application of overhead is:

   a.   Manufacturing Overhead..   214,000
          Cash   214,000

   b.   Manufacturing Overhead..   214,000
          Cash   158,000
          Accumulated Depreciation   50,000
          Prepaid Insurance   6,000

   c.   Work in Process Inventory   240,000
          Manufacturing Overhead...   240,000

   d.   Manufacturing Overhead..   240,000
          Cash   184,000
          Prepaid Insurance   6,000
          Accumulated Depreciation   50,000

3. The amount of over- or underapplied overhead is:

   a. $ 10,000 overapplied.
   b. $ 26,000 overapplied.
   c. $ 26,000 underapplied.
   d. $225,000 overapplied.
   e. $214,000 underapplied

Use the following information for the next two questions.

Earl Company uses a job-order costing system with perpetual inventories. The following transactions were completed.

4. Labor costs for the period were $70,000, of which $10,000 were indirect. The journal entry is:

   a.   Work in Process Inventory   60,000
        Manufacturing Overhead..   10,000
          Payroll Summary   70,000

   b.   Work in Process Inventory   10,000
        Manufacturing Overhead..   60,000
          Payroll Summary   70,000

   c.   Finished Goods Inventory...   70,000
        Indirect Labor..   2,000
          Payroll Payable..   72,000

   d.   Direct Labor   60,000
        Indirect Labor..   10,000
          Payroll Summary   70,000

5. Overhead was applied to production using a rate of $2.50 per machine-hour. Assuming 18,720 machine-hours were charged, the journal entry is:

   a. Work in Process Inventory 46,800
          Manufacturing Overhead 46,800

   b. Factory Overhead Applied 46,800
          Factory Overhead Control 46,800

   c. Work in Process Inventory 54,600
          Manufacturing Overhead 54,600

   d. Finished Goods Inventory 46,800
          Manufacturing Overhead 46,800

   e. Finished Goods Inventory 18,000
          Manufacturing Overhead Applied 18,000

6. Finished goods costing $33,600 were sold for $84,000 cash. Using perpetual inventory procedure, the journal entry(ies) is (are):

   a. Cash 84,000
          Sales 84,000

   b. Cost of Goods Sold 33,600
          Finished Goods Inventory 33,600

   c. Cost of Goods Sold 84,000
          Finished Goods Inventory 84,000

   d. Both a and c are necessary
   e. Both a and b are necessary

7. Job order costing is commonly used in:

   a. construction.
   b. motion pictures.
   c. other industries where many similar products are produced.
   d. All of the above are correct.
   e. Two of the above are correct.

8. Information recorded on the work ticket includes:

   a. job number.
   b. employee number.
   c. number of hours worked.
   d. All of the above are correct.
   e. Two of the above are correct.

9. Predetermined overhead rates are set at the _____ of the year in which they will be used.

   a. end
   b. beginning
   c. middle
   d. All of the above are correct.

10. If an overhead balance remains at year-end, it can be allocated to:

   a. Finished Goods Inventory.
   b. Work in Process Inventory.
   c. Cost of Goods Sold.
   d. All of the above are correct.
   e. Two of the above are correct.

11. A predetermined overhead rate is calculated by:

a. dividing estimated total overhead costs for a period by an expected level of activity.
b. dividing actual total overhead costs for a period by an expected level of activity.
c. dividing actual total overhead costs for a period by an actual level of activity.
d. None of the above is correct.

Solutions/Chapter 14

Completion and Exercises

1. A job order cost system is a cost accounting system in which the costs incurred to produce a product are accumulated for each individual job. It is generally used when the products being manufactured can be separately identified or when goods are produced to meet a customer's particular needs.

2. direct materials; direct labor; manufacturing overhead; job order sheet; Work in Process

3. Materials requisition; work (or labor time) tickets; predetermined overhead rate

4. They are entered as the unit costs of the finished goods on the finished goods perpetual inventory stock cards and used in financial reporting and for other actions such as pricing.

5. The predetermined rate is calculated by dividing estimated total overhead costs for a period by an expected level of activity.

6. to determine before year-end the unit costs of the products being manufactured.

7. The total of the costs charged to a job is divided by the number of units comprising the job to obtain a unit cost.

8. a. $155,000 ($20,000 + $30,000 + $45,000 + $10,000 + $20,000 + $30,000)

   b. $120,000 [150 percent of ($20,000 + $20,000 + $40,000)]. (From the relationship observed in the beginning inventory between manufacturing overhead and direct labor, the overhead rate can be seen to be 150 percent of direct labor cost.)

   c. $150,000 ($20,000 + $30,000 + $45,000 + $5,000 + $20,000 + $30,000)

   d. $280,000 (the cost of Job No. 505 which is $150,000 plus the cost of Job No. 506 which equals $10,000 + $20,000 + $30,000 + $20,000 + $20,000 + $30,000)

   e. $120,000 ($20,000 + $40,000 + $60,000)

   f.
Work in Process Inventory	45,000	
Materials Inventory		45,000
To record requisitioning of direct materials.		
Work in Process Inventory	80,000	
Payroll Summary		80,000
To charge direct labor costs to production.		
Work in Process Inventory	120,000	
Manufacturing Overhead		120,000
To assign overhead to production.		
Finished Goods Inventory	280,000	
Work in Process Inventory		280,000
To record transfer of completed goods.		

9. Overapplied overhead

10. Underappled overhead

11. Cost of Goods Sold

12. close it to the Cost of Goods Sold account; idle capacity; inefficiency

13. practical capacity; normal activity; expected activity

14. a. practical capacity: 50,000 × ($120,000/120,000) = $ 50,000
    b. normal capacity: 50,000 × ($120,000/100,000) = $ 60,000
    c. expected capacity: 50,000 × ($120,000/ 60,000) = $100,000

15. Rates based on expected activity: Year 1—$3 per unit ($150,000/50,000);
    Year 2—$5 per unit ($150,000/30,000).

16. service center

17. predetermined overhead rate

Multiple-Choice Questions

1. b. Actual manufacturing overhead is accumulated as a debit to the Manufacturing Overhead account. Credits are made to various other accounts.

2. c. Manufacturing overhead is applied through a debit to the Work in Process Inventory account and a credit to Manufacturing Overhead.

3. b. $240,000 applied overhead less $214,000 actual overhead leaves $26,000 overapplied.

4. a. Direct labor costs that are charged to jobs are debited to Work in Process Inventory and indirect costs are charged to Manufacturing Overhead.

5. a. $2.50 × 18,720 machine-hours = $46,800 overhead applied.

6. e. Under perpetual inventory procedure, Finished Goods Inventory must be credited at the time of sale in addition to recording the increase in cash and revenue.

7. e. Answer (c) is incorrect because job order costing is used in other industries where many *dissimilar* products are produced.

8. d. Answers (a), (b), and (c) can be found on the work ticket.

9. b. Predetermined overhead rates are set at the beginning of the year in which they will be used.

10. d. An overhead balance at year-end can be allocated to finished goods inventory, work in process inventory or cost of goods sold.

11. a. The predetermined overhead rate can be calculated by dividing estimated total overhead costs for a period by an expected level of activity.

Name _____

PINSON COMPANY
GENERAL JOURNAL

DATE	ACCOUNT TITLES AND EXPLANATION	POST. REF.	DEBIT	CREDIT

Name _____

_____

PINSON COMPANY
GENERAL JOURNAL

DATE	ACCOUNT TITLES AND EXPLANATION	POST. REF.	DEBIT	CREDIT	

(a) and (b)   WARD CORPORATION

		JOB NUMBER			
		401	402	403	404

(c)

(d)

(a)

BENSON COMPANY

(b)

(a)   CLOUD COMPANY

(b)

Name _____

_____

(a) _____

WRIGHT, INC.
GENERAL JOURNAL

DATE	ACCOUNT TITLES AND EXPLANATION	POST. REF.	DEBIT	CREDIT

Name _____

_____

WRIGHT, INC.
GENERAL JOURNAL

DATE	ACCOUNT TITLES AND EXPLANATION	POST. REF.	DEBIT	CREDIT
(b)				

(c)

	Using Direct Labor Costs			
	FIRST QUARTER	SECOND QUARTER	THIRD QUARTER	FOURTH QUARTER

15

Process Costing

Understanding the Learning Objectives

1. Describe the types of operations for which a process cost system is used.

    *   Process cost systems are used for businesses that manufacture large quantities of a single product or similar products on a continuous basis over long periods of time.

2. Distinguish between process and job order costing systems.

    *   Although both process and job order cost systems have the same basic cost flows, under a process cost system, products are usually partially completed in one department and then transferred out to another department for further processing. Costs are accounted for in each department and accumulated as the product flows through departments. Accordingly, each department will usually have its own Work in Process Inventory account that contains costs transferred in and costs incurred by the current department.

3. Discuss the determination of unit costs and the concept of equivalent units in a process cost system.

    *   At the most basic level, unit costs can be determined by dividing the total of direct materials, direct labor, and applied manufacturing overhead by the number of units transferred out. This computation will give the average unit cost. A complication arises, however, whenever partially completed inventories are present, which is usually the case. In this situation, equivalent units must be computed to arrive at the unit cost figure.

    *   Basically, the concept of equivalent units involves expressing a number of partial units as a smaller number of complete units. As a simple example, two glasses of water which are half full are equivalent to one whole glass. In manufacturing, the degree of completion is estimated for a group of products with respect to materials and conversion costs (direct labor and overhead). The concept of equivalent units is based on the fact that about the same amount of costs must be incurred to partially complete a large number of units as to totally complete a smaller number of units.

4. Compute equivalent units of production under an average cost procedure.

    *   The following production data are used to compute equivalent units of production under an average cost procedure:

Department A

Units started, completed, and on hand	12,000
Units on hand, 50% complete as to materials; 60% complete as to conversion costs	5,000
Total units on hand	17,000

	Materials	Conversion
Units completed and transferred	12,000	12,000
Units on hand	2,500*	3,000*
Equivalent units of production	14,500	15,000

*Materials = 5,000 (.50); Conversion = 5,000 (.60)

Because Department A initiates the production process, there are no transferred-in units to consider. Department A began the process with 17,000 units in beginning inventory. Of these, 12,000 were fully completed and 5,000 were partially completed during the month. Of the 5,000 partially completed, 50% of materials had been added to production, and 60% of direct labor and overhead costs had been incurred. Therefore, to compute the equivalent units of production, the units completed and transferred out are multiplied by 100%. The remaining 5,000 units on hand are multiplied by 50% for materials and 60% for conversion costs, respectively. Adding both columns gives the equivalent units of production for materials and conversion costs. Of the initial 17,000 units (12,000 fully complete), 14,500 are considered complete with respect to materials, and 15,000 are considered complete with respect to conversion costs.

5. Prepare a production cost report for a process cost system and discuss its relationship to the Work in Process Inventory account.

   * A production cost report shows both the flow of units and the flow of costs through a processing center. The report is divided into two parts. The first part traces the physical flow of the units through the production department and converts actual units to equivalent units. The second part shows the costs to be accounted for, computes unit costs based on equivalent units as determined in the first part, and shows how the costs were accounted for by adding the costs completed and transferred out with the costs remaining in ending inventory. The costs to be accounted for and the costs accounted for must balance.

   * The production cost report provides a check on the Work in Process Inventory account. Because each processing department normally has it's own Work in Process Inventory account and related production cost report, the separate items which make up work in process inventory, i.e., direct labor, direct materials, applied overhead, and cost of units transferred in and out, can be traced from one to the other during a given period.

6. Define and use correctly the new terms in the glossary.

   The new terms introduced in the chapter are as follows:

   Average cost procedure—A method of computing equivalent units where the number of equivalent units for each cost element equals the number of units transferred out plus the number of equivalent units of that element in the ending inventory.

   Equivalent units—A method of expressing a given number of partially completed units as a smaller number of fully completed units; for example, bringing 1,000 units to a 75% level of completion is the equivalent of bringing 750 units to a 100% level of completion.

   Job order cost system—A manufacturing cost system in which costs incurred to produce a product are accumulated for each individual job.

   Process cost system (process costing)—A manufacturing cost system in which costs incurred to produce a product are accumulated according to the processes or departments a product goes through on its way to completion.

   Processing center—An individual process or department in a process system which serves as a "cost center" where costs are accumulated for the entire period in question.

   Production cost report—A report that shows both the flow of units and the flow of costs through a processing center and how those costs are divided between the cost of units transferred out and the cost of units still in the processing center's ending inventory.

   Transferred-in costs—Costs, associated with physical units, which were accumulated in previous processing centers.

Completion and Exercises

1. What is a process cost system? _____

_____

_____

2. The concept of _____ _____ _____ involves expressing a given number of partially completed units as a smaller number of fully completed units.

3. The key document is a process costing system is the _____ _____ _____.

4. Like in job order costing, the goal of a process cost system is _____.

_____

5. Explain in a general way how unit costs are determined in a process cost system. _____

_____

6. If there are no beginning or ending enventories, the unit cost for a period of completing a given process

can be determined in a process cost system simply by dividing _____ _____

charged to the department by the number of units _____ and _____. If there are partially completed units on hand at the end of the period, the computation of average unit costs first

involves the computation of _____ _____ _____.

7. Assume that you are given the following information:
   Number of units:

	Case 1	Case 2	Case 3
In beginning inventory	-0-	2,000	4,000
Started	10,000	20,000	30,000
In ending inventory	1,000	-0-	8,000

Compute the equivalent production for use in computing average conversion cost for the period in each of these three cases assuming, in each instance, that the inventories are 50 percent complete.

8. Compute the equivalent production for Case 3 in Question 7 for materials, assuming that average costs are to be computed and that materials are added only at the beginning of the production process.

9. Use the data in Case 1 in Question 7 and assume that materials are added only at the beginning of processing in the department and that the ending inventory is 50 percent complete as to conversion. Compute the average unit cost of completing a unit in Case 1 assuming the following costs were incurred during the period:

Direct materials	$33,000
Direct labor	4,180
Manufacturing overhead	6,270

10. In the X Department for June, 4,000 units were in the June 1 inventory complete as to materials, 50 percent complete as to conversion. A total of 30,000 units was transferred in, and materials for 30,000 units were entered into production in the X Department. The ending inventory consists of 8,000 units complete as to materials and 50 percent complete as to processing. Costs to be accounted for in the department are as follows:

	Transferred-in	Materials	Conversion	Total
In beginning inventory	$ 8,000	$ 4,000	$ 10,000	$ 22,000
Added in June	60,680	29,320	293,000	383,000
Total	$68,680	$33,320	$303,000	$405,000
Equivalent units	_____	_____	_____	
Units costs.....................	_____	_____	_____	_____

The total cost of the units transferred out is $ _____ .

Fill in the above blanks assuming average unit costs are to be computed.

11. Equivalent costs must be determined for (1) _____ _____ ,

(2) _____ , and (3) _____ .

Multiple-Choice Questions

1. Product costs, which "attach" to the product as units are transferred from one processing center to another, include:

   a. direct materials.
   b. direct labor.
   c. manufacturing overhead.
   d. All of the above are correct.
   e. None of the above are correct.

2. The production cost report shows:

   a. the flow of units through a processing center.
   b. the flow of costs through a processing center.
   c. how costs are divided between the cost of units completed and transferred out and the cost of units still in the processing center as ending inventory.
   d. None of the above are correct.
   e. All of the above are correct.

3. There are _____ steps in the preparation of the production cost report.

   a. two
   b. three
   c. four
   d. five

4. The Roberts Company uses average costing in its process costing system. The output of a department measured in equivalent units under the following assumptions is:

   (1) Goods transferred during the period, 60,100 units
   (2) Ending work in process inventory, 6,600 units, one-third completed

   a. 64,500.
   b. 66,700.
   c. 60,100.
   d. 58,200.
   e. 62,300.

5. In a processing department, the beginning inventory of 8,000 units was 30 percent complete as to material and conversion costs. A total of 40,000 units was transferred to the next department and ending inventory consisted of 10,000 units having all their material and 75 percent of their conversion cost. Using average costing, the equivalent units for material are:

   a. 47,500.
   b. 48,000.
   c. 58,000.
   d. 50,000.
   e. None of these.

Use the following information for the next two questions.

6. The cost accountant for York Company estimates total manufacturing overhead cost for Department A for the year at $270,000 and total machine-hours at 90,000. During January, actual manufacturing overhead cost totaled $24,900 and machine-hours incurred totaled 8,200.

   The correct entry to apply factory overhead to production for January is:

   a. Work in Process—Dept. A... 24,900
         Manufacturing Overhead—Dept. A.................................... 24,900
   b. Work in Process—Dept. A... 24,600
         Manufacturing Overhead—Dept. A.................................... 24,600
   c. Manufacturing Overhead Applied—Dept. A.......................... 24,600
         Work in Process—Dept. A... 24,600
   d. Manufacturing Overhead—Dept. A 24,900
         Cash, Vouchers Payable and various credits..................... 24,900
   e. None of the above.

7. In question 6 above, what is the balance of the account Manufacturing Overhead—Dept. A at January 31, after the entry in No. 6 is made?

   a. $300 credit
   b. $24,900 debit
   c. $24,600 credit
   d. $300 debit

8. When compared to job order systems, process cost systems have _____ cost flows.

   a. smaller
   b. larger
   c. the same
   d. None of the above.

9. Under a (an) _____ , the number of equivalent units for each cost of element equals the number of units transferred out plus the number of equivalent units of that cost element in the ending inventory.

   a. job order costing system
   b. average cost procedure
   c. equivalent cost procedure
   d. None of the above.

10. If the Finishing Department had no work in process at the beginning of the period, 4,000 units were transferred during the period, and 1,000 units were 50 percent completed at the end of the period, what was the number of equivalent units of production for the period?

   a. 4,000
   b. 500
   c. 4,500
   d. 5,000
   e. None of these.

Now compare your answers with the correct ones beginning on page 435.

Completion and Exercises

1. A process cost system is a manufacturing cost system in which costs incurred during production are accumulated according to the processes or departments that a product goes through on its way to completion.

2. equivalent units

3. production cost report

4. to determine before year-end the unit costs of the products being manufactured

5. The processes or departments serve as "cost centers" where costs are accumulated for the entire period. These costs are divided by the number of units produced to get an average unit cost.

6. total costs; completed; transferred; equivalent production

7. Number of units:

	Case 1	Case 2	Case 3
In beginning inventory	-0-	2,000	4,000
Started	10,000	20,000	30,000
Units to be accounted for	10,000	22,000	34,000
In ending inventory	1,000	-0-	8,000
Units transferred	9,000	22,000	26,000
Equivalent units in ending inventory	500	-0-	4,000
Equivalent units produced	9,500	22,000	30,000

8.
Units completed and transferred (as above)	26,000
Equivalent units in ending inventory (100 percent complete)	8,000
Equivalent units	34,000

9.
	Total cost	Equivalent units	Per unit cost
Direct materials	$33,000	10,000*	$3.30
Direct labor	4,180	9,500†	0.44
Manufacturing overhead	6,270	9,500	0.66
Total unit cost			$4.40

*9,000 transferred + 1,000 in inventory, which are 100 percent complete.
†9,000 transferred + 1,000 in inventory, which are 50 percent complete.

10.
	Transferred in	Materials	Conversion	Total
Total costs	$68,680	$33,320	$303,000	$405,000
Equivalent units	34,000	34,000	30,000	
Unit costs	$2.02	$0.98	$10.10	$13.10

Cost of transferred units is $117,900 (9,000 × $13.10).

11. costs transferred in (if the department receives products from another processing department); costs of materials; costs of conversion

435

. d.   Product costs include direct materials, direct labor, and manufacturing overhead.

2. e.   The production cost report shows the information on the flow of units through a processing center, the flow of costs through a processing center, and how costs are divided between the cost of units completed and transferred out and the cost of units still in the processing center as ending inventory.

3. c.   There are four steps in the preparation of the production cost report.

4. e.   60,100 units transferred plus 2,200 equivalent units in ending inventory.

5. d.   Because ending inventory has all of its materials, the entire 10,000 units are added to the 40,000 units transferred to give 50,000 equivalent units to divide into material costs in the computation of unit material cost.

6. b. $270,000/90,000 = $3 per machine-hour overhead application rate.
$3 × 8,200 = $24,600 overhead applied in January.

7. d. $24,900 actual overhead less $24,600 overhead applied equals a $300 debit or underapplied overhead. Actual overhead is accumulated as a debit and applied overhead as a credit in the account.

8. c.   Cost flows under process cost systems are the same as those under job order systems.

9. b.   The average cost procedure calculates the number of equivalent units for each cost element as the number of units transferred out plus the number of equivalent units of that cost element in the ending inventroy.

10. c.   4,000 units transferred plus 500 units (1,000 × 50% complete).

(a) _____

FRASER COMPANY
Department A
Production Cost Report
For the Month Ended May 31

Units	Actual Units	Equivalent Units	
		Materials	Conversion

Costs	Materials	Conversion	Total

Name _____

FRASER COMPANY
Department B
Production Cost Report
For the Month Ended May 31

Units	Actual Units	Transferred-In	Equivalent Units Materials	Conversion

Costs	Transferred-In	Materials	Conversion	Total

HAYES COMPANY
Production Cost Report
For the Current Period

Units	Actual Units	Equivalent Units	
		Materials	Conversion

Costs	Materials	Conversion	Total

(a)   TOPS MANUFACTURING COMPANY

(b)

16

Control through Standard Costs

Understanding the Learning Objectives

1. Discuss the nature of standard costs, including how standards are set.

    * A standard cost represents what a cost should be under stated conditions using a careful predetermined measure. As such, the standard cost represents a goal that, if properly set, represents a reasonably efficient level of performance if the standard is achieved.

    * Although standards are set in many ways, engineering studies and time and motion studies are usually undertaken to determine the amounts of materials, labor, and other services required to produce a product. In addition, general economic conditions should be considered when setting standards because these conditions affect the cost of materials and other services that must be purchased.

2. Discuss the advantages of using standard costs.

    * Benefits that can be derived from the use of standard costs include:

        1. improved cost control.
        2. more useful information for managerial planning and control.
        3. more reasonable inventory measurements.
        4. cost savings in record-keeping.
        5. possible reductions in production costs incurred.

3. Calculate the six variances from standard, and determine if each variance is favorable or unfavorable.

    Materials price variance = (Actual price − Standard price) × Actual quantity purchased

    Materials usage variance = (Actual quantity used − Standard quantity) × Standard price

    Labor rate variance = (Actual rate − Standard rate) × Actual hours

    Labor efficiency variance = (Actual hours − Standard hours) × Standard rate

    Overhead budget variance = Actual overhead − Budgeted overhead

    Overhead volume variance = Budgeted overhead − Applied overhead

    * A variance is designated as favorable when actual costs are less than standard, and unfavorable when actual costs exceed standard. However, appraisal of whether the variance is desirable or undesirable should only be made after the causes of the variance are known.

4. Discuss what each of the six variance accounts shows, and prepare journal entries to record the variances.

    * The *material price variance* account shows whether the actual price paid was higher (debit) or lower (credit) than the standard price set for materials. The *materials usage variance* shows only differences from standard caused by the quantity of materials used. If more materials were used than the standard allowed, the materials usage account would be debited.

    * The *labor rate variance* account shows whether a higher actual rate (debit) or a lower actual rate (credit) from the standard rate was paid to produce a product or complete a process. On the other hand, the *labor efficiency variance* shows that more (debit) or less (credit) than the standard amount of direct labor-hours was used to produce a product or complete a process.

447

* The *overhead budget variance* shows the difference between the actual overhead incurred and the amount that was budgeted for overhead. If actual overhead is greater, the variance account will show a debit.

* The *overhead volume variance* account shows whether plant assets produced more or fewer goods than expected, and is the difference between the budgeted overhead and the applied overhead. If budgeted overhead is less than applied, there will be a favorable (credit) variance.

5. Discuss the three selection guidelines used to investigate variances from standard.

   * The three possible guides include the (1) amount of the variance; (2) size of the variance relative to cost incurred; and (3) controllability of the cost associated with the variance.

6. Discuss the theoretical and practical methods for disposing of variances from standard.

   * Variances that remain in the accounts at the end of the year may be (1) viewed as losses due to inefficiency and closed to Income Summary; (2) allocated as adjustments to the recorded Work in Process Inventory, Finished Goods Inventory, and Cost of Goods Sold; or (3) closed to Cost of Goods Sold.

   * Theoretically, the alternative chosen should depend upon whether the standards set were reasonably attainable and whether the variances were controllable by employees.

   * As a practical matter, especially if they are small, variances are usually closed to Cost of Goods Sold.

7. Discuss how standard costs are applied in both job order and process cost systems (covered in Appendix).

   * In a job order system, the materials and labor variances are isolated rather routinely in the recording process. However, the overhead variances must be computed separately at the end of the period, unless the standard production for the period is known before then.

   * In a process cost system, work in process inventories are charged with actual quantities and actual costs, or alternatively, actual quantities at standard costs. The second practice will isolate some variances sooner.

8. Define and use correctly the new terms in the glossary.

   The new terms introduced in the chapter are as follows:

   Flexible budget—A budget that shows the expected amount of overhead for various levels of output; used in isolating overhead variances and setting standard overhead rates.

   Labor efficiency variance—A variance from standard caused by using more or less than the standard amount of direct labor-hours to produce a product or complete a process; computed as (Actual direct labor-hours − Standard direct labor-hours) × Standard rate per hour.

   Labor rate variance (LRV)—A variance from standard caused by paying a higher or lower average rate of pay than standard to produce a product or complete a process; computed as (Actual rate per hour − Standard rate per direct labor-hour) × Actual direct labor-hours worked.

   Materials price variance (MPV)—A variance from standard caused by paying a higher or lower price than standard for materials purchased; computed as (Actual price − Standard price) × Actual quantity purchased.

   Materials usage variance (MUV)—A variance from standard caused by using more or less than the standard amount of materials to produce a product or complete a process; computed as (Actual quantity used − Standard quantity allowed) × Standard price.

   Overhead budget variance (OBV)—A variance from standard caused by incurring more or less than the standard manufacturing overhead for the actual production volume achieved, as shown by a flexible budget; computed as Actual overhead − Budgeted overhead at actual production volume level.

   Overhead volume variance (OVV)—A variance from standard caused by producing at a level other than that used in setting the standard overhead rates; computed as Budgeted overhead − Applied overhead.

   Standard cost—A carefully predetermined measure of what a cost should be under stated conditions.

Standard level of output—A carefully predetermined measure of what the expected level of output should be for a specified period of time, usually one year.

Variance—The amount by which actual costs differ from standard costs; may be favorable or unfavorable. That is, actual costs may be less than or more than standard costs. Variances may relate to materials, labor, or manufacturing overhead.

Completion and Exercises

1. A _____ _____ is a model or a projection of what a cost should be; it is a target or goal that is sought.

2. The use of standard costs represents an application of the principle of _____ _____ _____ through the recording of deviations from standard in _____ accounts.

3. Although useful for other purposes, such as management planning, standard costs are primarily employed as a means of securing control over _____ .

4. Using the following information, compute the materials price variance and the materials usage variance. Indicate whether each is favorable or unfavorable.

   Purchased 150 units at $8.10 per unit.
   Used 98 units to produce finished products for which the standard quantity is 100 units.
   Standard price of the material is $8 per unit.

   _____

   _____

5. In order to secure effective cost control, variances should, as a general rule, be isolated (when?).

   _____

   _____

6. Explain how a favorable materials price variance might be the cause of an unfavorable materials usage variance.

   _____

   _____

   _____

   _____

7. From the following information, compute the labor rate variance and the labor efficiency variance and indicate whether each is favorable or unfavorable.

Standard labor time per unit	2 hours
Equivalent production for the period	10,000 units
Standard labor rate per hour	$5.50
Total direct labor wages paid	$126,400
Actual direct labor-hours received	23,200

   16,400 Un.
   3,200 Un.

   _____

   _____

8. Explain how an unfavorable labor rate variance may be the cause of a favorable labor efficiency variance.

_____

_____

_____

9. Of the labor variances, the _____ _____ _____ is more likely to be under the control of management.

10. The _____ _____ _____ is designed to show how effectively overhead costs were controlled in the sense of the prices paid and the amounts of indirect manufacturing services received.

11. An overhead volume variance will exist only if the applied overhead cost of the actual production for a period differs from _____ _____ _____ for the same period. The formula for computing the overhead volume variance is _____ _____ _____ minus _____ _____ _____ assigned to production.

12. From the following information, compute the overhead budget variance and the overhead volume variance and indicate whether each is favorable or unfavorable. Prove the accuracy of your computations by summing algebraically the two variances you computed and comparing this total with the total overhead variance.

Standard production, in units	100,000
Budgeted variable overhead, per unit	$0.60
Budgeted fixed overhead, per month	$80,000
Actual variable overhead for the month	$38,300
Actual fixed overhead for the month	$78,100
Actual production for the month, in units	60,000

_____

_____

_____

_____

_____

_____

_____

_____

_____

13. When goods are completed, they are transferred to the Finished Goods Inventory account at _____ _____ cost.

14. Once variances are isolated, management must decide which ones should be _____ .

15. Possible guides in determining which variances to investigate include the _____ size of the variance, the size of the variance _____ to the cost incurred, whether the cost is _____ or _____ , and _____ analysis.

16. Although theoretically standard cost variances should be analyzed individually to determine the reasons(s) for their existence and treated accordingly, as a practical matter, they are usually closed to the

_____ _____ _____ _____ account.

(The remaining questions are based on the chapter Appendix.)

17. Assume that a given company has one job in process, Job No. 216, which has a standard labor cost of 4,000 hours at $4 per hour, and which has already been charged with 1,950 standard labor-hours. The factory payroll for the week ending June 7 showed direct labor of 6,000 hours at a total cost of $24,600, and $5,000 of indirect labor. Of the 6,000 hours, 2,000 were used to complete Job No. 216, while the other 4,000 hours were used to complete Job No. 217, which has a standard labor cost of 5,000 hours at $4 per hour. Under these circumstances, give the journal entry needed to distribute the payroll for the week ending June 7.

18. Normally, in both a job order cost system and a process cost system into which standard costs are introduced, the overhead variances cannot be isolated until the end of the period (usually a month)

because _____

_____

_____ .

19. The standard specifications of a product manufactured by the Adams Company as regards its first processing in Department B are as follows:

Materials—4 pounds @ $1	$ 4
Direct labor—2 hours @ $5	10
Overhead—2 hours @ $3	6
Total standard cost	$20

During the month of June the Adams Company charged the following actual quantities and actual costs to the Work in Process Inventory account for Department B:

Direct materials (32,050 pounds @ $1.02 per pound)................	$ 32,691
Direct labor (14,020 hours @ $4.95)	69,399
Actual fixed overhead	30,410
Actual variable overhead..	14,200
Total costs charged to production	$146,700
Less: Standard cost of completed units (6,000 @ $20)	120,000
Balance, June 30..	$ 26,700

At 15,000 hours—the normal activity level—fixed overhead is budgeted at $30,000 and variable overhead at $15,000. A total of 6,000 units of product was completed and transferred. There was no beginning inventory in the department, and the ending inventory consisted of 2,000 units, 100 percent complete as to materials and 50 percent complete as to processing.

a. The equivalent production for June for materials is _____ units.

b. The equivalent production for June for conversion is _____ units.

19. (concluded)

Compute each of the following variances and indicate whether favorable or unfavorable:

c. Materials price variance _____

d. Materials usage variance _____

e. Labor rate variance _____

f. Labor efficiency variance _____

g. Overhead budget variance _____

h. Overhead volume variance _____

Multiple-Choice Questions

For each of the following questions, indicate the single best answer by circling the appropriate letter.

1. A standard cost represents:

   a. a projection of what a cost should be.
   b. the results of scientific measurements.
   c. the costs which should be required to produce a unit of product.
   d. (b) and (c).
   e. all of the above.

2. Among the advantages claimed for standard costs are that they (choose the *incorrect* statement):

   a. require less clerical effort.
   b. help establish control over costs.
   c. provide information useful in budgeting.
   d. solve the period cost-product cost controversy.

3. The following are benefits resulting from a standard cost system:

   a. happier labor force since there is less pressure on them to perform.
   b. useful information is available for planning and control purposes.
   c. inventory measurements are improved.
   d. (b) and (c) above
   e. All of the above

4. In a standard cost system, exceptions or variances:

   a. represent instances where things are not going as planned.
   b. are always viewed as unfavorable.
   c. must all be investigated to determine what factors caused the variance.
   d. are the total responsibility of top management.
   e. (a) and (c)

5. In a standard cost system, units in inventory are:

   a. valued at FIFO, LIFO, or weighted average costing.
   b. all valued at LIFO costing.
   c. all carried at the same unit cost based on standard.
   d. not valued until the end of operations when variances are determined.
   e. None of the above

6. Regarding a standard cost system, which of the following statements is *false*?

    a.   If an employee works at a slower pace than standard, an unfavorable labor efficiency variance will result.
    b.   If a higher paid employee is assigned to a task that is normally performed by a lower paid employee, an unfavorable labor rate variance will result.
    c.   If the company operated at a higher rate of volume for a period than that budgeted, an unfavorable volume variance will result.
    d.   If the purchasing department is able to acquire materials at a lower price than standard, a favorable price variance will result.
    e.   If more indirect material is used than expected at the actual level of operations, an unfavorable budget variance will result.

The following information relates to questions 7 through 10. MDA, Inc. manufactures red widgets and has established standard costs for its production. In 1990 the following information has been extracted from MDA's financial records.

Standard labor cost...............	$7.85/hr.
Standard labor per unit	.6 hr./unit
Standard material cost	$25/lb.
Standard material per unit.........	4.2 lbs./unit
Units produced in 1986	145,000 units
Total hours in 1986	94,250 hrs.
Total cost for labor in 1985	$752,115
Total material used in 1986	623,500 lbs.
Total material cost in 1986	$15,275,750

7. The material price variance for 1990 is:

    a. $311,750 F
    b. $311,750 U
    c. $50,750 U
    d. $362,500 U

8. The material usage variance for 1990 is:

    a. $355,250 U
    b. $362,500 U
    c. $50,750 U
    d. $50,750 F

9. The labor rate variance for 1990 is:

    a. $600,010 U
    b. $12,252.50 U
    c. $56,912.50 U
    d. $11,310 U

10. The labor efficiency variance for 1990 is:

    a. $600,010 U
    b. $12,252.50 U
    c. $56,912.50 F
    d. $56,912.50 U

11. A firm budgets its overhead at $60,000 plus $4 per unit based on standard activity of 20,000 units. If the firm actually produced 18,000 units, the overhead volume variance would be:

    a. $2,000 favorable.
    b. $2,000 unfavorable.
    c. $6,000 favorable.
    d. $6,000 unfavorable.

12. If the standard overhead is $27,000 plus $1 per direct labor hour based on a volume of 10,000 units per period, actual production is 10,500 units, standard labor per unit is one hour, actual fixed overhead is $26,000, and actual variable overhead is $9,700, which of the following is a true statement?

   a. The overhead volume variance is $2,000 unfavorable.
   b. The overhead budget variance is $1,800 favorable.
   c. The total overhead variance is $1,750 unfavorable.
   d. Standard overhead applied to production is $35,000.

13. Assume the following data concerning overhead for the Brown Company:

   Actual overhead incurred..................................... $90,000
   Budgeted overhead for actual work performed.............. 95,000
   Standard overhead applied to actual work performed........ 88,000

   The overhead volume variance and the overhead budget variance are:

   Unfavorable = U   Favorable = F

   a. Volume variance—$7,000 U; budget variance—$5,000 F
   b. Volume variance—$2,000 U; budget variance—$7,000 F
   c. Volume variance—$7,000 F; budget variance—$5,000 U
   d. Volume variance—$5,000 F; budget variance—$7,000 U
   e. Volume variance—$2,000 U; budget variance—$5,000 F

14. The data concerning overhead for the Thomson Company are:

   Actual overhead incurred..................................... $102,400
   Budgeted overhead for actual work done.................... $105,000
   Standard overhead applied to actual work done............. $108,200

   The overhead budget variance and the overhead volume variance are:

   a. Overhead budget variance = $4,500 Unfavorable; Overhead volume variance = $3,000 Favorable.
   b. Overhead budget variance = $4,500 Favorable; Overhead volume variance = $3,000 Unfavorable.
   c. Overhead budget variance = $2,600 Unfavorable; Overhead volume variance = $3,200 Unfavorable.
   d. Overhead budget variance = $2,600 Favorable; Overhead volume variance = $3,200 Favorable.

15. (Based on Appendix) The following production and cost data relate to the Bennington Company for the month of June in its assembly department:

   Standard cost of product

Materials	$12
Labor (5 hours at $4)	20
Overhead................	20
	$52

   The above standard cost was established at the beginning of the current calendar year. The beginning inventory in the department consisted of 4,000 units complete as to materials and 50 percent completed as to processing. A total of 12,000 units was completed during the period, and the ending inventory consists of 6,000 units complete as to materials and 50 percent complete as to processing. Which of the following statement is *false* (use average cost method)?

   a. The standard cost of the completed production for the month was $624,000.
   b. The standard cost of the labor for the work done in the month was $300,000.
   c. If 65,200 hours of direct labor services were received during the month, the standard overhead for the work done in the month is $260,800.
   d. The standard cost of the beginning inventory when completed would be $208,000.

Now compare your answers with the correct ones beginning on page 455.

Solutions/Chapter 16

Completion and Exercises

1. standard cost

2. management by exception; variance

3. costs

4. Materials price variance = 150 × ($8.10 − $8.00) = $15 Unfavorable

   Materials usage variance = $8 × (98 − 100) = $16 Favorable

5. As soon as possible (generally, the sooner corrective action can be taken, the more effective it is).

6. The purchase of cheaper than standard quality material may yield a favorable materials price variance, but the cheaper quality material may cause more waste and, thus, an unfavorable materials usage variance.

7. Labor rate variance = $126,400 − (23,200 × $5.50) = $−1,200 Favorable
   Labor efficiency variance = (23,200 − 20,000) × $5.50 = $17,600 Unfavorable

8. An unfavorable labor rate variance usually results from using employees with a higher than standard labor rate in a given job. These employees may be more skilled than those carrying a standard labor rate and this, in turn, may result in greater productivity per hour of labor activity.

9. labor efficiency variance

10. overhead budget variance

11. budgeted overhead; budgeted overhead; applied overhead

12. Overhead budget variance =
    $38,300 − (60,000 × $0.60) + ($78,100 − $80,000) = $400 Unfavorable
    Overhead volume variance = $116,000 − (60,000 × $1.40) = $32,000 Unfavorable
    Total overhead variance = $400 + $32,000 = $32,400 Unfavorable
    Actual total overhead = $38,300 + $78,100 = $116,400; Actual overhead minus applied overhead in production = $116,400 − (60,000 × $0.60) − (60,000 × $0.80) = $32,400 Unfavorable

13. standard

14. investigated

15. absolute; relative; controllable; noncontrollable; statistical

16. Cost of Goods Sold

17.

Work in Process [(2,050 + 4,000) × $4]	24,200	
Labor Rate Variance [$24,600 − (6,000 × $4)]	600	
Manufacturing Overhead	5,000	
Payroll Summary		29,600
Labor Efficiency Variance [(4,000 − 4,050) × $4]		200

    To distribute factory payroll and to isolate labor variances.

18. the actual production for the period and the actual costs for the period are not known until the end of the period

19. a. 8,000
    b. 7,000 [6,000 + (0.50 × 2,000)]
    c. Materials price variance = 32,050 × ($1.02 − $1.00) = $641 Unfavorable
    d. Materials usage variance = (32,050 − 32,000) × $1 = $50 Unfavorable
    e. Labor rate variance = ($4.95 − $5.00) × 14,020 = −$701 Favorable
    f. Labor efficiency variance = (14,020 − 14,000) × $5 = $100 Unfavorable
    g. Overhead budget variance = [$14,200 − (14,000 × $1)] + ($30,410 − $30,000) = $610 Unfavorable
    h. Overhead volume variance = $44,000 − (14,000 × $3) = $2,000 Unfavorable

1. e.

2. d. There is nothing conceptual in standard costs that will lead to the solution of this problem.

3. d.

4. a.

5. c.

6. c.

7. a. ($15,275,750 ÷ 623,500) − $25 = −$0.50; −$0.50 × 623,500 = $−311,750

8. b. 623,500 − (4.2 × 145,000) = 14,500 × $25 = $362,500

9. b. ($752,115 ÷ 94,250) − $7.85 = $0.13; $0.13 × 94,250 = $12,252.50

10. d. 94,250 − (145,000 × .6) = 7,250; 7,250 × $7.85 = $56,912.50

11. d. The overhead volume variance is computed as the difference between applied overhead and budgeted overhead. In this case, overhead is budgeted at $132,000 [$60,000 + ($4 × 18,000)] while applied overhead is only $126,000 (18,000 × $7). The variance is unfavorable because less overhead was applied than budgeted.

12. b. The budget variance is:

Actual: $26,000 + $9,700   = $ 35,700
Budgeted: (10,500 × $1) + $27,000 =   37,500
                                $− 1,800 Favorable

13. a. Volume variance is: $95,000 − $88,000 = $7,000 unfavorable
Budget variance is: $90,000 − $95,000 = $5,000 favorable

14. d. The overhead budget variance is equal to:

Actual overhead incurred .... $ 102,400
Less: Budgeted overhead for actual work done 105,000
                                      $− 2,600 (Favorable)

The overhead volume variance is equal to:

Budgeted overhead for actual work done .... $ 105,000
Less: Standard overhead applied to actual work done 108,200
                                      $− 3,200 (Favorable)

15. (c) The standard overhead for the work done is equal to the equivalent production for the period multiplied by the standard overhead cost per unit of product. This is 15,000 units (12,000 + 3,000) at $20 per unit, or $300,000. Standard overhead would not be assigned to production for the direct labor hours in excess of standard hours allowed.

Name _____

_____

CLANCY COMPANY

(a)

Materials	Materials Price Variance	Accounts Payable

Work in Process Inventory	Materials Usage Variance

(b)

GENERAL JOURNAL

DATE	ACCOUNT TITLES AND EXPLANATION	POST. REF.	DEBIT	CREDIT

Name _____

_____

REPUBLIC COMPANY

(a)

(b)

GENERAL JOURNAL

DATE	ACCOUNT TITLES AND EXPLANATION	POST. REF.	DEBIT	CREDIT	

Work in Process Inventory

Labor Rate Variance

Labor Efficiency Variance

Payroll Summary

Name _____

_____

(a)

RLA COMPANY
Houston Plant

(b)

Name _____

WILDER COMPANY

(a) (concluded)

DATE	ACCOUNT TITLES AND EXPLANATION	POST. REF.	DEBIT	CREDIT

(b)

DATE	ACCOUNT TITLES AND EXPLANATION	POST. REF.	DEBIT	CREDIT

Name _____

MARKOV COMPANY
GENERAL JOURNAL

(a)

DATE	ACCOUNT TITLES AND EXPLANATION	POST. REF.	DEBIT	CREDIT

(b)   GENERAL JOURNAL

DATE	ACCOUNT TITLES AND EXPLANATION	POST. REF.	DEBIT	CREDIT
(c)				
(d)				

Responsibility Accounting and Segmental Analysis

Understanding the Learning Objectives

1. Explain responsibility accounting and its use in a business entity.

   * Responsibility accounting makes reference to an accounting system that collects, summarizes, and reports accounting data relating to the responsibilities of individual managers.

   * The responsibility accounting system provides information that is used to evaluate each manager for revenue and expense items over which he or she has primary control.

   * To use a responsibility accounting system, a business entity must be organized so that responsibility is assignable to individual manager (i.e., have an organization chart).

2. Prepare responsibility accounting reports.

   * A unique feature of a responsibility accounting report is the condensation of data that occurs in successive levels of management reports.

   * Two basic methods of preparing the reports are:

     1. Only items over which a manager has direct control are included in the responsibility report.
     2. Items over which a manager has direct or indirect control are included in the responsibility report.

3. Prepare a segmental income statement using the contribution margin format.

   * The contribution margin format is so named because it does show the contribution margin. The contribution margin is defined as sales revenue less variable expenses.

   * Two basic methods of preparing the statement using the contribution margin format are:

     1. All expenses are allocated between the segments.
     2. All expenses, with the exception of indirect fixed expenses, are shown for the segments. Indirect fixed expenses are only shown in the total column for the computation of net income for the entire company.

4. Calculate return on investment, margin, and turnover for a segment.

   * Return on investment (ROI) is calculated by dividing the income by the investment.

   * Margin is calculated by dividing income by sales.

   * Turnover is calculated by dividing sales by the investment.

5. Calculate the residual income of a segment.

   * Residual income (RI) is calculated as follows:

     $$RI = \text{Income} - (\text{Investment} \times \text{Desired minimum ROI})$$

6. Define and correctly use the new terms in the glossary.

The new terms introduced in the chapter are as follows:

Budget variance—The difference between the budgeted and actual amounts of an item.

Contribution margin—Sales revenues less variable expenses.

Contribution margin format—An income statement format that shows the contribution margin (Sales − Variable expenses) for a segment.

Contribution to indirect expenses—The income of a segment remaining after direct expenses are deducted from segmental revenues.

Controllable profits of a segment—Profit of a segment when expenses under a manager's control are deducted from revenues under that manager's control.

Cost objective—A segment, product, or other item for which costs may be accumulated.

Current replacement cost—The cost of replacing the present assets with similar assets in the same condition as those now in use.

Decentralization—The dispersion of decision-making authority among individuals at lower levels of the organization.

Direct cost (expense)—A cost that is directly traceable to a given cost objective.

Expense center—A responsibility center producing only expense items and producing no direct revenue from the sale of goods or services. Examples include the accounting department and the maintenance department.

Indirect cost (expense)—A cost that is not traceable to a given cost objective but has been allocated to it.

Investment center—A responsibility center having revenues, expenses, and an appropriate investment base.

Management by exception—The principle that upper-level management does not need to examine operating details at lower levels unless there appears to be a problem (an exception).

Margin (as used in ROI)—The percentage relationship of income (or profits) to sales.

$$\text{Margin} = \frac{\text{Income}}{\text{Sales}}$$

Original cost—The price paid to acquire an asset.

Original cost less accumulated depreciation—The book value of an asset—the amount paid less total depreciation taken.

Profit center—A responsibility center having both revenue and expense items.

Relative control—Means the manager has control over most of the factors that influence a given budget item.

Residual income (RI)—The amount of income a segment has in excess of a desired minimum ROI. Residual income is equal to income − (Investment × Desired minimum ROI).

Responsibility accounting—Refers to an accounting system that collects, summarizes, and reports accounting data according to the responsibilities of the individual managers. A responsibility accounting system provides information to evaluate each manager on revenue and expense items over which that manager has primary control.

Responsibility Center—A segment of an organization for which a particular executive is responsibile.

Return on investment (ROI)—Calculates the return (income) as a percentage of the assets employed (investment).

$$\frac{\text{Return on}}{\text{investment}} = \frac{\text{Income}}{\text{Investment}} \text{ or } \frac{\text{Income}}{\text{Sales}} \times \frac{\text{Sales}}{\text{Investment}}$$

472

Segment—A fairly autonomous unit or division of a company.

Segmental net income—Final total in the income statement; segmental revenues less all expenses (direct expenses and allocated indirect expenses).

Suboptimization—A situation that occurs when a segment manager takes an action that is in the segment's best interest but is not in the best interest of the company as a whole.

Transfer price—An artificial price used when goods or services are transferred from one segment to another segment within the same company.

Turnover (as used in ROI)—The number of dollars of sales generated by each dollar of investment.

$$\text{Turnover} = \frac{\text{Sales}}{\text{Investment}}$$

Completion and Exercises

1. A responsibility accounting system charges a given manager only with those items over which the manager has primary _____ .

2. Items which are not controllable at one level are controllable at some _____ _____ .

3. Allocated expenses are almost never _____ by the segment manager.

4. Responsibility centers may be _____ centers, _____ centers, or _____ centers.

5. The goal of an expense center should be to _____ long-run expenses for any given _____ _____ _____ .

6. Direct costs of a center tend to be _____ , while indirect costs tend to be _____ .

7. Profit centers have both _____ and _____ , and therefore permit a calculation of earnings for a given segment.

8. A _____ _____ may be established in order to convert a producing segment from an expense center to a profit center.

9. The goal of a profit center is to maximize _____ within that segment, assuming that this goal is _____ with overall company goals.

10. Investment centers calculate _____ and divide these by an appropriate _____ base.

11. The logic for using investment centers is that segments with larger _____ should produce larger _____ .

12. In a responsibility accounting system the _____ from one management level are carried forward in the report to the next higher _____ _____ .

13. Noncontrollable items at a given level may be _____ from the report prepared for the manager of that segment or they may be _____ from the controllable items.

14. The more _____ the decision making in an organization, the more applicable is the investment center concept.

15. Some of the advantages of decentralized decision making include the following:

   a. _____

   b. _____

   c. _____

   d. _____

16. A cost is a direct cost of a segment if it is _____ to that segment. If the segment were eliminated, a direct cost would be likely to _____ .

17. An indirect cost of a segment cannot be _____ to it and only becomes a cost of the segment through _____ .

18. The contribution margin is equal to _____ less _____ _____ .

19. The contribution to indirect expenses is equal to the contribution margin less _____ _____ _____ or gross margin less _____ _____ _____ .

20. Net income of a segment is equal to _____ _____ _____ less _____ _____ _____ .

21. a. Given the following data, prepare a statement which shows the contribution margin, contribution to indirect expenses, and net income (or loss) of the segment:

Sales......................................	$150,000
Variable expenses.........................	70,000
Fixed Expenses:	
Direct..................................	45,000
Indirect	60,000

   b. The amount which the segment contributes to company income is _____ .

   c. Should the segment be eliminated (yes/no)? _____ Why? _____

   _____

   _____

   _____

22. Methods of allocating indirect expenses to a segment include _____ , _____ , or some other method which seems reasonable in the circumstances. The very process of allocation can be termed _____ .

23. Since allocations of indirect expenses are often so arbitrary some companies do not _____ them to their _____ .

24. The basic formula for return on investment is (fill in the numerator and denominator):

ROI = _____

25. The ROI formula can be divided into parts as follows (supply the names of the two parts):

ROI = _____ × _____

26. Margin is equal to _____ ÷ _____ . Turnover is equal to _____

÷ _____ .

27. To evaluate the earning power of an entire company the ROI formula is (supply the numerator and denominator):

ROI = _____   or   ROI = _____

28. For evaluating the rate of income contribution of a segment the ROI formula is (supply the numerator and denominator):

ROI = _____

29. To evaluate the earnings performance of the manager of the segment the ROI formula is (supply the numerator and denominator):

ROI = _____

30. Three possible valuation bases for plant assets in investment center computations are:

a. _____

b. _____

c. _____

31. The most frequently used valuation base probably is _____ _____

_____ _____ _____ .

32. The preferred valuation base to use is _____ _____

_____ , but often reliable data are _____ to obtain.

33. Residual income is found as follows:

Residual income = _____ – (_____ ×

_____ _____ _____)

34. Assume that a segment has the opportunity to undertake a new activity. Relevant data are:

	Before new activity	After new activity
Contribution to indirect expenses	$ 20,000	$ 23,400
Assets directly used by and identified with the segment	100,000	130,000

a. The return on investment (ROI) before the new activity is _____ .

The ROI after the new activity is _____ .

34. (concluded)

    b.   Assuming the minimum desired ROI is 10 percent, the residual income (RI) before the new

        activity is _____ .

        The residual income after the new activity is _____ .

    c.   Should the segment undertake the new activity (yes/no)? _____

        Why? _____

        _____

        _____

35. When an outside market for the part or service produced by the supplying segment exists, the outside market price might be used as the _____ _____ .

36. When an outside price exists, a downward adjustment in the transfer price might be appropriate if:

    a. _____

    b. _____

37. After the transfer price is established:

    a.   The buying segment should be required to buy internally as long as the transfer price _____

        _____ .

    b.   The selling segment should be required to sell internally as long as the transfer price _____

        _____ .

38. If no outside price exists and negotiation fails, the transfer price may have to be _____ by an impartial board.

39. If the establishment of a transfer price would create hard feelings among the personnel of the segments, the parts or services should be transferred at _____ cost of supplying the parts or services (actual or standard) and the supplying segment should be treated as an _____ center rather than as an _____ center.

Multiple-Choice Questions

For each of the following questions, indicate the single best answer by circling the appropriate letter.

1. In a responsibility accounting system:

    a.   each accounting report contains all items allocated to a responsibility center.

    b.   organized and clear lines of authority and responsibility are only incidental.

    c.   all managers at a given level have equal authority and responsibility.

    d.   each accounting report contains only (or clearly segregates) those items which are controllable by the responsible manager.

2. In determining whether or not to include an item in a responsibility report, which statement is *true*?

   a. The manager must have absolute control of the item included in the report.
   b. All direct costs of a segment are automatically included in the report.
   c. All indirect costs of a segment are automatically included in the report.
   d. The manager must be able to exercise relative control over an item included in the report.

3. Which of the following statements is *true*?

   a. Noncontrollable and controllable expense items at the manager level are *always* included in the manager's report.
   b. Responsibility reports should be prepared as soon as possible after the end of the performance measurement period.
   c. Responsibility reports should only be issued when the manager is aware of a problem. This is the management by exception concept.
   d. Reports should be relatively simple; thus eliminating any data on budgets and variances.

4. The theoretical requirement with regard to the control a manager should have before being held responsible for an item is:

   a. an imperative that must be followed in all responsibility accounting systems.
   b. often compromised since many revenue and expense items have some noncontrollability in them.
   c. isolated from the effects of internal and external factors.
   d. the same idea expressed in the relative control concept.
   e. none of the above.

5. A *responsibility center:*

   a. consists of all members of one particular management level.
   b. may be an expense center, a profit center, or an investment center.
   c. may be defined according to function or product line.
   d. (b) and (c) only.

6. Which of the following statements is *true*?

   a. In an expense center, managers are responsible for revenues and expenses over which they have control.
   b. The appropriate goal of an expense center is the long-run minimization of expense.
   c. Since an appropriate investment base is not determinable, only absolute earnings are used to evaluate expense centers.
   d. (a) and (c) only.

7. A transfer price is most effective when:

   a. it represents full cost of the units transferred.
   b. it is established by market researchers based on supply and demand in the market environment because these prices become the price outside buyers pay.
   c. it represents the purchase price from an outside party.
   d. it represents full cost less variable unit costs.

8. When a division or segment only sells its output to other segments of the same company, a transfer price:

   a. will result in "revenue" for the division so that it may be treated as a profit center rather than an expense center.
   b. should be equal to the market "price" if such a figure is available.
   c. may require arbitration if two segments cannot agree on the price.
   d. all of the above.

9. To use the investment center concept, a segment manager must have control over:

    a. revenues.
    b. expenses.
    c. assets.
    d. (a), (b), and (c) above.

10. When a company is highly decentralized:

    a. the most appropriate evaluation method is absolute earnings.
    b. the bulk of the decision making is made by the vice president.
    c. managers have added responsibility and authority which often result in the use of the investment center concept and increased job satisfaction and motivation.
    d. top management is highly involved in everyday problem solving.

11. The advantages of decentralized decision making include:

    a. decisions can be made at the point where problems arise.
    b. top management can use the management-by-exception principle.
    c. the investment center concept can be used.
    d. all of the above.

12. Which of the following statements is *true?*

    a. The classification of costs as direct or indirect is relative.
    b. The salary of a manager of a segment is an indirect cost to the segment since the manager has no control over the cost.
    c. Direct costs are controllable costs and indirect costs are noncontrollable costs.
    d. A direct cost becomes an expense of a cost objective through allocation.

13. Indirect fixed expenses may be allocated to a segment on the basis of:

    a. benefit received.
    b. responsibility for incurring.
    c. net sales.
    d. all of the above.

14. Ames Company has three different segments: A, B, and C. All three segments use the company's computer facilities. The total expense for 1990 for running the computer is $640,000. Segment A used 10,000 computer hours, Segment B used 24,000 computer hours, and Segment C used 20,000 computer hours. What would be the cost to segments A, B, and C, in that order, if the expense was allocated based on computer hours used?

    a. $213,332; $213,334; $213,334
    b. $284,444; $213,336; $138,220
    c. $118,519; $284,444; $237,037
    d. $10,000; $24,000; $20,000

15. The contribution to indirect expenses shows:

    a. revenues less all expenses of a segment.
    b. the amount by which earnings of the company will decline if the segment is eliminated.
    c. the amount which should be used as earnings when evaluating the earnings performance of the segment manager.
    d. all of the above.

16. Companies frequently use return on investment (ROI) in evaluating segments in which the manager has control over revenues, expenses, and assets. In computing ROI:

    a. the total amount of revenue is divided by the investment base.
    b. it is necessary to determine the desired definition of earnings and investment.
    c. only the rate of earnings contribution of a segment may be evaluated, not the earnings performance of the manager of a segment.
    d. it is first necessary to determine a desired minimum rate of return.

17. In a period of rising prices, which of the following (if used to value plant assets) would be likely to result in the highest ROI in the later years of the life of those assets?

    a. Current replacement cost
    b. Original cost less depreciation
    c. Original cost
    d. Original cost adjusted for the changing price level

18. Assume that a segment of a company last year had the following amounts of sales, earnings and assets:

    Sales $500,000
    Assets 200,000
    Earnings 40,000

    Its margin, turnover, and ROI are:

    a. 12.5 percent $\times$ .4 times = 5 percent.
    b. 20 percent $\times$ .4 times = 8 percent.
    c. 8 percent $\times$ 2.5 times = 20 percent.
    d. 20 percent $\times$ 1 time = 20 percent.

19. Residual income is equal to:

    a. Income − (Investment $\times$ Actual ROI).
    b. Income − (Desired investment $\times$ Actual ROI).
    c. Desired income − (Investment $\times$ Desired minimum ROI).
    d. Income − (Investment $\times$ Desired minimum ROI).

20. Assume that Segment A of Company W has earnings of $200,000, investment of $800,000, and a desired minimum ROI of 20 percent. Its residual income is:

    a. $120,000.
    b. $ 24,000.
    c. $ 80,000.
    d. $ 40,000.

21. If a segment is to be treated as an investment center, all but which one of the following might be used as a transfer price in a given situation?

    a. External market price
    b. Actual variable cost
    c. Standard full cost plus profit margin
    d. Standard variable cost plus profit margin

Now compare your answers with the correct ones beginning on page 480.

Completion and Exercises

1. control

2. higher level

3. controllable

4. expense; profit; investment

5. minimize; level of output

6. controllable; noncontrollable

7. revenues; expenses

8. transfer price

9. profits; congruent (or harmonious)

10. income; investment

11. resources; income

12. totals; management level

13. eliminated; segregated

14. decentralized

15. a. Decentralized decision making gives segment managers experiences which train them for top-management positions.
    b. Top management is freed from day-to-day decision making at the lower echelons of the company.
    c. Decisions can be made at the point where problems arise.
    d. The investment center concept may be applied.

16. traceable; disappear

17. traced; allocation

18. sales; variable expenses

19. direct fixed expenses; other direct expenses

20. contribution to indirect expense; indirect fixed expenses

21. a.
Sales	$150,000
Less: Variable expenses	70,000
Contribution margin	$ 80,000
Less: Direct fixed expenses	45,000
Contribution to indirect expenses	$ 35,000
Less: Indirect fixed expenses	60,000
Net Loss	$ (25,000)

    b. $35,000
    c. No. Because company earnings would decline by $35,000 if the segment were eliminated (unless a more profitable alternative activity could be pursued with the resources now devoted to this segment).

22. responsibility; benefit; arbitrary

23. allocate; segments

24. $\text{ROI} = \dfrac{\text{Income}}{\text{Investment}}$

25. ROI = Margin × Turnover

26. Income ÷ Sales; Sales ÷ Investment

27. $\text{ROI} = \dfrac{\text{Net income}}{\text{Total assets}}$ or $\text{ROI} = \dfrac{\text{Net operating income}}{\text{Operating assets}}$

28. $\text{ROI} = \dfrac{\text{Contribution to indirect expenses}}{\text{Assets directly used by and identified with the segment}}$

29. $\text{ROI} = \dfrac{\text{Controllable income}}{\text{Assets under the control of the segment manager}}$

30. (a) original cost less accumulated depreciation; (b) original cost; (c) current replacement cost

31. original cost less accumulated depreciation

32. current replacement cost; difficult

33. Residual income = Income − (Investment × Desired minimum ROI)

34. a.

Before	After
$\text{ROI} = \dfrac{\$20,000}{\$100,000} = \underline{20\text{ percent}}$	$\dfrac{\$23,400}{\$130,000} = \underline{18\text{ percent}}$

b.

Before	After
RI = $20,000 − ($100,000 × 0.10)	$23,400 − ($130,000 × 0.10)
$20,000 − $10,000 = $10,000	$23,400 − $13,000 = $10,400

c. Yes. By undertaking the new activity, residual earnings are increased by $400. Use of ROI could lead to suboptimization because ROI goes down if the new activity is performed.

35. transfer price

36. (a) there are cost savings from selling internally; (b) there would be idle capacity in the supplying segment if the other segment does not acquire the goods internally.

37. (a) is not above some bona fide available outside price; (b) allows the selling segment to earn as much on internal "sales" as on external sales

38. arbitrated

39. full; expense; investment

Multiple-Choice Questions

1. d. This is the fundamental principle of responsibility accounting. As a result, clear lines of authority and responsibility are essential. Each level of responsibility only receives condensed data from the level beneath it.

2. d. The manager must be able to exercise relative control over an item in order to include it in a report. Absolute control is rare. The important factor is primary control by the manager. Direct costs and indirect costs may or may not be controllable by the manager.

3. b. Reports should be regular and timely. They may contain both controllable and noncontrollable items but frequently only include controllable items. Simplicity in terminology is desirable, but variance and budget data should be included in the report.

4. b. Controllability is often difficult to identify precisely.

5. d. A responsibility center may be organized according to function or product lines. There are three basic types: expense center, profit center, and investment center.

6. b. Expense centers do not generate revenue, therefore they are evaluated through the minimization of expenses, not absolute earnings.

7. c. Ideally, an outside price can be used in setting the transfer price.

8. d. All of the statements are correct.

9. d. The investment center concept is concerned with the return in relation to the amount of investment.

10. c. Decentralization refers to the extent to which management decision making is dispersed to lower levels of the organization. The more decentralized the decision making is in an organization, the more applicable is the *investment* center concept. The advantages of decentralization include the removal of top management from everyday problem solving and "job enrichment" for managers.

11. d. Any of these are advantages of decentralized decision making.

12. a. A cost is a direct cost of a cost objective if it is traceable to that cost objective; it is an indirect cost if it is not traceable but has been allocated to the cost objective. Direct costs are not necessarily controllable costs and indirect costs are not necessarily noncontrollable costs.

13. d. Any of these methods of allocation may be used.

14. c. The computer expense is allocated to each segment based on its percentage of total computer hours used.

    Segment A is allocated 10/54 $\times$ \$640,000 = \$118,519
    Segment B is allocated 24/54 $\times$ \$640,000 = \$284,444
    Segment C is allocated 20/54 $\times$ \$640,000 = \$237,037

15. b. To the extent that direct expenses will disappear if the segment is eliminated, this is the correct statement.

16. b. ROI is computed as income divided by investment. Since three possible definitions of income and investment are available, the desired definition must be determined. The various definitions allow different aspects of the firm to be evaluated.

17. b. The investment base would shrink the most with this method. Accumulated depreciation reduces the book value of the asset each year.

18. c. The answer is found as follows:

$$\text{ROI} = \text{Margin} \times \text{Turnover}$$

$$\text{ROI} = \frac{\text{Income}}{\text{Sales}} \times \frac{\text{Sales}}{\text{Investment}}$$

$$\text{ROI} = \frac{\$40,000}{\$500,000} \times \frac{\$500,000}{\$200,000}$$

$$\text{ROI} = 8.0 \text{ percent} \times 2.5$$
$$= 20\%$$

19. d. Each of the other formulas misstates the relationship in some way.

20. d. Residual income are formed as follows:

    RI = Income − (Investment $\times$ Minimum desired ROI)
    RI = \$200,000 − (\$800,000 $\times$ 20 percent)
    RI = \$200,000 − \$160,000
    RI = \$40,000

21. b. If actual variable cost were used, there would be no earnings in the supplying segment. Thus, the investment center concept could not be used. The segment should be treated as an expense center.

McMILLAN COMPANY
Plant Manager

	AMOUNT		OVER OR
	ACTUAL	BUDGET	(UNDER) BUDGET

Vice President of Manufacturing

	AMOUNT		OVER OR
	ACTUAL	BUDGET	(UNDER) BUDGET

President

	AMOUNT		OVER OR
	ACTUAL	BUDGET	(UNDER) BUDGET

Name _____

_____

TURNER CORPORATION

(a)

	Plant A	Plant B	Plant C
(b)			

(c)

18

The Budget—for Planning and Control

Understanding the Learning Objectives

1. Define a budget and name several kinds of budgets.

   * A budget is a plan showing a company's objectives and proposed ways of attaining the objectives.

   * Responsibility budgets are designed to judge the performance of an individual segment or manager. Capital budgets evaluate long-term capital projects. The master budget contains the planned operating budget, which helps plan future earnings, and a financial budget, which helps plan the financing of assets.

2. List several benefits of a budget.

   * Budgets help a company plan for future profitability.

   * A budget also shows how management intends to control the acquisition and use of resources in the coming period(s).

   * Budgets may be used to motivate individuals so that they strive to achieve stated goals.

   * Business activities are better coordinated; managers become aware of other managers' plans; employees may become cost conscious and try to conserve resources; the organizational plan of the company may be reviewed more often and changed where necessary; and a breadth of vision is fostered.

3. List five general principles of budgeting.

   * All management must be aware of the budget's importance to the company. [Top Management Support]

   * Employees are more likely to strive toward organizational goals if they participate in setting them. [Participation in goal setting]

   * Individuals should be aware of management's expectations. [Responsibility accounting]

   * People should be informed of their progress promptly and clearly. [Communication of results]

   * If the basic assumptions underlying the budget change during the year, the budget should be restated. [Flexibility]

4. Prepare a planned operating budget and its supporting budgets, such as the sales budget, production and purchases budget, and other expense budgets.

   * The sales budget is prepared first.

   * Then planned cost of goods sold is calculated.

   * Then other expenses are estimated.

5. Prepare flexible operating budgets.

  * A flexible operating budget provides detailed information about budgeted expenses at various levels of output.

  * The difference between actual costs incurred and the budgeted amount for that same level of operations is called a budget variance.

6. Prepare a financial budget and its supporting budgets.

  * Each balance sheet must be analyzed.

  * Many balance sheet accounts will be affected by items shown in the planned operating budget, by cash inflows and outflows, and by policy decisions of the company.

7. Define and use correctly the new terms in the glossary.

  The new terms introduced in the chapter are as follows:

  Budget—A plan showing a company's objectives and proposed ways of attaining the objectives. Two major types of budgets are the (1) master budget and (2) control, or responsibility, budget.

  Budgeting—The coordination of financial and nonfinancial planning to satisfy an organization's goals.

  Budget variance—The difference between an actual cost incurred (or revenue earned) at a certain level of operations and the budgeted amount for that same level of operations.

  Cash budget—A plan indicating expected inflows (receipts) and outflows (disbursements) of cash; it helps management decide whether enough cash will be available for short-term needs.

  Financial budget—The projected balance sheet portion of a master budget.

  Fixed costs—Costs that are unaffected by the relative levels of production or sales.

  Flexible operating budget—Provides detailed information about budgeted expenses and revenues at various levels of output.

  Master budget—The projected income statement and projected balance sheet showing the organization's objectives and proposed ways of attaining them; includes supporting budgets for such areas as cash, sales, costs, and production; also called the master profit plan. It is the overall plan of the enterprise and ideally consists of all of the various segmental budgets.

  Participatory budgeting—A method of preparing the budget that includes the participation of all levels of management responsible for actual performance.

  Planned operating budget—The projected income statement portion of a master budget.

  Production budget—Takes into account the units in the sales budget and the company's inventory policy.

  Variable costs—Costs that vary directly with production or sales and are a constant dollar amount per unit of output over different levels of output or sales.

  _____

  *Some terms defined in earlier chapters are repeated here for your convenience.

Completion and Exercises

1. A tool widely used in planning and controlling the use of scarce resources is a _____ .

2. The projected income statement in budgetary terminology is often referred to as the planned

   _____ budget, while the projected balance sheet is called the _____ budget.

3. The _____ budget contains estimates of costs at various levels of output.

4. _____ budgeting involves charging the individual supervisor or department head with only those costs over which he or she has authority to control.

494

5. The process of budget preparation that involves all levels of management that are responsible for operations is known as _____ _____ .

6. Supplies are considered a directly variable cost. At 50,000 units supplies are budgeted for $12,500. What would the flexible budget for supplies be at a level of 40,000 units?

   Budgeted supplies $_____ .

7. A _____ _____ is the deviation of actual performance from expected performance at the actual level of operations.

8. When should a flexible budget be used? _____

   _____

   _____

   _____

   _____

   _____

   _____

   _____

9. Cost of goods sold (including $120,000 of fixed charges) are budgeted at $560,000 for an expected output of 240,000 units. Actual output was 220,000 units, while actual costs were $530,000. What is the budget variance?

   _____

   _____

   _____

   _____

   _____

   _____

   _____

   _____

10. Four main advantages of budgets are the following:

    a. _____

    b. _____

    c. _____

    d. _____

11. The _____ _____ is the starting point for the preparation of a budget.

12. The Kager Company has decided to produce 100,000 calculators at a uniform rate in 1990. The sales department has estimated sales for 1990 according to the following schedule:

	Sales in units
First quarter	20,000
Second quarter	30,000
Third quarter	25,000
Fourth quarter	35,000
Total for 1990	110,000

If the December 31, 1989 inventory is estimated to be 5,000 calculators, prepare a schedule of planned sales and production (in units) for the first two quarters of 1990.

13. The Perry Company plans to sell 40,000 units of Wheelies next quarter at a price of $40 per unit. Production costs (all variable) are $15 per unit. Selling and administrative expenses are variable, $3 per unit, and fixed, $300,000 per quarter. Budgeted income is $ _____ . (Ignore income taxes.)

14. The Palmer Company has predicted sales for the first three months of 1990 as follows: January, $300,000; February, $250,000; and March, $350,000. Eighty percent of sales are collected in the month of sale, and 20 percent of sales are collected in the following month. The Palmer Company's expected cash receipts for March 1990 are $_____ .

15. The Ewing Corporation has a December 31, 1990 accounts receivable balance of $140,000 of which $108,000 are from December's sales. Sales for January 1991 are budgeted at $400,000. Seventy percent of sales are collected in the month of sale, 20 percent in the following month, and 10 percent in the second following month. Collections of receivables during January will be $_____ , and the January 31, 1991 accounts receivable balance will be $_____ .

For each of the following questions, indicate the single best answer by circling the appropriate letter.

1. Budgets can be used for all of the following purposes *except* which one?

    a. A plan revealing how management intends to acquire and use assets.
    b. A comparison of a company's operations with individual statistics for the industry as a whole for the same period.
    c. A tool used to motivate individuals by indicating what performance is expected of them.
    d. Means of coordination of activities of the enterprise in its efforts to meet overall goals.
    e. Method of appraising performance of individual company segments and the overall company.

2. Which of the following statements is *true*?

    a. The more stable the business and economic conditions, the more necessary and desirable is budgeting.
    b. The more stable the business and economic conditions, the less reliable is past experience as a basis for budgeting.
    c. In preparing a budget, both past experience and expected future conditions are considered.
    d. Assumptions used in making a budget are stable and unchanging.

3. General principles of budgeting include which of the following?

    a. Employees are encouraged to participate in goal setting
    b. Responsibility accounting is utilized
    c. Flexibility and timely communication of results
    d. (a) and (c)
    e. All of the above

4. The relationship between an "imposed" budget and a "participatory" budget is:

    a. since budgets are prepared under similar conditions, these are identical terms.
    b. these terms refer to the process of comparing budgeted performance and actual performance.
    c. an imposed budget implies that all levels having control or responsibility for a given performance level are involved in the budgetary process while the participatory budget indicates that it is prepared at the top and handed down for employees to examine.
    d. a participatory budget implies that all levels having accountability or responsibility for certain revenue or expense items are encouraged to provide input into the budgeting process while an imposed budget is handed down by top management and employees are expected to perform within the budgeted level.

5. The accountant's role in budgeting includes the following:

    a. preparing budget data for review by top management only.
    b. preparing budget data for review by all levels of operating personnel.
    c. coordinating efforts throughout the budgeting process.
    d. compiling data forwarded from various operating levels of management.
    e. (b) and (d).
    f. (c) and (d).

6. Indicate which of the following statements is *false* concerning budgets for purchases of items for sale directly to customers (purchases budgets).

   a. Similar techniques are used in their preparations for a manufacturer.
   b. The estimates of cost of goods to be sold during the next period and the inventory required at the end of the quarter must be estimated when budgets are prepared.
   c. The sales budget and the company's inventory policy provide input into preparation of the purchases budget.
   d. Company management's desires concerning the amount of inventory it wishes to have on hand at the end of operations must be determined.
   e. None of the above.

7. Which of the following statements is *true*?

   a. A financial budget is just a simple cash budget that shows planned cash receipts and disbursements.
   b. A master budget consists of an operating budget and a capital budget.
   c. The amounts shown on individuals' responsibility budgets always equal the amount shown in the master budget for the entire firm.
   d. A budget shows how management intends to control the acquisition and use of resources in a coming period.

8. When preparing the sales budget:

   a. it is first expressed in units and eventually in dollars.
   b. it should only be expressed in dollars because this provides input for the production budget.
   c. reliance is made on the information contained in the previously-prepared production budget for the budgeted period.
   d. no allowance should be made for external factors as these are reflected in the production budget.
   e. none of the above.

9. Sales volume is expected to be $120,000 for Brown Company. Its cost of goods sold averages 60 percent of sales. Management expects to begin operations with an $80,000 inventory and end the period with an $88,000 inventory. Based on these data, what purchases are required?

   a. $88,000
   b. $72,000
   c. $160,000
   d. $80,000
   e. None of the above

10. At 100,000 budgeted units of production, labor cost is expected to be $400,000 and materials cost is budgeted to be $150,000. A flexible budget for labor and materials for possible production levels of 125,000 and 87,500 units would result in what budgeted costs?

   a. $400,000 for labor and $150,000 for materials at each level of 125,000 units and 87,500 units
   b. Labor—$500,000 at 125,000 units and $350,000 at 87,500 units; materials—$187,500 at 125,000 units and $131,250 at 87,500 units
   c. Labor—$500,000 at 125,000 units and $400,000 at 87,500 units; materials—$175,000 at 125,000 units and $160,000 at 87,500 units
   d. Labor—$400,000 at both levels of operation and materials—$187,500 at 125,000 units and $131,250 at 87,500 units
   e. Impossible to compute materials costs and labor costs at the two levels because of lack of information.

11. The Goddard Company estimates that next quarter it would be operating at 100 percent capacity with sales of $300,000, cost of goods sold of $180,000, and variable administrative costs of $40,000. The actual results were: sales, $290,000; cost of goods sold, $162,000; and variable administrative costs, $34,000. Operations were at 90 percent of capacity. The budget variances for sales, cost of goods sold, and variable administrative expenses were, respectively:

a. $20,000 over; $0; $2,000 under.
b. $10,000 under; $18,000 under; $6,000 under.
c. $10,000 under; $0; $2,000 under.
d. $10,000 over; $18,000 over; $6,000 over.

12. Repair materials were budgeted at the beginning of a given period to be $50,000. At the end of the period, repair materials used amounted to $55,000. Indicate which of the following statements is correct with regard to the efficient or inefficient use of materials.

a. Repair materials were inefficiently used because the budget was exceeded by $5,000.
b. Repair materials were efficiently used because the repair supervisors indicated they carefully managed the issuance of repair materials.
c. The data given are not sufficient to allow a conclusion because actual production may have exceeded planned production by more than 10 percent.
d. There is an unfavorable variance relative to the use of repair materials.
e. There is a favorable variance relative to the use of repair materials.

13. Clay Corporation has a December 31, 1990, accounts receivable balance of $50,000 of which $40,000 applies to December's sales. Sales for January 1991, are budgeted at $200,000. Seventy-five percent of sales are collected in the month of sale, 20 percent in the following month, and 5 percent in the second following month. Which of the following statements is *true*?

a. Sales for December 1990 were $160,000.
b. Sales for November 1990 were $200,000.
c. Collections of receivables during January will be $192,000.
d. (a), (b), and (c) are true.

14. The following report compares budgeted and actual costs and production for the cutting department of the Kline Corporation for the month of April:

	Planned	Actual
Units of production........	100,000	98,000
Materials	$300,000	$296,400
Direct labor	100,000	100,600
Supplies	40,000	40,200
Maintenance	20,000	22,000
Taxes	1,000	1,100

Materials, direct labor, and supplies are considered variable costs. Maintenance was originally budgeted at $6,000 plus $0.14 per unit of output. For the cutting department in April, which of the following is true?

a. There is an unfavorable variance for materials of $2,400.
b. There is an unfavorable variance for direct labor of $2,600.
c. There is an unfavorable variance in maintenance costs incurred of $2,280.
d. All of the above.

15. Selected balance sheet balances of the Ottley Company at December 31, 1990, are:

Accounts payable	$ 30,000
Wages payable	2,800
Accounts receivable	36,000
Prepaid expenses	4,400
Taxes payable	22,000

For the month of January 1991, the following estimates have been compiled:

Net sales	$110,000
Purchases	80,000
Wages expense	30,000
Rent expense	2,200
Taxes expense	2,000

All sales are on a credit basis, with approximately 70 percent collected in the month of sale and the balance in the following month. Purchases are paid for one half in month of purchase and the balance in the following month. Wages are paid 90 percent in month of incurrence and the balance in the following month. Rent expense results from the amortization of the prepaid rent (shown as prepaid expenses of $4,000). Property taxes are due in February.

Which of the following statements correctly describes one of the items relating to the cash forecast for the month of January 1991? (Choose the one best answer.)

a. Expected cash receipts from customers total $113,000.
b. Expected cash disbursements to suppliers for merchandise total $70,000.
c. Expected cash disbursements to employees amount to $29,800.
d. All of the above statements are true.

Now compare your answers with the correct ones beginning on page 502.

Solutions/Chapter 18

Completion and Exercises

1. budget

2. operating; financial

3. flexible

4. Responsibility

5. participatory budgeting, or budget participation

6. $10,000. Obtained either by multiplying $12,500 × 0.80, or 40,000 × $0.25 cost per unit.

7. budget variance

8. A flexible budget should be used whenever the actual level of operations differs from that originally expected; or whenever basic assumptions regarding operations or cost behavior change.

9. $560,000 − $120,000 = $440,000 variable cost
   $440,000 ÷ 240,000 = $1.83 per unit variable cost.

   Budgeted cost at 220,000 units:

220,000 × $1.83 = ...	$402,600
Fixed costs	120,000
	$522,600
Actual costs	530,000
Unfavorable budget variance	$ 7,400

10. (a) planning for future earnings; (b) controlling earnings through timely variance analysis and responsibility accounting; (c) motivating employees and evaluating performance; (d) allows for management by exception

11. sales forecast

12.
KAGER COMPANY
Planned Sales and Production

	Quarter ending	
	March 31, 1990	June 30, 1990
	(in units of product)	
Sales forecast	20,000	30,000
Production planned...	25,000	25,000
Increase (decrease) in finished goods inventory	5,000	(5,000)
Planned beginning finished goods inventory	5,000	10,000
Planned ending finished goods inventory	10,000	5,000

13. $580,000 (computed below):

Sales (40,000 × $40)		$1,600,000
Cost of goods sold (40,000 × $15)		600,000
Gross margin		$1,000,000
Selling and administrative expenses:		
Variable (40,000 × $3)...................................	$120,000	
Fixed	300,000	420,000
Net Income		$ 580,000

14. $330,000 (computed below):

From February sales ($250,000 × 0.2)	$ 50,000
From March sales ($350,000 × 0.8)	280,000
Total cash receipts	$330,000

15. $384,000; $156,000

Beginning balance		$140,000
January sales		400,000
Total		$540,000
Projected collections:		
From January sales ($400,000 × 70%)	$280,000	
From December sales ($108,000 × 2/3)	72,000	
From November sales ($140,000 − $108,000)	32,000	384,000
Ending balance		$156,000

Multiple-Choice Questions

1. b. Budgets fulfill the purposes listed in a, c, d, and e; however, while the comparison of a company's operations with the industry can reveal important information, this activity is not part of budgeting.

2. c. Both past experience and future conditions are considered in preparing the budget.

3. e. All of the items are principles of budgeting.

4. d. Participatory budgets give those affected some say in its preparation.

5. f. Accountants are not preparers of budgeting data; instead they coordinate efforts and compile data prepared by operating management levels.

6. a. A manufacturer does not prepare a purchases budget for goods to sell, although it may have one for raw materials; instead a production budget is prepared for a manufacturer.

7. d. The budget is a plan for the coming period.

8. a. It is easier to initially plan sales in units rather than dollars.

9. d.
$ 88,000 Ending inventory desired
 72,000 Cost of goods sold (.60 × $120,000)
$160,000
 80,000 Beginning inventory
$ 80,000 Purchases required

10. b. The unit cost is $4 ($400,000/100,000) for labor and $1.50 ($150,000/100,000) for materials.
Labor: $4 × 125,000 = $500,000 and $4 × 87,500 = $350,000
Materials: $1.50 × 125,000 = $187,500 and $1.50 × 87,500 = $131,250

11. a.

	Flexible budget	Actual	Over (under*)
Sales	$270,000	$290,000	$20,000
Cost of goods sold	162,000	162,000	-0-
Variable administrative expenses	36,000	34,000	(2,000*)

12. c. The budgeted amount at the actual level of operations may have been greater than $55,000.

13. d.

   (a) $40,000/.25 = $160,000
   (b) ($50,000 − $40,000)/.05 = $200,000
   (c) November sales .... $ 10,000 - (1.)
       December sales ....   32,000 - (2.)
       January sales ....   150,000 - (3.)
       Total collections $192,000

     1. The remaining accounts receivable from November.
     2. $160,000 × .20 = $32,000
     3. $200,000 × .75 = $150,000

14. d.

   (a) $300,000/100,000 = $3/unit
       $3 × 98,000 = $294,000; $294,000 − $296,400 = $2,400 U
   (b) $100,000/100,000 = $1
       $1 × 98,000 = $98,000; $98,000 − $100,600 = $2,600 U
   (c) $0.14 × 98,000 = $13,720
                   6,000
            $19,720; $19,720 − $22,000 = $2,280 U

15. d.

   (a) $ 36,000 Balance in Accounts Receivable
        77,000 ($110,000 × .7)
     $113,000

   (b) $ 30,000 Balance in Accounts Payable
        40,000 ($80,000 × 1/2)
     $ 70,000

   (c) $ 2,800 Balance in Wages Payable
        27,000 ($30,000 × .9)
     $ 29,800

Name _____

_____

SUNSET COMPANY

Projected Income Statement

For January 1990

Schedule 1

Name _____

_____

THOMAS COMPANY
Planned Production and Cost of Goods Sold
For April, May and June 1990

	April	May	June
(a)			
(b)			

(a)

BAKER COMPANY
Comparison of Actual and Budgeted Operations
For the Year 1991

	Budget	Actual	Over(Under*)

(b)

BAKER COMPANY
Comparison of Actual and Budgeted Operations
For the Year 1991

	Flexible Budget	Actual	Over(Under*)

(c)

Name _____

_____

T. K. ANDERSON COMPANY

(a)

Projected Income Statement

For the Year Ending December 31, 1990

(b)

T. K. ANDERSON COMPANY
Comparison of Actual and Budgeted Operations
Year Ended December 31, 1990

	Flexible Budget	Actual	Over(Under*)

Analysis of Results

Name _____

_____

HOLLY COMPANY
Sales Department Budget
For the Three Months Ended March 31, 1991

Name _____

MDA MANUFACTURING COMPANY
Schedule of Production in Units

	Quarter	
	3/31/90	6/30/90
Planned Cost of Goods Manufactured and Sold		

(a)

A & K CORPORATION

Projected Income Statement

Quarter Ending March 31, 1991

Schedule I

Name _____

(a) (cont.)

A & K CORPORATION   Schedule I-a

Planned Merchandise Purchases and Ending Inventory

Quarter Ending March 31, 1991

A & K CORPORATION   Schedule I-b

Planned Operating Expenses

Quarter Ending March 31, 1991

(b)

A & K CORPORATION   Schedule II
Projected Balance Sheet
March 31, 1991

Name _____

(b) (continued)

A & K CORPORATION

Schedule II-A

Analysis of Accounts Credited for Purchases and Expenses

Quarter Ending March 31, 1991

	TOTAL	ACCOUNTS PAYABLE	ACCRUED LIABILITIES	PREPAID EXPENSES	ALLOWANCE FOR DOUBTFUL ACCOUNTS	ACCUMULATED DEPRECIATION

(b) (concluded)

A & K CORPORATION

Schedule II-b

Planned Cash Flow and Cash Balance

Quarter Ending March 31, 1991

A & K CORPORATION

Schedule II-c

Planned Collections on Accounts and Accounts Receivable Balance

Quarter Ending March 31, 1991

(c)

MAHARIS COMPANY
Cash Budget
For the Quarter Ending June 30, 1990

(a)

(b)

19

Short-Term Decision Making

Understanding the Learning Objectives

1. Explain and describe the different cost behavior patterns.

   * Variable costs vary directly with changes in volume of production or sales. Examples of variable costs are direct materials, direct labor, and sales commissions.

   * Fixed costs remain constant over some relevant range of output, and are often described as time-related costs. Examples of fixed costs are depreciation, insurance, property taxes, and administrative salaries.

   * Mixed costs contain a fixed portion of costs that will be incurred even when the plant is completely idle and a variable portion that will increase directly with production volume. An example of a mixed cost is electricity.

   * Step costs remain constant in total over a range of output (or sales), but then increase in steps at certain points.

2. Calculate the break-even point for a company.

   * The break-even point is that level of operations at which a company realizes no net income or loss.

   * The break-even point is calculated using cost-volume-profit (CVP) analysis (sometimes called break-even analysis).

   * The break-even point can be expressed as:

     Sales = Fixed costs + Variable costs

   * The break-even point is computed by:

   $$BEP_{dollars} = \frac{Fixed\ costs}{Contribution\ margin\ rate} \quad or \quad BEP_{units} = \frac{Fixed\ costs}{Contribution\ margin\ per\ unit}$$

3. List the assumptions underlying cost-volume-profit analysis.

   * Selling price, variable cost per unit, and total fixed costs remain constant throughout the relevant range.

   * The number of units produced equals the number of units sold.

   * In multiproduct situations, the product mix is known in advance.

   * Costs can be accurately classified into their fixed and variable portions.

4. Calculate the various applications of cost-volume-profit analysis.

   * One application is the calculation of the break-even point. The formula for the break-even point is given under Objective 2.

* Another application is the calculation of the sales volume needed for desired net income. The formula for this application is:

Sales = Fixed costs + Variable costs + Desired net income

* In addition, an application is the calculation of the effect on net income of changing price. This effect can be calculated by:

Sales = Fixed costs + Variable costs + Net income

* Lastly, an application is the calculation of the sales needed to maintain the net income when costs change. This formula is the same as above:

Sales = Fixed costs + Variable costs + Net income

5. Explain differential analysis and describe its various components.

* Differential analysis involves analyzing the different costs and benefits that would arise from alternative solutions to a particular situation.

* The components are as follows:

Relevant revenues or costs are future revenues or costs that differ depending on which alternative course of action is selected.

Differential revenue is the difference in relevant revenues between two alternatives.

Differential cost or expense is the difference between relevant costs for two alternatives.

Sunk costs, or past costs, are not relevant in decision making because the costs have already been incurred and, therefore, cannot be changed no matter which alternative is selected.

6. Calculate the various applications of differential analysis.

* One application involves the setting of the price for a product. When selecting a price, the goal is to select the price that has the greatest total contribution margin, where total future revenues exceed the total future variable costs by the greatest amount.

* Another application involves accepting or rejecting special orders. Special orders may be accepted at prices lower than average unit costs because the only relevant costs are the future additional costs that will be incurred. One must appraise the pricing of the additional business in light of the long-range effects on company and industry price structures.

* Elimination of products, segments, or customers is another application of differential analysis. One must simply assume elimination and compare the reduction in revenues with the eliminated costs.

* In addition, processing or selling joint products is an application. One must compare the differential revenue of further processing the product with the differential cost of further processing to get the net advantage/disadvantage of further processing the product.

* Lastly, an application is the decision to make or buy. The price that would be paid for the part if it were purchased is compared with only the additional costs that would be incurred if the part were manufactured to get a net advantage/disadvantage of making.

7. Compare and contrast absorption costing and direct costing.

* Under absorption costing, all production costs, including fixed manufacturing overhead, are accounted for as product costs and are allocated to the units of product produced during a period.

* On the other hand, direct costing includes only variable manufacturing costs as product costs. All fixed manufacturing overhead costs are charged to expense in the period in which they are incurred.

* Comparison of income statements under both of these methods shows differences in the net income before taxes and in ending inventory valuation. The differences are due to the treatment of the fixed manufacturing overhead costs.

* Selling and administrative expenses are treated as period costs under both methods.

8. Define and use correctly the new terms introduced in the chapter.

The new terms introduced in the chapter are as follows:

Absorption (or full) costing—A concept of costing under which all production costs, including fixed manufacturing overhead, are accounted for as product costs and allocated to the units produced during a period.

Break-even analysis—See Cost-volume-profit analysis.

Break-even chart—A graph that shows the relationships between sales, costs, volume, and profit and also shows the break-even point.

Break-even point—That level of operations at which revenues for a period are equal to the costs assigned to that period so that there is no net income or loss.

By-products—The waste materials (which sometimes have a small market value compared to the main product) that result from the production of a product or products.

Committed fixed costs—Costs relating to the basic facilities and organization structure that a company must have to continue operations. An example is depreciation on the factory building.

Contribution margin—The amount by which revenue exceeds the variable costs of producing that revenue.

Contribution margin rate—Contribution margin per unit divided by selling price per unit.

Cost-volume-profit (CVP) analysis—An analysis of the effects that any changes in a company's selling prices, costs, and/or volume will have upon income (profits) in the short run. Also called break-even analysis.

Differential analysis—An analysis of the different costs and benefits that would arise from alternative solutions to a particular problem.

Differential cost or expense—The difference between the amounts of relevant costs for two alternatives.

Differential revenue—The difference between the amounts of relevant revenues for two alternatives.

Direct (or variable) costing—A concept of costing under which only variable manufacturing costs are accounted for as product costs and charged to the units produced during a period. All fixed manufacturing overhead is charged to expense in the period in which it is incurred.

Discretionary fixed costs—Fixed costs that are subject to management control from year to year. An example is advertising expense.

Fixed costs—Costs that remain constant (in total) over some relevant range of output.

High-low method—A method used in dividing mixed costs into their fixed and variable portions. The high plot and low plot of actual costs are used to draw a line representing a total mixed cost.

Joint costs—Those costs incurred up to the point where joint products split off from each other.

Joint products—Two or more products resulting from a common raw material or manufacturing process.

Make-or-buy decision—Concerns whether to manufacture or purchase a part or material used in the manufacture of another product.

Margin of safety—Amount by which sales can decrease before a loss will be incurred.

Margin of safety rate—Margin of safety expressed as a percentage; is equal to (Current sales − Break-even sales) ÷ Current sales.

Mixed cost—Contains a fixed portion of cost that will be incurred even when the plant is completely idle and a variable portion that will increase directly with production volume.

Opportunity cost—The potential benefit that is foregone from not following the next best alternative course of action.

Product mix—The proportion of the company's total sales attributable to each type of product sold. Product mix may be defined either in terms of sales dollars or in terms of the number of units sold.

Relevant range—The range of production or sales volume over which the basic cost behavior assumptions will hold true.

Relevant revenues or costs—Revenues or costs that will differ in the future depending on which alternative course of action is selected.

Scatter diagram—A diagram that shows plots of actual costs incurred for various levels of output or sales; it is used in dividing mixed costs into their fixed and variable portions.

Short run—The period of time over which it is assumed that plant capacity and certain costs are fixed; often determined to be one year or less.

Step cost—A cost that remains constant in total over a range of output (or sales) but then increases in steps at certain points.

Sunk costs—Past costs about which nothing can be done; they are not relevant in decision making because the costs have already been incurred.

Variable cost rate—Variable costs expressed as a percentage of sales; used to find the break-even point.

Variable costs—Costs that vary (in total) directly with changes in volume.

Completion and Exercises

1. _____ costs are constant in total over an entire range of output, while _____ costs vary directly in total with changes in volume.

2. Costs that are fixed over a certain range of output and increase in steps at certain points of output are called _____ _____ costs.

3. _____ costs are a mixture of fixed and variable components.

4. Indicate whether each of the following is true or false.

    ____ a. Fixed cost per unit remains constant as output varies.

    ____ b. Total fixed cost does not vary with output.

    ____ c. Total variable cost varies directly with output.

    ____ d. Variable cost per unit remains constant as output changes.

5. What is meant if a company is said to break even? _____

_____

6. From the following information compute the break-even point in sales dollars and number of units.

    Fixed costs for period $120,000
    Sales price per unit   20
    Variable costs per unit   8

7. The contribution margin is the difference between sales revenue for a period and _____

_____ for that period.

8. In the break-even chart shown below, label the axes, the lines, the shaded areas, and indicate the break-even point.

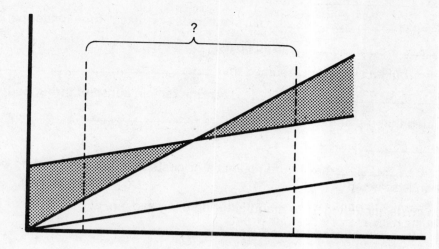

9. The greatest amount of net income will be obtained by a price which provides the greatest total contribution margin over _____ _____ .

10. Fixed costs exist only in a _____-_____ time period.

11. The formula to calculate the break-even point in units is (insert the numerator and denominator):

BEP in units = _____

12. Assume a company has fixed costs of $50,000, a contribution margin per unit of $20, and desired income of $40,000. The number of units it would have to sell to achieve the desired income amount is:

13. To calculate the break-even point for a multiproduct firm you need to know the _____ _____ for the future period.

14. The _____ diagram may be used to separate _____ costs into their _____ and _____ components.

15. The _____-_____ method of drawing the cost line for a mixed cost uses only two actual cost amounts.

16. The _____-_____ method utilizes statistical methods to draw the cost line for a mixed cost.

17. Fixed costs may be divided into two categories: _____ and _____ fixed costs.

18. _____ fixed costs are "fixed" for a longer period of time than are _____ fixed costs.

19. In cost-volume-profit analysis, it is assumed that _____ _____ and _____ _____ per unit remain constant throughout the relevant range.

20. It is also assumed that the number of units _____ equals the number of units _____ .

21. _____ _____ are future revenues or costs that differ depending on which alternative course of action is selected.

22. All production costs, including fixed manufacturing overhead, are accounted for as product costs and are allocated to the units of product produced during a period under _____ _____ .

23. Under _____ _____ , all variable costs af production are treated as product costs.

24. The difference in net income before taxes under absorption costing and direct costing can be related to the _____ in inventories.

Multiple-Choice Questions

For each of the following questions, indicate the single best answer by circling the appropriate letter.

1. Which of the following items would probably be properly classifiable as a step variable cost?

   a. Depreciation computed on a time basis
   b. Depreciation computed on a usage basis
   c. Supervisory salaries
   d. Real estate taxes

2. Given the following data regarding the revenue and costs of the Brandenburg Corporation, which of the following is the break-even point?

Sales		$200,000
Cost of goods manufactured and sold:		
Materials................................	$32,000	
Labor....................................	30,000	
Variable manufacturing overhead..........	24,000	
Fixed manufacturing overhead	20,000	106,000
		$ 94,000
Selling expenses:		
Variable	$14,000	
Fixed	18,000	32,000
		$ 62,000
General and administrative expense:		
Variable	$16,000	
Fixed	24,000	40,000
Net Operating Income		$ 22,000

   a. S = $62,000 + .69S = $200,000
   b. S = $62,000 + .58S = $147,619
   c. S = $42,000 + .68S = $131,250
   d. S = $22,000 + .58S = $ 52,381

524

3. Break-even analysis could be used by management:

   a. to determine the additional sales volume required to cover a contemplated expenditure on advertising, all other factors remaining constant.
   b. to determine the effect of a change in selling price on net income at various levels of sales.
   c. to analyze the effect of substituting a production method which would decrease fixed costs but would at the same time increase variable costs per unit.
   d. to accomplish all of the above.

4. Fixed costs are $1,000,000 and variable costs are 50 percent of sales. The break-even point is:

   a. $2,400,000.
   b. $2,000,000.
   c. $1,000,000.
   d. $ 500,000.

5. Using the facts in question 4, what sales are required to realize a before-tax income of $200,000?

   a. $2,400,000
   b. $2,000,000
   c. $ 400,000
   d. $1,400,000

6. Wagner Company sells a single product at $150 per unit. For output up to 40,000 units, its fixed costs are $450,000. Variable costs are $50 per unit. If 10,000 units are sold, the firm has net income (loss) of:

   a. $1,000,000.
   b. $1,150,000.
   c. $ 50,000.
   d. $ 550,000.

7. The break-even point is the point at which:

   a. fixed costs equal variable costs.
   b. sales equals fixed costs plus variable costs.
   c. variable costs equal sales.
   d. all of the above are true.

8. The P & M Corporation produces and sells belts. The selling price is $22 per belt. Fixed costs are $8,000. Variable costs are $14 per belt. What is the break-even point in units?

   a. 10,000 units
   b. 1,000 units
   c. 5,000 units
   d. 4,000 units

9. If sales are $400,000, net income $40,000, and sales at break-even point are $300,000, what is the margin of safety for this company expressed as a percentage of actual sales?

   a. 25 percent
   b. 50 percent
   c. 75 percent
   d. 10 percent
   e. None of these

Questions 10-11.

For the past year Russell Company had sales of $1,200,000, a margin of safety of 30 percent, and a contribution margin ratio of 40 percent.

10. The variable costs are:

    a. $840,000.
    b. $336,000.
    c. $720,000.
    d. $144,000.

11. The break-even point is:

    a. $840,000.
    b. $336,000.
    c. $720,000.
    d. $144,000.

12. The break-even point in sales for the following case is:

    Fixed expenses $336,000
    Percent of variable expense to sales 70%

    a. $ 840,000.
    b. $1,120,000.
    c. $ 820,000.
    d. $1,060,000.

13. Which of the following is *true* regarding a multiproduct situation?

    a. Break-even analysis cannot be used.
    b. The historical product mix must be used in the analysis.
    c. If product mix is expected to change, then projected product mix should be used in the analysis.
    d. The break-even point may be computed in units.

14. Assume that a company uses the high-low method in drawing the cost line for a mixed cost. The low and high points are as follows:

Volume	Cost
40,000	$16,000
200,000	$24,000

    The variable cost per unit is:

    a. $5.
    b. $0.05.
    c. $0.50.
    d. $1.

15. Assume that the company uses the high-low method in drawing the cost line for a mixed cost. What would be the amount of fixed costs for the company in question 14?

    a. $ 8,000
    b. $10,000
    c. $12,000
    d. $14,000

16. An example of a committed fixed cost is most likely to be:

    a.   depreciation on administrative office building.
    b.   employee training expense.
    c.   research and development expense.
    d.   advertising expense.

17. Selling and administrative expenses are treated as period costs:

    a.   under direct costing only.
    b.   under absorption costing only.
    c.   under both costing methods.
    d.   under neither direct costing or absorption costing.

18. Variable selling and administrative expenses are:

    a.   part of product cost under direct costing.
    b.   part of product cost under absorption costing.
    c.   part of product cost under both methods.
    d.   not part of product cost under either method.

Now compare your answers with the correct ones beginning on page 528.

Solutions/Chapter 19

Completion and Exercises

1. Fixed; variable

2. step variable

3. Mixed

4. (a) F; (b) T; (c) T; (d) T

5. A company is said to break even for a period if total revenues equal total costs for that period.

6. Sales (S) = Fixed costs (FC) + Variable costs (VC)
   $$S = \$120,000 + 0.4S$$
   $$0.6S = \$120,000$$
   $$S = \$120,000 \div 0.6$$
   $$S = \$200,000$$

   Units to be sold = $\$200,000 \div \$20$ per unit = 10,000 units

7. variable costs

8.

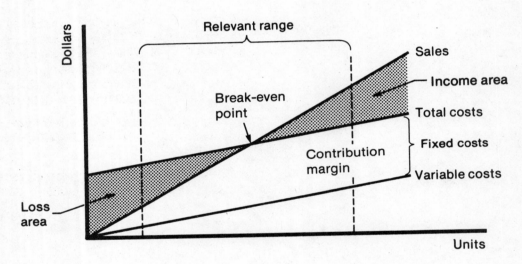

9. fixed costs

10. short-run

11. BEP in units = $\dfrac{\text{Fixed costs}}{\text{Contribution margin per unit}}$

12. Units = $\dfrac{\text{FC + Desired earnings}}{\text{Contribution margin per unit}}$

    Units = $\dfrac{\$50,000 + \$40,000}{\$20}$ = 4,500 units

13. product mix

14. scatter, mixed; fixed; variable

15. high-low

16. least-squares

17. committed; discretionary

18. Committed; discretionary

19. selling price; variable costs

20. produced; sold

21. Relevant revenues (costs)

22. absorption costing

23. direct costing

24. change

Multiple-Choice Questions

1. (c) Of the costs listed, supervisory salaries best fit the classification of a step variable cost. It is a well-known fact that an executive cannot supervise the activities of an unlimited number of employees. At some time, additional supervisory personnel will be required.

2. (b) The fixed costs are $62,000: $20,000 plus $18,000 plus $24,000 for manufacturing, selling, and administrative expenses. Variable costs are $116,000. Thus, the break-even point is determined as: $S = \$62,000 + .58S = \$147,619$.

3. (d) To demonstrate that (a), (b) and (c) are true, assume that a company has fixed costs of $40,000 and that its variable costs are equal to 50 percent of sales. Then for (a), assume that a one-time advertising program having a cost of $10,000 is planned. If sales prior to the one-time advertising program are $200,000, the net income is: $200,000 − $40,000 − $100,000 (50 percent of $200,000), or $60,000. To find the level of sales which will just cover the additional cost of the advertising, the formula is: Sales = $50,000 + .5S + $60,000. Thus, $.5S = \$110,000$ and $S = \$220,000$.

   For (b), assume sales prices are increased 10 percent with no change in volume. Variable costs then are 5/11 of sales. Net income then is: Sales of $200,000 + $20,000 (or $220,000) − $40,000 − 5/11 of sales of $220,000 (or $100,000) = $80,000.

   For (c), assume that fixed costs are decreased to $30,000 but variable costs are increased to 60 percent of sales. With sales of $200,000, net income would be $200,000 − $30,000 − $120,000, or $50,000.

4. (b) $\$1,000,000/.50 = \$2,000,000$

5. (a) $(\$1,000,000 + \$200,000)/.50 = \$2,400,000$

6. (d) Computation of amount:

$$S = FC + VC + NI$$
$$(\$150 \times 10,000) = [\$450,000 + (\$50 \times 10,000)] + NI$$
$$\$1,500,000 = \$450,000 + \$500,000 + NI$$
$$NI = \$550,000$$

7. (b) When sales equal total costs, no net income exists. This is the break-even point.

8. (b) Computation of amount:

$$BEP = \frac{\text{Fixed costs}}{\text{Contribution margin per unit}}$$

$$BEP = \frac{\$8,000}{\$22 - \$14}$$

$$BEP = \frac{\$8,000}{\$8}$$

$$BEP = 1,000 \text{ units}$$

9. (a) $100,000/\$400,000 = 25\%$

10. (c) $100\% - 40\% = 60\% \times \$1,200,000 = \$720,000$

11. (a) $100\% - 30\%$ margin of safety $= 70\%$
    $70\% \times \$1,200,000 = \$840,000$ break-even sales

12. (b) $S = \$336,000 + .70S$
        $.3S = \$336,000$
          $S = \$1,120,000$

13. (c) If historical product mix is not expected to hold in future periods, projected product mix should be used.

14. (b) The variable cost per unit is found as follows:

$$\frac{\text{Change in cost}}{\text{Change in volume}} = \frac{\$8,000}{160,000} = \$0.05 \text{ per unit}$$

15. (d) This is found as follows:

$\$16,000 = (40,000 \times .05) + FC$
$\$16,000 = \$2,000 + FC$
$\$14,000 = FC$

16. (a) The depreciation on the administrative office building is an example of a cost associated with the basic facilities which a company must have to continue operations.

17. (c) Selling and administrative expenses are treated as period costs under both direct costing and absorption costing.

18. (d) Variable selling and administrative expenses are not part of product cost under either method.

Name _____

_____

(a) _____ TUCKER COMPANY _____

(b)

(c)

(a)   CALDWELL CORPORATION

(b) _____
_____
_____
_____
_____
_____
_____
_____

(c) _____
_____
_____
_____
_____
_____
_____
_____
_____
_____
_____

Name _____

_____

(a)

(b)

(a)   WIDNER COMPANY

(b)

(c)

(d)

Name _____

_____

(e) _____

Name _____

_____

SPENCER COMPANY

(a)

PRODUCTS

	A		B		C		D		TOTAL	
	AMOUNT	%	AMOUNT	%	AMOUNT	%	AMOUNT	%	AMOUNT	%
Sales										
Less Variable Expenses										
Contribution Margin										

(b)

PRODUCTS

	A		B		C		D		TOTAL	
	AMOUNT	%	AMOUNT	%	AMOUNT	%	AMOUNT	%	AMOUNT	%
Sales										
Less Variable Expenses										
Contribution Margin										

ELLIS COMPANY

(a)

_____

_____

_____

_____

_____

_____

_____

_____

_____

_____

_____

_____

_____

_____

_____

_____

_____

_____

_____

_____

_____

_____

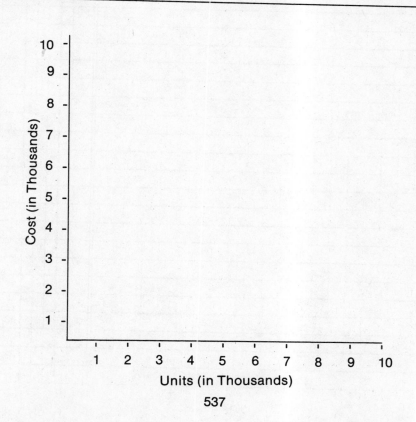

Name _____

_____

(a)

FOWLER COMPANY

Income Statement

For the Year Ended December 31, 1990

(b)

FOWLER COMPANY

Income Statement

For the Year Ended December 31, 1990

Name _____

_____

(c)

(a)   DAVIS COMPANY

(b)

(c)

(a)   MEAD COMPANY

(b)

(c)

(d)

20

Capital Budgeting: Long-Range Planning

Understanding the Learning Objections

1. Define capital budgeting and explain the effects of making poor capital budgeting decisions.

   * Capital budgeting is the process of considering alternative capital projects and selecting those alternatives that provide the most profitable return on available funds, within the framework of company goals and objectives.

   * Poor capital-budgeting decisions can have many effects, such as the following:

      They can be very costly because of the large sums of money and relatively long time periods involved.

      They can cause morale and unemployment problems.

      Alternative investment opportunities are lost once any decisions are made. This opportunity cost may be very great.

2. Determine the net cash inflows, after taxes, for both an asset addition and an asset replacement.

   * Net cash inflows are the net cash benefits expected from a project in a period. They are the difference between the periodic cash inflows and the periodic cash outflows for a proposed project.

   * The net cash inflows after tax can be found by the following formula:

$$\begin{array}{c} \text{Net cash inflow} \\ \text{after tax} \end{array} = \left[\begin{array}{c} \text{Net cash inflow} \\ \text{before tax} \end{array} \times (1 - \text{Tax rate}) \right] + \left[\begin{array}{c} \text{Depreciation} \\ \text{expense} \end{array} \times \begin{array}{c} \text{Tax} \\ \text{rate} \end{array} \right]$$

3. Evaluate projects using the payback period.

   * The payback period is the period of time it takes for the cumulative sum of the annual net cash inflows from a project to equal the initial net cash outlay.

   * The payback period answers the question: How long will it take the capital project to recover, or pay back, the initial investment?

   * The formula for the payback period is:

$$\text{Payback period} = \frac{\text{Initial cash outlay}}{\text{Annual net cash inflows (or benefits)}}$$

4. Evaluate projects using the unadjusted rate or return.

   * The unadjusted rate of return is an approximation of the rate of return on investment of a capital project.

   * The formula for the unadjusted rate of return is:

$$\text{Unadjusted rate of return} = \frac{\text{Average annual income after taxes}}{\text{Average amount of investment}}$$

   * The average investment is the original cash outlay divided by 2.

545

5. Evaluate projects using the net present value.

   * The net present value of the proposed investment is the difference between the present value of the annual net cash inflows and the present value of the required cash outflows.

   * Under the net present value method, all expected after-tax cash inflows and outflows from the proposed investment are discounted to their present values using the company's required minimum rate of return as the discount rate.

   * In general, a proposed capital investment is acceptable if it has a positive net present value.

6. Evaluate projects using the profitability index.

   * A profitability index is the ratio of the present value of the expected net cash benefits (after taxes) divided by the initial cash outlay (or present value of cash outlays if future outlays are required).

   * The profitability index method provides information by which to rank the projects in order of contribution to income or desirability under limited financial resources.

7. Evaluate projects using the time-adjusted rate of return.

   * The time-adjusted rate of return equates the present value of expected after-tax net cash inflows from an investment with the cost of the investment by finding the rate at which the net present value of the project is zero.

   * If the time-adjusted rate of return equals or exceeds the cost of capital or target rate of return, then the investment should be considered further. Similarly, if the time-adjusted rate of return is less than the minimum rate, the proposal should be rejected.

   * Present value tables can be used to approximate the time-adjusted rate of return.

   * The first step in determining the rate is to compute the payback period. Then, look at the applicable present value tables to find the present value factor that is nearest in amount to the payback period. The row looked at will be the years that the investment is expected to yield returns.

8. Determine, for project evaluation, the effect of an investment in working capital.

   * The increases in the current assets—accounts receivable and inventory—are investments in working capital that usually are recovered in full at the end of a capital project's life.

   * The net present value is recomputed to include the considerations of investing in working capital as follows:

Net cash inflows (years 1 − the useful life of the asset) × P.V. Factor	$XXXX
+ Recovery of investment in working capital × P.V. Factor	XXXX
= Present value of cash inflows	$XXXX
− Initial cash outlay	XXXX
= Net present value	$ XX

   * If the project has a positive net present value, it is acceptable. Similarly, if the project has a negative net present value, it is not acceptable.

9. Define and correctly use the new terms in the glossary.

   The new terms introduced in the chapter are as follows:

   Annuity—A series of equal cash inflows.

   Capital budgeting—Process of considering alternative capital projects and selecting those alternatives that provide the most profitable return on available funds, within the framework of company goals and objectives.

   Capital project—Any long-range endeavor to purchase, build, lease, or renovate buildings, equipment, or other major items of property.

   Cost of capital—The cost of all sources of capital (debt and equity) employed by a company.

Initial cost of an asset—Any cash outflows necessary to acquire an asset and place it in a position and condition for its intended use.

Net cash inflow—The periodic cash inflows from a project less the periodic cash outflows related to the project.

Net present value—A project selection technique that discounts all expected after-tax cash inflows and outflows from the proposed investment to their present values using the company's minimum rate of return as a discount rate. If the amount obtained by this process exceeds or equals the investment amount, the proposal is considered acceptable for further consideration.

Opportunity cost—The benefits or returns lost by rejecting the best alternative investment.

Out-of-pocket cost—A cost requiring a future outlay of resources, usually cash.

Payback period—The period of time it takes for the cumulative sum of the annual net cash inflows from a project to equal the initial net cash outlay.

Profitability index—The ratio of the present value of the expected net cash inflows (after taxes) divided by the initial cash outlay (for present value of cash outlays if future outlays are required).

Sunk cost—Costs that have already been incurred. Nothing can be done about sunk costs at the present time; they cannot be avoided or changed in amount.

Tax shield—The total amount by which taxable income is reduced due to the deductibility of an item.

Time-adjusted rate of return—A project selection technique that finds a rate of return that will equate the present value of future expected net cash inflows (after taxes) from an investment with the cost of the investment.

Unadjusted rate of return—The rate of return computed by dividing average annual income after taxes from a project by the average amount of the investment.

Completion and Exercises

1. Capital expenditures usually involve very _____ sums of money, are not as

    _____ _____ as are other expenditures, and commit a firm to a

    _____-_____ course of action.

2. The final step in the capital budgeting process is the _____ to see how well the

    implemented proposal compared to _____.

3. Match the terms in the left-hand column with their proper meanings in the right-hand column:

    a. Sunk cost
    b. Net cash benefit
    c. Cost of capital
    d. Initial cost
    e. Out-of-pocket cost

    1. The cost of all sources of capital employed by a firm.
    2. A cost which as of the present moment would require a future cash outflow.
    3. Includes any cash outflow necessary to acquire an asset and place it in a position and condition for its intended use.
    4. The annual cash inflows less the annual cash outflows from a proposal.
    5. A cost about which nothing can be done at the present time.
    6. None of the descriptions fit this term.

4. To determine the payback period the _____ cost is divided by the annual _____

    _____ benefits when these benefits are uniform from year to year.

5. Assuming the initial cost is $92,000 for a given project and the annual net cash benefits are $16,000, what is the payback period?

6. If a proposal has an initial cost of $120,000 with annual net cash benefits expected to be $24,000, $20,000, $30,000, $34,000, and $24,000, respectively, what is the payback period? (The benefits occur evenly throughout the year.)

_____

_____

_____

_____

_____

_____

_____

_____

7. The unadjusted rate of return is calculated by dividing the average increase in future annual _____ _____ from a project by the average amount of the _____ .

8. Assuming that the investment of $80,000 in a project will increase average annual earnings by $15,000 over the period of the project, what is the unadjusted rate of return? _____

9. There is a serious weakness in both the payback and unadjusted rate-of-return methods. They both ignore the _____ _____ of money.

10. A project with an initial outlay of $45,000 has expected annual benefits of $18,000, $20,000, $14,000, and $9,000 respectively. The required rate of return is 14 percent. Is this project considered acceptable for further consideration? (The present value factors at 14 percent are 0.87719, 0.76947, 0.67497, and 0.59208, respectively.)

_____

_____

_____

_____

_____

_____

_____

_____

_____

11. Under the net present value method, if the present value of the _____ exceeds the _____ _____ , the proposal is considered acceptable for further consideration.

12. Under the net present value method, the minimum required rate of return should be no lower than the _____ _____ _____ .

13. If in Question 10 the required rate of return had been 20 percent, would the project have been eligible for further consideration? (The present value factors at 20 percent are 0.83333, 0.69444, 0.57870, and 0.48225, respectively.)

_____

_____

_____

_____

_____

_____

_____

_____

_____

14. The _____ _____ is calculated by dividing the present value of the benefits by the initial cost.

15. To qualify for further consideration a project must have a profitability index greater than _____ .

16. In Question 10 what was the profitability index? [Refer to the answer to Question 10 to find the relevant data.]

17. In Question 13 what was the profitability index? [Refer to the answer to Question 13 to find the relevant data.]

18. Is it true that the proposal described in Question 10 would, on the basis of the calculation, automatically be accepted for implementation? Explain.

_____

_____

_____

_____

19. Is it true that the proposal with the characteristics as described in Question 13 would be automatically rejected in most cases? Why?

_____

_____

_____

_____

20. Under the time-adjusted rate-of-return method the required minimum rate of return is used as a _____

_____ point in accepting projects for further consideration. This method involves finding the

rate of return which will _____ the present value of future expected net cash

_____ (after tax effects) from a proposal with the _____

_____ of the investment.

21. Assume a proposal has an initial cost of $84,000 and has annual net cash benefits of $14,000 for a ten-year period. If the minimum required return is 16 percent, will the project be accepted for further consideration?

_____

_____

_____

_____

_____

_____

22. When a proposal does not have level benefits (the same each year), a _____ _____

_____ approach must be used to determine the time-adjusted rate of return.

Multiple-Choice Questions

For each of the following questions, indicate the single best answer by circling the appropriate letter.

1. Capital expenditures differ from ordinary expenditures in that they:

   a. involve small sums of money.
   b. occur frequently.
   c. involve large sums of money which are committed for a long period of time.
   d. are used to pay for daily expenses such as maintenance and repair.

2. Applying appropriate capital budgeting techniques is especially important because:

   a. capital budgeting is similar to accepting or rejecting a special order because both involve only short-run income.
   b. after a capital budgeting decision is made, the company has less flexibility with regard to plant operations.
   c. capital budgeting decisions affect only the funds originally invested, which are often significant.
   d. poor capital budgeting decisions may harm the firm's competitive position and image.
   e. (b) and (d).
   f. all of the above.

3. Indicate which of the following statement(s) concerning net cash benefits is/are true.

   a. Net cash benefit is used in capital budgeting to represent the net cash inflow expected from a project in a period.
   b. Net cash benefit is affected by the tax shield provided by depreciation.
   c. Net cash benefit represents the difference between the periodic cash inflows and the periodic cash outflows for a proposed project.
   d. (a) and (b) above.
   e. All of the above.

4. Which one of the following statements best describes the relationship between sunk costs and out-of-pocket costs in capital budgeting decisions?

   a. There is no relationship because neither costs are used in capital budgeting decisions.
   b. Sunk costs represent future commitments for funds while out-of-pocket costs represent past commitments of funds.
   c. Out-of-pocket costs differ from sunk costs because they represent a future outlay of resources while sunk costs have already been incurred.
   d. Out-of-pocket costs cannot be avoided or changed in amount while sunk costs can.
   e. Future repair and material costs associated with a capital project are typical sunk costs while depreciation on the capital project represents an out-of-pocket cost.

5. The payback period as a means of project selection:

   a. ignores the time value of money.
   b. considers the period of time that the capital project may operate after recovering its original cost.
   c. represents the period of time during which net cash benefits from an investment must continue in order to earn the desired percentage return indicated by management.
   d. represents the period of time during which net cash benefits from an investment must continue in order to earn the cost of capital percentage.

6. The payback period measures:

   a. the cash flow per year for the proposed investment.
   b. the amount of depreciation to be considered for tax purposes.
   c. how quickly the dollars invested in the capital project will be recovered.
   d. the economic life of the investment.

7. When using the net present value method of analysis for capital projects, which one of the following is not important?

   a. Required rate of return indicated by management
   b. The method of financing the project—whether notes or bonds
   c. Firm's cost of capital
   d. Timing of the cash flow
   e. Amount of the cash flows per year

Questions No. 8-9.
Milker Company is evaluating a project requiring a capital expenditure of $160,000. The project has an estimated life of 4 years and no salvage value. The estimated net income and net cash flow from the project are as follows:

Year	After-tax Net Income	Net Cash Flow
1	$ 32,000	$ 48,000
2	22,000	56,000
3	42,000	60,000
4	50,000	60,000
	$146,000	$224,000

The company's minimum desired rate of return for discounted cash flow analysis is 10 percent. The present value of 1 at compound interest of 10 percent for 1, 2, 3, and 4 years is .90909, .82645, .75131, and .68301 respectively. The present value of an ordinary annuity for 4 years at 10 percent is 3.16987.

8. What is net present value of the project?

   a. $175,977
   b. $160,000
   c. $224,000
   d. $ 15,977
   e.   None of these

9. What is the unadjusted rate of return on the investment?

   a.   22.81%
   b.   48.75%
   c.   24.38%
   d.   45.625%
   e.   None of these

10. The Randall Investment Company is considering the possibility of investing $250,000 in a special project. This venture will return $62,500 per year for five years in cash. Depreciation on the project is $50,000 per year using straight-line depreciation. The payback period is:

   a.   6 years.
   b.   5 years.
   c.   2 years.
   d.   4 years.
   e.   none of those listed.

Questions 11-13.
A company is considering the addition of a new product to its line. Production of the product will make use of factory space not presently in use and will require the purchase of new machinery costing $180,000, having a 12 year life, and no salvage value. The following additional information is available:

Estimated annual sales of the new product.....................	$165,000
Estimated costs:	
Materials	51,000
Direct labor	35,000
Overhead including depreciation on the new machinery	22,500
Selling and Administrative expenses.........................	14,500
State and federal income taxes...............................	40%

11. The annual depreciation is:

    a. $60,000.
    b. $70,000.
    c. $15,000.
    d. none of these.

12. The payback period on the investment in the new machine is:

    a. 6 years.
    b. 4.5 years.
    c. 2.5 years.
    d. 5.5 years.

13. The unadjusted rate of return is:

    a. 28 percent.
    b. 21.5 percent.
    c. 14 percent.
    d. 25.8 percent.

14. The present value of 1 due in four years at 10 percent is .68301 and the present value of an annuity of 1 at 10 percent for four years is 3.16987. The Namath Company is considering a capital project that will involve a $40,000 investment in equipment and a $25,000 investment in working capital. The project will have a life of four years and will provide an annual net cash inflow (after taxes) of $15,000. The $25,000 investment in working capital will be recovered at the end of four years. The Namath Company's cost of capital is 10 percent. The net present value of the proposed project is:

    a. $(24,625).
    b. $(7,175).
    c. $(377).
    d. $ 7,550.

15. A company is considering purchasing a new machine to be used for making motors. It is expected that the machine will have a useful life of at least 10 years and it will greatly reduce material and labor costs. The company's cost of capital is about 15 percent and it desires some analysis of cost-benefit relationships. The most relevant quantitative technique for evaluating the investment is:

    a. payback period analysis.
    b. net present value analysis.
    c. cost-volume-profit analysis.
    d. unadjusted rate of return.
    e. none of the above.

Questions 16-17.

A company is considering the addition of a new product to its line. It estimates it can sell 25,000 units of the product annually at $4.80 per unit; but to manufacture the units will require new machinery having an estimated ten-year life, no salvage value, and costing $50,000. This additional information is also available: (a) material cost per unit of product, $1.50; (b) direct labor cost per unit, $0.70; (c) annual manufacturing overhead other than depreciation on the new machinery, $18,000; (d) selling and administrative expenses per unit, $0.80; and (d) assume the income tax rate is 50 percent for federal and state taxes.

16. The payback period on the investment in new machinery is:

a.   3.1 years.
b.   4.5 years.
c.   7.5 years.
d.   5.0 years.
e.   10 years.

17. The unadjusted rate of return on the new machinery is:

a. $25,000.
b. $22,000.
c.   22 percent.
d.   44 percent.
e.   both (b) and (c) are correct above.

Now compare your answers with the correct ones beginning on page 555.

Solutions/Chapter 20

Completion and Exercises

1. large; regularly recurring; long-term

2. postaudit; expectations

3. (a) 5; (b) 4; (c) 1; (d) 3; (e) 2

4. initial; net cash

5. $\dfrac{\$92,000}{\$16,000} = 5.75$ years

6. $24,000 + $20,000 + $30,000 + $34,000 = $108,000. Since the flow in the next year is $24,000 and only $12,000 more is needed to equal the initial cost (of $120,000), the payback period is 4.5 years. This means that halfway through the fifth year the cumulative benefits would equal the initial cost.

7. earnings; investment

8. $\dfrac{\$15,000}{\$80,000 \times 0.50} = \dfrac{\$15,000}{\$40,000} = 37.5$ percent

   The average amount of the investment is the gross investment divided by 2.

9. time value

10.

Year	Annual benefit	Present value factor	Present value
1	$18,000	0.87719	$15,789
2	20,000	0.76947	15,389
3	14,000	0.67497	9,450
4	9,000	0.59208	5,329
Total			$45,957

Yes, since the present value of the benefits ($45,957) exceeds the initial outlay ($45,000), the project is eligible for further consideration.

11. benefits; initial cost

12. cost of capital

13.

Year	Annual benefit	Present value factor	Present value
1	$18,000	0.83333	$15,000
2	20,000	0.69444	13,889
3	14,000	0.57870	8,102
4	9,000	0.48225	4,340
Total			$41,331

No. The higher required rate of return reduces the present value of the benefits below the initial outlay.

14. profitability index

15. 1.00

16. $\dfrac{\$45,957}{\$45,000} = 1.02$

17. $\dfrac{\$41,331}{\$45,000} = 0.92$

18. No. Further analysis would be necessary. Nonquantitative factors (such as the impact on the environment) would be considered. Also, there may be a computing project with even a higher profitability index.

19. Yes. It does not meet the required rate of return. (Of course, one can envision a circumstance in which very desirable nonquantifiable factors associated with the project would change this, but these situations are likely to be very rare.)

20. cutoff; equate; benefits; initial cost

21. To find the approximate rate of return, first calculate the payback period: $84,000/$14,000 = 6 years. Then look in Table III in Appendix C of the text and look along the 10 periods row and find the factor closest to 6. Notice that it is in the 10.5 percent column (6.01477). Also notice that the factor in the 11 percent column is 5.88923. This means that the rate of return of this project is between 10.5 and 11 percent. Thus the project would not be considered further since it does not meet the required return of 16 percent.

22. trial and error

Multiple-Choice Questions

1. c. Capital expenditures differ from ordinary expenditures in that they do not occur as often as ordinary expenditures and involve substantial sums of money which are committed for a long period of time.

2. e. Capital budgeting is a long-run decision because it affects not only day-to-day operations, but also future years.

3. e. All of the statements are true.

4. c. Out-of-pocket costs are relevant to capital budgeting decisions because they can be changed in the future while sunk costs cannot.

5. a. The payback period is the period of time during which net cash benefits from an investment must continue in order to recover the initial cost of the project. The time value of money, cost of capital, and percentage return desired by management are ignored.

6. c. The payback period is the time it takes to recover the initial investment.

7. b. Notes and bonds both involve interest expense which is deductible for tax purposes. It does not matter whether the interest resulted from notes or bonds.

8. d.

Year	Present Value	Net Cash Flow	Present Value of Net Cash Flow
1	.90909	$ 48,000	$ 43,636
2	.82645	56,000	46,281
3	.75131	60,000	45,079
4	.68301	60,000	40,981
		$224,000	$175,977
Investment—original			160,000
Excess present value			$ 15,977

9. d. $146,000/4 years = $36,500 average income
$160,000/2 = $80,000 average investment
$36,500/$80,000 = 45.625%

10. d. $250,000/$62,500 cash flow yearly = 4 years payback period

11-13. Solution material:

Sales		$165,000
Estimated expenses:		
Materials	$51,000	
Direct labor	35,000	
Overhead including depreciation on machinery	22,500	
Selling and administrative expenses	14,500	123,000
Income before state and federal income taxes		$ 42,000
State and federal income taxes (40% × $42,000) ..		16,800
Net income		$ 25,200

11. c. $180,000/12 years = $15,000 depreciation

12. b. $180,000/$40,200 = 4.5 years payback period. (The $40,200 is equal to $25,200 net income + $15,000 depreciation.)

13. a. $180,000/2 = $90,000 average investment
$25,200/$90,000 = 28% return

14. c. The net present value is $(377) computed below:

$15,000 (3.16987) = ...	$47,548
$25,000 (.68301) = ...	17,075
Present value of net cash inflows	$64,623
Initial cash outlay	65,000
Net present value	$ (377)

15. b. Net present value analysis takes into account the time value of money; the other methods listed do not.

16. a.

Sales ($4.80 × 25,000 units)..		$120,000
Estimated costs:		
Direct materials ($1.50 × 25,000 units)	$37,500	
Direct labor ($.70 × 25,000 units)	17,500	
Manufacturing overhead other than depreciation	18,000	
Selling and administrative expenses ($.80 × 25,000 units)	20,000	
Machinery depreciation ($50,000/10 years)	5,000	98,000
Income before income taxes		$ 22,000
State and federal income taxes..		11,000
Net income		$ 11,000

Payback period: $50,000/$16,000 = 3.1 years. (The $16,000 is equal to $11,000 + $5,000.)

17. d. $11,000/$25,000 average investment = 44% return

(a)   COURTNEY COMPANY

		TO COMPUTE INCOME	TO COMPUTE CASH FLOW

(b)

Name _____

_____

ABILENE COMPANY

		TO COMPUTE	
		TAX	CASH FLOWS

(a)   ALMA MANUFACTURING COMPANY

	PER UNIT		PER YEAR	
	OLD MACHINES	NEW MACHINES	OLD MACHINES	NEW MACHINES

(b)

(c)

Name _____

_____

(a)   COLUMBIA CANNING COMPANY

(b)

(c)

(d)

COUGAR COMPANY

(a) Unadjusted rate of return:

	(a)	(b)	(c)	(b) − (c) = (d)	(d/a)
		Average		Average	
	Average	Annual Net	Average	Annual	Rate of
Proposal	Investment	Cash Inflow	Depreciation*	Income	Return
1					
2					
3					

(b) Payback period:

	(a)	(b)	(a/b)
		Annual	Payback
Proposal	Investment	Cash Flow	Period
1			
2			
3			

(c) Time-adjusted rate of return:

Proposal	Rate
1	
2	
3	

(d) Profitability index:

	(a)	(b)	a × b = (c)	(d)	(c/d)
			Present		
		Present	Value of		
	Annual	Value	Annual		
	Net Cash	Factor	Net Cash	Initial	Profitability
Proposal	Inflow	at 12%	Inflow	Outlay	Index
1					
2					
3					

Name _____

SCOTTSDALE COMPANY

PRESCOTT SPORTS COMPANY

Name _____

WOODRUFF COMPANY

	CASH FLOW BEFORE TAX	CASH FLOW AFTER TAX	PRESENT VALUE FACTOR	PRESENT VALUE

Name _____

HOLLAND COMPANY

Proceeds if sold:					
Returns if not sold:					

RICE COMPANY

(a) Invest- ment	(a) Expected After-tax Net Cash Inflow per Year	(b) Present Value Factor at 15%	a × b = (c) Present Value of Annual Net Cash Inflow	(d) Initial Outlay	(c/d) Net Present Value

(b)

TRAPP COMPANY

(a)

(b)

Name_____

SMITH COMPANY

21

Personal and Corporate Income Taxes

Understanding the Learning Objectives

1. Compute gross income, adjusted gross income, and taxable income for personal tax returns.

    *   Gross income includes wages, interest (but not interest earned on an IRA), dividends, tips, bonuses, gambling winnings, gains from property sales, and prizes (including noncash prizes).

    *   Adjusted gross income involves certain items that taxpayers may deduct from gross income in arriving at the adjusted gross income.

    *   Taxpayers may take additional deductions, such as standard and personal deductions and exemptions, to arrive at their taxable income. Personal deductions must exceed the standard deduction and include such items as taxes, interest, charitable contributions, medical expenses, and personal casualty losses.

2. Compute the tax liability on personal returns.

    *   Though marginal tax rates are applied to the taxable income to determine the tax liability, the effective rate should be used as a measure of total taxes to be paid.

    *   Certain capital gains and losses and tax credits may be applied to this tax liability. The tax liability must be paid by April 15 of the year following a calendar year.

3. Compute the tax liability for corporations.

    *   Taxable income is computed by subtracting all allowable deductions from the corporation's gross income. Once taxable income is determined, a tax rate is applied to find the amount of tax liability.

4. Illustrate the use of tax loss carrybacks and carryforwards.

    *   If a corporation suffers a net loss in a given year, the tax law provides that the corporation can apply this loss to its taxable income from prior years and recover some or all of the taxes paid during those years up to three years. The corporation may then carry the remaining, unused loss forward for up to 15 years to reduce its taxable income in those future years.

5. Calculate the depreciation allowance for tax purposes using modified ACRS (Modified Accelerated Cost Recovery System).

    *   Capital assets are grouped into one of eight different classes. Each class has an assigned life over which the costs of the assets (not reduced by salvage) are depreciated.

    *   Once the asset has been classified, the depreciation schedule for the life of the asset can be completed.

6. Identify the nature of permanent and temporary differences between taxable income and accounting pre-tax income.

    *   The tax treatment for some items is completely different from the accounting treatment and never change or reverse themselves, resulting in permanent differences.

    *   A temporary difference is the difference between taxable income and financial statement income caused by items that affect both taxable income and pre-tax income, but in different periods.

7. Account for temporary differences using interperiod allocation.

   * Normally a credit balance will develop in the Deferred Income Tax account at first and then later be eliminated.

8. Define and use correctly the new terms in the glossary.

   The new terms introduced in the chapter are as follows:

   Adjusted gross income—Gross income less deductions for adjusted gross income such as business expenses, certain payments to an individual retirement account (IRA), and certain other deductions.

   Capital assets—All items of property other than inventories, trade accounts and notes receivable, copyrights, government obligations due within one year and issued at a discount, and real or depreciable property used in a trade or business. Examples include investments in capital stocks and bonds.

   Deductions for adjusted gross income—Expenses of carrying on a trade, business, or practice of a profession, certain payments to an IRA or Keogh plan, and alimony paid.

   Deductions from adjusted gross income—Specified by law; either standard deduction amount or itemized deductions.

   Effective tax rate—Average rate of taxation for a given amount of taxable income.

   Estimated tax—A tax that must be paid in four installments by persons having amounts of income above a certain level that are not subject to withholding.

   Exemptions—A fixed amount, $1,950 in 1988 and $2,000 in 1989 due to indexing, that a taxpayer may deduct from adjusted gross income for the taxpayer, the spouse, and one more for each dependent.

   Gross income—All items of income from whatever source derived, except for those items specifically excluded by law.

   Head of household—Certain unmarried or legally separated persons who maintain a residence for a relative or dependent.

   Interperiod income tax allocation—A procedure whereby the tax effects of an element of expense, revenue, loss or gain, that will affect taxable income is allocated to the period in which the item is recognized for accounting purposes, regardless of the period in which the element is recognized for tax purposes.

   Itemized deductions—Deductions from adjusted gross income for items such as contributions, mortgage interest paid, taxes, casualty losses, limited medical expenses, and other employment related expenses.

   Marginal tax rate—The tax rate that will be levied against the next dollar of taxable income.

   Modified ACRS—A tax method of depreciation that assigns assets into particular groups that have specified lives for depreciation purposes. The 1986 Tax Reform Act modified the Accelerated Cost Recovery System.

   Permanent differences—Differences between taxable income and financial statement pre-tax income caused by tax law provisions that exclude an item of expense, revenue, gain, or loss as an element of taxable income.

   Standard deduction amount—An amount that can be taken in lieu of all itemized deductions. For 1988 the amount is $3,000 for single persons, $4,400 for heads of households, and $5,000 for married persons filing joint returns. An additional $750 (or $600 if married) is allowed for each individual over 65 or blind.

   Tax credit—A direct reduction from the amount of taxes to be paid, resulting largely from certain expenditures made.

   Tax loss carryback—Provision in tax law permitting corporation to apply a loss to their taxable income from three prior years and recover some or all of the taxes paid during those years.

Tax loss carryforward—Provision in tax law permitting corporations to carry any remaining, unused loss forward for up to 15 years to reduce their taxable income in future years.

Taxable income—Adjusted gross income less deductions and exemptions.

Temporary (or timing) differences—Differences between taxable income and financial statement pre-tax income caused by items that affect both taxable income and pre-tax income, but in different periods.

Total (gross) income—See Gross income.

Completion and Exercises

1. Determine the amount of tax due for a married couple filing a joint return if taxable income is $65,000, using Illustration 21.2 in the text.

2. The following data are for Sally Jones, who is single.

   Salary earned, $20,000; interest income, $2,000; long-term capital gain, $1,250; contribution to an IRA, $1,000; itemized deductions, $2,475; income taxes withheld, $4,800.

   a. What is her taxable income?

   b. Using Illustration 21.2 in the text, determine the amount of taxes due or the overpayment of taxes.

3. Net income and taxable income _____ _____ (must agree/may differ).

4. Corporate income is taxed to the _____ , and dividend distributions are taxed to the _____ .

5. Interest on municipal bonds is an example of a _____ difference between net income before taxes and taxable income.

6. Different depreciation methods for accounting and for tax purposes result in _____ differences.

7. Income tax allocation procedures must be used for _____ differences but not for _____ differences.

8. Under income tax allocation procedures any difference between the amount shown on the income statement as income tax expense and the actual amount payable is debited or credited to a _____ _____ _____ _____ _____ account.

9. Taxable income for an individual taxpayer is determined as follows (fill in the blanks):

Total (gross) income
|
less
↓

a. _____

|
equals
↓

b. _____

|
less
↓

c. _____

|
less
↓

d. _____

|
equals
Taxable income

10. Certain direct credits may be taken (deducted directly from tax due) for the following:

a. _____

b. _____

c. _____

d. _____

574

11. Allowable itemized duductions may be taken for the following items:

    a. _____

    b. _____

    c. _____

    d. _____

    e. _____

    f. _____

12. An exemption can be claimed for each of the following:

    a. _____

    b. _____

    c. _____

13. A person claimed as a dependent must have less than _____ gross income during the year unless
    he/she is under _____ years of age or a full-time _____ . The person must also, in
    most cases, receive more than _____ _____ of support from the taxpayer to
    qualify as a dependent.

14. Taxpayer, husband and wife, with three dependent children, have adjusted gross income of $36,000 for
    1988. They file a joint return. Payments for medicines totaled $390 and for other unreimbursed medical
    expenses totaled $1,492. Determine the amount of their allowable deductions for medical expense.

15. A pre-tax income of the Arriva Corporation for a given year amounts to $400,000; while its taxable income
    is only $320,000. If the current income tax rate is 40 percent, give the entry to record the income taxes
    chargeable to the year and the tax liability for the year.

DATE	ACCOUNT TITLES AND EXPLANATION	POST. REF.	DEBIT	CREDIT

16. _____ _____ is a tax paid in four installments by persons having income above a certain level that is not subject to _____.

17. A(n) _____ _____ (tax credit/itemized deduction) is generally of greater value to taxpayer than a(n) _____ _____ (tax credit/itemized deduction).

Multiple-Choice questions

For each of the following questions, indicate the single best answer by circling the appropriate letter.

1. Which of the following are required to file an income tax return?

      1.   College student, 20 years old supported by father; gross income of $5,000.
      2.   Child, 14 years old; gross income of $6,100 from investments.
      3.   Unmarried man, 70 years old, gross income of $1,100.
      4.   Married man, 45 years old; gross income of $15,000.
      5.   Wife of the man in (4) 40 years old; gross income of $300.

   a.   1, 2, 4, 5 are required to file an income tax return.
   b.   1, 2, 4 are required to file an income tax return.
   c.   1, 2, 3, 4 are required to file an income tax return.
   d.   2, 4, 5 are required to file an income tax return.
   e.   All are required to file an income tax return.

2. Which of the following is true regarding loss carrybacks and carryforwards?

   a.   A company can carry losses back 5 years and forward 15 years.
   b.   A company can carry losses back 3 years by applying the loss to the newest year first, then the next newest, and finally to the third year or oldest year.
   c.   If the loss carryforward is not used up by the end of the 15th year, the remaining portion may be carried forward at 1/2 rate for 5 additional years.
   d.   A company has the option of carrying the loss back 3 years and forward 15 years or carrying the loss forward only.
   e.   None of the above statements is true.

3. Itemized deductions should be used only if they exceed a specified amount called the standard deduction. The standard deductions in 1988 are:

   a. $1,950 for each exemption claimed.
   b. $3,400 for each taxpayer.
   c. $3,000 for single persons, $5,000 for joint returns, and $2,500 for married persons filing separately.
   d. $3,000 for each taxpayer.
   e. $4,950 for single and head of household returns and $8,900 for joint returns.

4. The following could account for the fact that net income on the income statement and taxable income may differ.

   a.   Interest on state and municipal bonds is excluded in the computation of taxable income.
   b.   Cash received for magazines and newspapers to be supplied next year by a cash-basis taxpayer. Revenue is recognized for financial accounting purposes according to generally accepted accounting principles.
   c.   Use of different depreciation methods for accounting and tax purposes
   d.   a and c only
   e.   All of the above

5. The income before income tax for the year as reported on the income statement is $200,000. The taxable income for the same year is $150,000. Assuming an income tax rate of 50 percent, what is the amount of the deferred income tax liability?

   a. $200,000
   b. $25,000
   c. $50,000
   d. $75,000

6. If a married taxpayer who is 65 years of age and blind files a tax return, how many exemptions is he entitled to assuming his wife is 63 years old?

   a. 1
   b. 2
   c. 3
   d. 4
   e. 5

7. The adjusted gross income of a sole proprietorship for the year was $10,000. The owner withdrew $3,000 out of this income. The owner had invested an additional $5,000 at the beginning of this fiscal year. What amount of income from the business enterprise must the owner report in his income tax return?

   a. $3,000
   b. $2,000
   c. $7,000
   d. $10,000
   e. $8,000

8. A taxpayer is entitled to an exemption for a person as long as which of the following are satisfied?

   a. Closely related to the taxpayer or lived as a member of the taxpayer's family for the entire year
   b. Received more than half of his/her support from the taxpayer and if married does not file a joint return with a spouse for the taxable year
   c. Has an income of less than $1,950 unless he/she is under 19 or enrolled as a full-time student
   d. a and b
   e. All of the above

The following applies to questions 9-10

Mr. X is married, with dependent son and daughter. How much do each of the following items add to his adjusted gross income?

9. Cash bequest provided by his uncle's will, $2,000, and money borrowed from bank to help finance son's education, $1,500.

   a. $2,000
   b. $1,500
   c. $3,500
   d. 0
   e. None of these

10. Withdrawals from X and Y, a partnership, of $10,000. Mr X's distributive share of the net income amounted to $19,500. His partner withdrew $13,000 and his partner's share of net income amounted to $20,000.

   a. $10,000
   b. $19,500
   c. $9,500
   d. $23,000
   e. None of these

11. Mary Douglas is subject to an income tax on the income reported for her business. After an audit of her records, an internal revenue agent reports that she owes an *additional* amount of tax. Which of the following errors would reasonably account for the underpayment of the tax?

   a. Recording unearned revenue in a revenue account by mistake.
   b. A failure to record depreciation of the period.
   c. An understatement of the inventory of supplies on hand at the end of the period.
   d. A failure to record an accrued expense at the end of the period.

12. Identify the following items as includible or excludible by an individual in determining his or her taxable income.

   1. Interest on municipal bonds
   2. Cash received from a friend in repayment of a non-interest-bearing loan
   3. Dividends on stock
   4. Wages received for labor
   5. Scholarship received from a university by a freshman for which no services are required

   a. 1, 4, 5 are includible
   b. 1, 2, 5 are includible
   c. 3, 4, 5 are includible
   d. All 5 items are includible
   e. 3, 4 are includible

13. Which of the following items are included in determining a taxpayer's gross income?

   1. Dividends on Coca-Cola stock
   2. A tax credit for child care expenses
   3. Interest on a home mortgage
   4. $100 from Uncle Joe as a birthday present
   5. $100 won in a Friday night poker game

   a. All 5 are includible
   b. 1, 2, 3, 5 are includible
   c. 1, 5 are includible
   d. 1, 2, 3 are includible
   e. 1, 3, 4 are includible

14. The last deductions taken in computing taxable income are:

   a. deductions from gross income.
   b. exemptions.
   c. standard deduction.
   d. itemized deductions

Now compare your answers with the correct ones beginning on page 579.

Solutions/Chapter 21

Completion and Exercises

1. Tax due = ($29,750 × .15) + ($35,250 × .28)
   = $ 4,462.50 + $9,870
   = $14,332.50

2. a.

Salary		$20,000
Interest income		2,000
Capital gain		1,250
		$23,250
Contribution to an IRA		1,000
Adjusted gross income		$22,250
Itemized deductions	$2,475	
Standard deduction	3,000	
Higher of itemized or standard deduction	$3,000	
Exemption	1,950	4,950
Taxable income		$17,300

   b.

Income taxes	$ 2,595
Less: Taxes withheld	4,800
Tax overpayment	$ 2,205

3. may differ

4. corporation; stockholders

5. permanent

6. temporary

7. temporary; permanent

8. Deferred Federal Income Taxes Payable

9. (a) Deductions for adjusted gross income; (b) Adjusted gross income; (c) Itemized deductions or standard deduction; (d) Exemptions.

10. (a) child and dependent care expenses; (b) low income levels; (c) the elderly; (d) income taxes paid to foreign countries.

11. (a) charitable contributions; (b) mortgage interest paid; (c) certain taxes; (d) casualty and theft losses adjusted for the excess of $100 for each occurrence and the sum total of all adjusted casualty losses exceeding 10 percent of adjusted gross income, (e) limited medical expenses; (f) certain "nonbusiness" expenses.

12. (a) one for the taxpayer; (b) one for the spouse; (c) one more for each dependent.

13. $1,950; 19; student; one half

14.

Medicines	$ 390	
Other medical	1,492	
Total medical		$1,882
Less 7.5% × $36,000		2,700
Amount deductible		$ -0-

15. Federal Income Tax Expense 160,000
      Federal Income Taxes Payable 128,000
      Deferred Federal Income Taxes Payable 32,000
  To record income tax expense.

16. Estimated tax; withholding

17. Tax credit; itemized deduction

Multiple-Choice Questions

1. d.

2. d. If the company chooses to carry the loss back, the company must apply the loss to the oldest year first, then the next oldest year, and so on. At the end of the 15th year, the remaining portion of any loss carryforward is lost.

3. c.

4. e.

5. b. $200,000 − $150,000 = $50,000 difference × 50% = $25,000

6. b. One for husband and one for wife

7. d.

8. e.

9. d. Neither of these items is includible; inheritances are specifically excluded and loans are not income.

10. b.

11. c.

12. e. Interest on municipal bonds and scholarships received are excludible along with repayment of loan from a friend.

13. c.

14. b.

JUNE REDDY

ARTHUR ROSS

JILL AND ERNEST YOUNG

Name_____

(a)

BONANZA CORPORATION
Computation of Taxable Income and Income Taxes
For the Year Ended December 31, 1988

(b)

Name_____

BUCK AND JANE ROGERS
Computation of Taxable Income and Income Taxes
For the Year Ended December 31, 1988

(a)

PARADE COMPANY

Computation of Taxable Income and Income Taxes

For the Year Ended December 31, 1988

(b)

Name_____

ALLEN COMPANY
Taxable Income

(a)

Year	at 15%	at 25%	Total

(b)

Year	Taxable Income	Offset by Loss Carryforward*	Taxed Income	Tax

(c)

Year	Taxable Income	Offset by Loss Carryforward*	Taxed Income	Tax

(d)

Name

CLEO CORPORATION

(a)	1988	1989	1990	1991	TOTAL

(b)			TOTAL FOR EACH YEAR	TOTAL FOR FOUR YEARS

CLEO CORPORATION
GENERAL JOURNAL

(c)

DATE	ACCOUNT TITLES AND EXPLANATION	POST. REF.	DEBIT	CREDIT
1988				
1989				
1990				
1991				

HARRIS COMPANY
Taxable Income

(a)

Year	at 15%	at 25%	Total

(b)

Year	Taxable Income	Offset by Loss Carryforward*	Taxed Income	Tax

(c)

Year	Taxable Income	Offset by Loss Carryforward*	Taxed Income	Tax

(d)

CROSS ENTERPRISES

	YEAR ONE	YEAR TWO	YEAR THREE	YEAR FOUR
Cash flow before income taxes (a)				
Present Value of Net Cash Flows at 18 percent:				

Appendix A

Inflation Accounting

Understanding the Learning Objectives

1. Describe how inflation affects information presented in conventional financial statements.

   * Until recently, no attempt was made to report the effects of inflation on the financial statements.

   * Failure to adjust for the impact of inflation may lead to conclusions that are not valid.

2. Apply the two basic approaches to income statement adjustment under inflationary conditions.

   * The two approaches are current cost accounting and constant dollar accounting.

   * Current cost accounting measures net income from continuing operations by deducting the current cost of replacing the goods sold and the other expenses from current revenues.

   * Constant dollar accounting measures net income from continuing operations by restating all items on the income statement into dollars expressed in comparable terms—end-of-year dollars. A price level index is used.

3. Discuss the FASB requirements regarding inflation accounting.

   * In 1979 the FASB issued *FASB Statement No. 33*, which required certain companies to report both current cost information and constant dollar information in supplemental financial statements.

   In 1984 the FASB issued *FASB Statement No. 82*, which required that only current cost information be reported in supplemental financial statements.

   * In 1987, *FASB Statement No. 89* was issued, which *encourages* but does not require companies to disclose the effects of inflation in supplementary financial statements.

4. Define and use correctly the new terms in the glossary.

   The new terms introduced in the appendix are as follows:

   Constant dollar accounting—A recommended approach :   ..l with the problem of accounting for inflation by changing the unit of measure from the actual histo: .. ,.ominal) dollar to a dollar of constant purchasing power.

   Current cost—The amount that would have to be paid currently to acquire an asset.

   Current cost accounting—A recommended approach to deal with the problem of accounting for inflation by showing current cost or value of items in the financial statements.

   Deflation (period of)—Exists when prices in general are falling.

   Historical cost—The amount paid, or the fair value of a liability incurred or other resource surrendered, to acquire an asset.

   Historical cost accounting—Conventional accounting in which accounting measurements are in terms of the actual dollars expended or received.

   Inflation (period of)—Exists when prices in general are rising.

Monetary items—Cash and other assets and liabilities that represent fixed claims to cash, such as accounts and notes receivable and payable.

Nonmonetary items—All items on the balance sheet other than monetary items; examples are inventories, plant assets, capital stock, and owner's equity.

Price index—A weighted average of prices for various goods and services. A base year is chosen and assigned a value of 100 for comparative purposes.

Purchasing power gain—The gain that results from holding monetary liabilities during inflation or monetary assets during deflation.

Purchasing power loss—The loss that results from holding monetary assets during inflation or monetary liabilities during deflation.

Completion and Exercises

1. In preparing a constant dollar balance sheet, the restated amount for retained earnings is derived _____ _____ .

   In converting sales and other operating expenses and taxes (excluding depreciation), these items are multiplied by a ratio of the _____ index over the _____ index for the year. Inventory and depreciation are restated by means of a ratio of the _____ index over the index at _____ . (Assume restatement into end-of-current-year dollars.)

2. Assume that you held cash of $50,000 and accounts payable of $20,000 during a period in which the general price index increased 2 percent. You would have an inflation gain or loss (state which) of $_____ for the period. If, at the end of the period you had cash of $60,100 and accounts payable of $20,000, you would have an inflation gain or loss (state which) of $_____ .

3. If cost of goods sold at historical cost is $312,000 and the price index rose from 104 when the goods were acquired to 110 at the end of the period in which they were sold, the converted cost of goods sold is $_____ .

4. With regard to the impact of inflation upon financial statements, *FASB Statement No. 33* required certain large companies to disclose income from continuing operations on both a _____ _____ and a _____ _____ basis. These companies also were required to disclose _____ gains and losses on net monetary items. Also required was a _____-_____ _____ of selected financial data such as sales, net assets, and dividends per share.

5. The requirements referred to in Question 4 also called for the disclosure of the increases or decreases in the _____ _____ for the current fiscal year of inventory and property, plant, and equipment, net of the effects of _____ _____ .

6. If you purchased a product for $100, sold it for $115 after a period in which the general level of prices rose 20 percent, you would have actually experienced a _____ of $_____ . In this situation, it can be argued that you have not recovered your _____ , therefore _____ do not exist.

7. Vance Company's plant assets at December 31, 1990, had a historical cost of $150,000 and accumulated depreciation of $50,000 (15 percent annual depreciation rate). There were no additions or retirements in 1990. The current cost of the plant assets on December 31, 1990, was $175,000 and on December 31, 1991, was $190,000. Compute the current cost depreciation for 1991.

8. In each of the situations given, determine the amount of purchasing power gain or loss.

   a.   You hold cash of $45,000 during a year in which prices in general rose 20 percent.
   b.   You hold cash of $30,000 during a year in which prices in general dropped 5 percent.
   c.   You are in debt $20,000 during a year in which prices in general rose 9 percent.

   _____

   _____

   _____

   _____

   _____

   _____

   _____

   _____

Multiple-Choice Questions

1. Roberts Corporation purchased merchandise for $5,000 when an index of the general level of prices stood at 110. It sold these goods some time later when their replacement cost was $5,700 and the index of the general level of prices was 121 and received $6,000 cash. The increase in specific prices was:

   a. $1,000.
   b. $ 700.
   c. $ 300.
   d. $ -0-.

2. In adjusting a set of conventional financial statements for the effects of the general price level change, a purchasing power gain or loss will be recognized only from the existence of which one of the following?

   a.   Bonds payable
   b.   Capital stock
   c.   Retained earnings
   d.   Merchandise inventory

3. Assume an index of the general level of prices rose gradually through the year 1990 from 120 to 140. In adjusting the conventional income statement for 1990 into constant end-of-1990 dollars, a company's wages expense would be converted through use of a conversion ratio of:

   a.   140/130.
   b.   120/140.
   c.   130/120.
   d.   120/130.

4. In adjusting conventional financial statements for the effects of the general price level change, the presence of which of the following in a period of inflation gives rise to a purchasing power loss?

   a. Cash
   b. Prepaid expense
   c. Bonds payable
   d. Retained earnings

5. B Company was organized on January 1, 1990. It issued stock for $80,000 cash and borrowed $20,000 on a long-term note (which to simplify the problem is assumed to be noninterest-bearing). The $100,000 was then paid for a tract of land. There were no further transactions in 1990. An index of the general level of prices rose from 100 to 105 during the year, and the land was worth $115,000 at year-end. The December 31, 1990, balance sheet when adjusted into end-of-1990 constant dollars would show:

   a. Land at $115,000 and Notes Payable at $21,000.
   b. Land at $105,000 and Notes Payable at $20,000.
   c. Land at $105,000 and Notes Payable at $21,000.
   d. Land at $115,000 and Notes Payable at $20,000.

6. Which of the following is true assuming that the base year index is 100?

   a. When the index is 103, the dollar has more purchasing power than it did in the base year.
   b. When the index is 50, the value of the dollar has dropped to one-half of the base year dollar.
   c. When the index is 300, a current dollar would have purchased $2.67 worth of goods in the base year.
   d. If the index rose 15 percent, then the value of the dollar fell to approximately 87¢.

7. Which of the following terms represents the concept of accounting which had to be used in the primary financial statements according to *FASB Statement No. 33?*

   a. General price-level accounting
   b. Historical cost accounting
   c. Constant dollar accounting
   d. Current cost accounting

8. The Great Southeast Weaving Company purchased 50 acres of property in 1985 for $1,500 an acre. Plans for building a new plant on the property did not materialize and in 1990 the company sold the land for $4,000 an acre. The general price level index stood at 78 when the property was acquired but stood at 156 at the time of sale. What was the real gain in terms of 1990 dollars?

   a. $ 50,000
   b. $125,000
   c. $ 25,000
   d. $ 75,000

9. On September 1, 1990, when the price level stood at 110, Madison Furriers, Ltd., opened for business with an inventory recorded on the books at $250,000. Even though furs retailed for 300 percent of cost, business was booming and three-fourths of the inventory was sold before the holiday season ended. No purchases were made during the period. Expenses amounted to $35,000. Assume that sales and expenses were incurred uniformly throughout the year. The index stood at 100 on January 1, 1990, and at 116 on December 31. What was the net income from operations on the constant dollar financial statements dated December 31, 1990?

   a. $343,778
   b. $349,027
   c. $365,185
   d. $368,847

Now compare your answers with the correct ones beginning on page 597.

Solutions/Appendix A

Completion and Exercises

1. as the amount needed to balance the balance sheet; current; average; current; acquisition

2. loss; $600 [($50,000 − $20,000) × 1.02] − ($50,000 − $20,000)
   loss; $700 [($50,000 − $20,000) × 102/100 = $30,600]; $30,600 + (Increase for the year of $10,100 × 102/100) = $40,800; $40,800 − Actual net monetary items of $40,100 [$60,100 − $20,000] = $700

3. $330,000 [$312,000 × 110/104]

4. current cost; constant dollar; purchasing power; five-year summary

5. current cost; general inflation

6. loss; $5; capital; earnings

7. Current cost depreciation is:

$$\frac{\$175,000 + \$190,000}{2} \times .15 = \$27,375$$

8. a. $45,000 × 120/100 = $54,000; $45,000 − $54,000 = $9,000 purchasing power loss
   b. $30,000 × 95/100 = $28,500; $30,000 − $28,500 = $1,500 purchasing power gain
   c. $20,000 × 109/100 = $21,800; $20,000 − $21,800 = $1,800 purchasing power gain

Multiple-Choice Questions

1. b. $5,700 − $5,000 = $700.

2. a. Of the items listed, only bonds payable is a monetary item. Purchasing power gains and loss can result only from monetary items.

3. a. The index at the end of the year is 140 and the index is assumed to average 130 [(140 + 120)/2] for the year.

4. a. A purchasing power loss results from holding monetary assets during inflation.

5. b. Land would be converted to current constant dollars by a conversion ratio of 105/100. Notes Payable is a monetary item which is always expressed in terms of the number of dollars at the current price level.

6. d. The index would be 115. The value of the dollar would fall to approximately 87¢ (100/115 = .8696).

7. b. The primary financial statements are to be based on historical cost. The supplementary statements are to report the effects of inflation on both a constant dollar (general price level) and current cost basis.

8. a. To recover the original cost, the land would have to be sold for $150,000 ($75,000 cost × 156/78). The difference between $200,000 and $150,000 is the gain in 1990 dollars.

9. a.

	Historical Dollars		Conversion Ratio	Constant Dollars
Sales [($250,000 × .75) × 300%]	$562,500	×	116/113	$577,434
Cost of Goods Sold ($250,000 × .75)	187,500	×	116/110	197,727
Gross margin				379,707
Expenses	35,000	×	116/113	35,929
Income from continuing operations				$343,778

597

(a)   KNIGHT COMPANY

Partial Statement of Current Cost Income from Continuing Operations

In December 31, 1990 Dollars

For the Year Ended December 31, 1990

Sales	
Cost of good sold	
Depreciation	
Other expenses	
Income from continuing operations	

(b)   KNIGHT COMPANY

Partial Statement of Constant Dollar Income from Continuing Operations

For the Year Ended December 31, 1990

Sales	
Cost of good sold	
Depreciation	
Other expenses	
Income from continuing operations	

Name _____

_____

(a)

Q COMPANY

Partial Statement of Current Cost Income from Continuing Operations

For the Year Ended December 31, 1990

Sales	
Cost of good sold	
Depreciation	
Other expenses	
Income from continuing operations	

(b)

Q COMPANY

Partial Statement of Constant Dollar Income from Continuing Operations

In December 31, 1990 Dollars

For the Year Ended December 31, 1990

Sales	
Cost of good sold	
Depreciation	
Other expenses	
Income from continuing operations	

OSBORN COMPANY

Restated Income for the Year Ended December 31, 1990

(in constant end-of-year 1990 dollars)

	Historical Dollars	Conversion Ratio	Constant Dollars

LUMPKIN COMPANY

Restated Income for the Year Ended December 31, 1990

(in constant end-of-year 1990 dollars)

	Historical Dollars	Conversion Ratio	Constant Dollars

Name _____

_____

(a)

McINTYRE CORPORATION

Partial Statement of Current Cost Income from Continuing Operations

For the Year Ended June 30, 1991

Sales		
Cost of good sold		
Depreciation		
Other expenses		
Income from continuing operations		

(b)

McINTYRE CORPORATION

Partial Statement of Constant Dollar Income from Continuing Operations

In June 30, 1991 Dollars

For the Year Ended June 30, 1991

Sales		
Cost of good sold		
Depreciation		
Other expenses		
Income from continuing operations		

Name _____

_____

(a)   BRITT HOME FURNISHINGS

Statement of Current Cost Income from Continuing Operations

For the Year Ended December 31, 1990

Sales	
Cost of good sold	
Depreciation	
Other expenses	
Income from continuing operations	

(b)   BRITT HOME FURNISHINGS

Statement of Constant Dollar Income from Continuing Operations

In December 31, 1990 Dollars

For the Year Ended December 31, 1990

Sales	
Cost of good sold	
Depreciation	
Other expenses	
Income from continuing operations	

OAKLAND CLEANING COMPANY

Restated Income for the Year Ended December 31, 1990

(in constant end-of-year 1990 dollars)

	Historical Dollars	Conversion Ratio	Constant Dollars
(a)			
Service revenue			
Supplies expense			
Rent expense			
Depreciation expense			
Other expenses			
Total expenses			
Income from continuing operations			
Purchasing power loss on net monetary items			
Net income			

(b)

Name _____

THE WRIGHT COMPANY
Work Sheet
For the Year Ended December 31, 1990

(a)

ACCOUNT TITLE	UNADJUSTED TRIAL BALANCE		ADJUSTMENTS		ADJUSTED TRIAL BALANCE		INCOME STATEMENT		STATEMENT OF RETAINED EARNINGS		BALANCE SHEET	
	DR.	CR.	DR.	CR.	DR.	CR.	DR.	CR.	DR.	CR.	DR.	CR.
Cash												
Accounts receivable												
Notes receivable												

Name _____

WELLS COMPANY

Work Sheet

For the Year Ended December 31, 1990

(a)

ACCOUNT TITLE	UNADJUSTED TRIAL BALANCE		ADJUSTMENTS		ADJUSTED TRIAL BALANCE		INCOME STATEMENT		STATEMENT OF RETAINED EARNINGS		BALANCE SHEET	
	DR.	CR.	DR.	CR.	DR.	CR.	DR.	CR.	DR.	CR.	DR.	CR.
Cash												
Accounts receivable												